THE MADNESS IN SPORTS

Arnold R. Beisser, M. D.

Director
Center for Training in Community Psychiatry
Los Angeles
State of California, Department of
Mental Hygiene

Clinical Professor
Psychiatry and Human Behavior
University of California
California College of Medicine

APPLETON-CENTURY-CROFTS
Division of Meredith Publishing Company
New York

THE MADNESS IN SPORTS

Psychosocial Observations on Sports

to RITA

PREFACE

*Thought is born of failure. Only when action fails to
satisfy human needs is there ground for thought.*

L. L. WHYTE
The Next Development in Man

This is a book about athletes, about athletic teams and
about sports fans. It differs from the more common journalistic
treatment of sports and seeks to go beyond the sports page. It
examines the thoughts and hearts of those who are caught up in
the swiftly moving current of American sports. They are so swift
and engulfing that only a unique series of events can cause one
to stop and wonder what it all means.

Such a series occurred in my life allowing me to synthesize an interpretation of sports from my varied experiences
as psychiatrist, athlete, fan and reporter. Today, there is a need
for greater awareness of the psychological significance of sports
since they strongly influence Americans throughout their lives.
Their impact begins with the growth and development of our
youth and, in adult life, they occupy much of the growing leisure
time available.

As I grew up, sports were of major importance to me.
As they are in the lives of many American boys, they were probably the most important single activity in my life. I fell asleep
each night with a fantasy of breaking away from the starting

blocks on the track, dashing into the foul circle to shoot a hook shot, or making a leaping catch of a long pass in the end zone. School, to me, was made up of sports, which were the reward, and studies which were the price I had to pay to play them.

My love of sports continued into my early adult life at college and later in medical school. As an intern in a busy general hospital there was little time for leisure, but what was available was spent in sports—in a makeshift basketball game after midnight or, if there was still some daylight, a quick set of tennis at the neighborhood court. There were always a few contemporaries who were eager to share these moments. I looked forward to these moments of sport at odd hours, for they carried with them a certain nostalgia after a hard day and were like coming home and relaxing.

When I was 24, the Korean Conflict had begun. Since I was a Naval Reserve Officer, I was alerted for recall into the military service. In the characteristic military fashion of "hurry up and wait," it was nearly four months before I received my orders. In the meantime I had resigned my hospital position for a week's vacation of playing in a tennis tournament. This extended into months of tournament play, climaxed when I reached a lifelong goal of winning a national championship. I wrote home that I had accomplished what I wanted in sports and I didn't think I'd play seriously any more, for there were more important things to do.

Two weeks later I got my orders, and on the day after I reported for active duty to the Navy, my life had changed more than I could ever have anticipated. Stricken with polio, housed in a tank that did my breathing, I was unable to move at all. The tank continued to do my breathing for nearly two years, and I was never again to walk or move very much. I had lost a major source of gratification. Now, physically limited, my principle activities became reflection and thinking.

My thoughts were of what had been familiar sources of pleasure and significant among them were thoughts about sports. I became aware that when action is blocked, the energy is transformed into thought. Although I was a half-century later than Freud in making this discovery, I doubt that it was any more dramatically demonstrated to him.

Had it not been for the suddenness of the cessation of my athletic activity, I believe that there would simply have been a gradual dissipation of the intensity of my interest in sports. Other activities which were becoming more important would have taken the place of sports. But I was not to experience this slow transition, for one day I played and the next I could not move at all.

As soon as I was able, I began to prepare myself for return to medical practice, now in the field of psychiatry. My study of the behavioral sciences led to a natural synthesis with my interest in sports and I became interested in understanding their psychological and sociological function and meaning. With my active participation in sports blocked and transformed into thought, I began to try to understand my own sports interest and experiences, and that of athletes I knew and heard about, now within the framework of my growing knowledge of existing facts and theories in the behavioral sciences.

I became increasingly aware of how an athlete competes well or poorly under pressure, of how a coach or a crowd may influence his performance, and the symbolic meanings of each. I realized that the psychological condition of the athlete is of equal importance to his physical readiness in determining his performance. Based on psychodynamic theory I became aware of the influences of parents and siblings during the athlete's developmental years on his choice of sports, his style and his ability. I began to understand how losing could be more important than winning to some athletes and how others constructed elaborate rituals when winning to ward off magically retaliation from dim, nearly forgotten figures.

During my years of active competition I had very little interest as a spectator in the performances of others and was bored by sports statistics. Now I became a fan. As a passive observer I enjoyed a vicarious excitement in competition. The psychology of the fan, as one who could gain pleasure from identification with the players without the actual dangers of competition, became clear to me.

The most profoundly revealing insights, however, came after I became a practicing psychiatrist, when I had opportunities to study athletes who became psychiatric patients. The intimate relationship of psychotherapy was the major method of investigation. A segment of my psychiatric practice became specialized as former athletes whom I had known or who knew of me sought help. They felt that their problems could best be understood by someone knowledgeable in sports, but I was surprised that they sought an athlete whose career had come to a sudden and final conclusion due to illness. I learned that the action-oriented athlete tends to equate emotional disorder with physical disability. Moreover, their emotional difficulties began with such factors as graduation from college, retirement due to age, or new responsibilities, which precluded continuation of their customary roles in sports.

Participation in sports served as an integrating personality force and when deprived of this their psychiatric symptoms appeared. In the course of psychotherapy the psychological meanings of their sports activities became clear. For some the athletic field was a place where they could act out certain desires that were unacceptable elsewhere. For others sports were a way of relating to people in what was otherwise a forbidding world. Sports were a way of pleasing or identifying with parents for some, whereas for others they were a way of rebelling, in a socially acceptable way, against parents or the culture in which they lived.

It has, of course, been necessary to disguise the identities of the athletes described, and some important case histories had to be left out entirely because widely known dramatic events would surely identify them. However, the illumination which their cases add is not lost, and in later sections of the book anecdotes which are public information, gleaned from the sports pages, are used to make specific points which were derived from more confidential information.

Two additional sources of information have added to my understanding. I have had opportunities to cover certain sports events as a reporter which gave me access to the opinions of other reporters and to still another view of the athlete. More recently, I have acted as a consultant to coaches on phychological problems of competition in athletes and teams.

The first half of the book reports several case histories and their significance. The second half relates these individual cases to psychological theories about play and work, and places them within the social matrix of contemporary America. Finally, I have tried to integrate all of these into a theoretical contribution on the psychosocial meanings of sports.

Colleagues, friends and patients, too numerous to mention, have been of direct assistance to me in writing this book and I gratefully acknowledge my debt to them. I am indebted to Marsha Grant Bohr, Connie Cozens, Hazel Jaworski, Daisy Johnson, Betty Ortiz, Barbara Ashworth and Connie Maziol for their work in the preparation of the manuscript. The encouragement and support of my wife has made the book possible.

Arnold R. Beisser

CONTENTS

Gerry Cranham   Rapho Guillumette

THE MADNESS IN SPORTS

1 THE PARADOX OF SPORTS

In World War II the attacking Japanese troops thought they knew what Americans hold most dear. They made their Banzai attacks not only with weapons but with shouted invectives meant to demoralize. One of those cries was, "To hell with Babe Ruth!" So far as I know they did not defame the religions of America, vilify our economic system, or condemn motherhood. Instead, they selected a sports hero as representative of what Americans held in highest esteem.

It is doubtful that the battlefield shout, "To hell with Babe Ruth," created more than mild amusement to the American troops, for in time of national peril, concern for basic rights and freedom was predominant. But to Japanese intelligence officers, the great amount of sports enthusiasm in the United States had led them to the conviction that this is what Americans loved most.

Not long ago, while on a visit to this nation, a European economist was strangely puzzled. Aware of America's proclamations to the world about the vigor of its commitment to the capitalistic economic system, he searched in vain for a financial section in the local newspapers. An American informant could easily have directed him to it, for in many newspapers it is, in deference to American reading practices, fastened to the end of the horse racing results at the back of the sports section. The priority, so casually accepted by Americans, can be puzzling for visitors.

Sometimes it can be bewildering even for a newspaperman. When The New York Times' political columnist, James Reston, came to California in 1962 to cover the heated gubernatorial race between Richard Nixon and "Pat" Brown, he was hard put to sample popular opinion. "When a political reporter asks around here who's going to win," he reported later,* "the answer is invariably 'the Dodgers.' " It may be fortunate that few political elections occur at the same time as major sports events. Otherwise perhaps the relatively small percentage of American voters who go to the polls would be even further reduced.

There is no lack of evidence, in all kinds of odd places, of the overwhelming importance of sports in American life. In many American newspapers the sports pages constitute the largest specialized daily section. One-tenth of The World Almanac is devoted to sports. In both newspapers and the Almanac the sports sections are greater in volume than the sections about politics, business, entertainment, or science.

Radio programming has become largely sports, music, and news, and even the news is filled with sports results. Prime television viewing time on weekends is filled with sports. Major networks compete for the privilege of showing sports events, so that frequently the three major networks simultaneously cover different events in the same sport. Major events such as the World's Series or the New Year's Day bowl games capture almost the entire viewing audience. A number of bowl games formerly played on New Year's Day have had to be rescheduled because network viewing time was filled.

Television programs are changed rapidly in an attempt to satisfy the insatiable public appetite, yet year after year football, baseball, golf, bowling, and boxing are among the most viable attractions. Few programs have survived longer than "The Fight of the Week," "The Game of the Week," or "All Star" this or that. Only old movies exceed old sports events in popularity as fillers.

It is not only in the mass communications that our dedication to sports is apparent. Americans take their sports

---

* "Scorecard," *Sports Illustrated,* October 8, 1962, p. 6.

any way they can get them—even live. Cumulative annual attendance figures for football, basketball, and baseball exceed a billion. Regular participants in golf, tennis, and bowling number many millions. Participation in school and club-team sports has been a part of almost every American life.

In education many public schools require more time in physical education, usually meaning sports, than in any other subject. From grammar school through high school, they are one-sixth or one-seventh of the curriculum. Team sports are, for many pupils, the most important aspect of their school life.

OF PLAY AND WORK

How could this remarkable state of affairs have come about? In the Puritan tradition, the early American churches vigorously opposed sports. As Thomas Macaulay neatly put it, "The Puritan hated bear-baiting, not because it gave pain to the bear, but because it gave pleasure to the spectators." Blue laws were passed forbidding sports participation at times when men were expected to be at worship. Today, the Sunday double header or the televised professional football "Game of the Week" has all but replaced the Sunday sermon. Churches now have gymnasiums and sponsor their own teams. The smiling face of Bob Richards, the former Olympic pole-vaulting champion, has become a symbol of the marriage of the former sworn enemies. Today he peripatetically shuttles between his two callings, the pulpit and the Wheaties Sports Foundation.

Recently, when Americans began to voice their concern about an inability to find meaning in traditional values, much was written about the need for a new national purpose. A widely circulated cartoon commented on this. It showed two baseball players standing before a cheering multitude of fans. One said to the other, "But I thought baseball was our national purpose." The joke, as I have already suggested, is not so far from expressing the true state of affairs.

In his classical work on wit and humor, Sigmund Freud observed that in jest truth emerges.* For various reasons of conscience, embarrassment, fear, and integrity, people tend to push certain issues out of their awareness. But these issues are not lost and, in fact, may reappear when the psychological guard is down. Sports interest is one of these. Indeed, Americans tend to be somewhat embarrassed by the intensity of their feelings about sports. They express concern about the priority of sports in schools and the idolization of sports heroes, but this concern does not seem to diminish their fervor.

Why should there be this inner doubt, this lurking sense of embarrassment? The answer, which I believe is to be found in the psychological understanding of sports, constitutes the subject of this book. In a preliminary way we can take our bearings at once. It is usual to explain modern sports as a complex outgrowth of play: to argue that the play of children and primitives, through cultural refinement, becomes what we know as sports. To play may be defined as "to engage in sport or diversion, to amuse oneself, to frolic or gambol. To act in a way which is not to be taken seriously." By definition, then, play is not a serious activity, and should not be considered too important. If this is so, we must conclude that Americans occupy themselves, to a large extent, with activities they consider unimportant.

We deepen our understanding of play by contrasting it with its traditional opposite: work—"continued exertion or activity directed to some purpose or end; especially manual labor; hence, opportunity for labor; occupation." Work is "an undertaking; task." In the very meaning of the words, work, in contrast to play, is clearly something to be taken seriously.

In the earlier history of America, the Protestant

---

* Sigmund Freud, "Wit and Its Relation to the Unconscious," *The Basic Writings of Sigmund Freud,* trans. and ed. A. A. Brill (New York: Random House, Inc., 1938), pp. 711–727.

ethic idealized work; play was one of its rewards. Every boy heard, "Get your work done so you'll have time to play," and play without work was a forbidden fruit. In the mid-twentieth century a shrinking work week, vacations, and retirement plans present problems for those still influenced by the spirit of the nineteenth century. The "Sunday neurosis has made its appearance: the person who is effective at work is depressed with his leisure. He can enjoy his play only when he "steals" time for it; otherwise, guilt interferes. As a clandestine activity he can enjoy it, but when it is allowed or expected, he cannot. The man who has worked hard for retirement finds time, which was so diligently sought, empty and devoid of meaning. In the ambivalent attitude toward the playboy—publicly scorned, privately envied —we find the traditional view of play.

Today the relationships between work and play are greatly changed.* A considerable part of unskilled and semiskilled labor has been replaced by automation, making steady work unattainable for many Americans. For many of the five to six million chronically unemployed, not working has become an acceptable state. During the great depression of the 1930's the unemployed worker was guilt-ridden and filled with an overriding sense of personal inadequacy.† Contemporary unemployment compensation lines are surprisingly different. There is "an unmistakable air of conviviality and easy spontaneity, almost approaching gaiety."‡ Unemployment does not, of course, preclude a man's interest in sports; the commitment which in other times would have been reserved for work may be focused instead on the team of his choice.

* There are also generational differences. Those born in the first part of this century carry with them the spirit of the previous century and idolize work. Those born later tend to doubt its purpose.

† Mirra Komarovsky, *The Unemployed Man and His Family: Effect of Unemployment upon the Status in 59 Families* (New York: Dryden Press, Inc., 1940).

‡ Gregory P. Stone, Ph.D., personal communication. Stone, a sociologist, joined unemployment lines to observe.

The complexity of modern technology and the mandatory retirement age have produced profound attitudinal changes, even in those who find steady work. Added educational requirements prolong the period of job preparation and diminish productive years. At the other end, increasingly early retirement seems to leave only a fleeting moment for production. Quite the reverse is true, however, of sports and play, which grow with every reduction in work. Even while we are at work, production sometimes seems to pale into insignificance when compared with extracurricular activities like the "coffee break," so sanctified that practically nothing has precedence over it.

While work diminishes, preoccupation with sports grows. In the footrace of time, work led the way, with play following slowly behind; but in this century, wearing the colors of sport, play has taken the lead.

Still the anachronistic definitions of work and play prevail, in part, because of "cultural lag": work is serious and important, but play is not. However, much contemporary behavior makes it appear that the opposite is more nearly true. A void is left as word and deed are fractured, a paradox symbolized by the beatnik who withdraws and wants nothing to do with either work or sports. But most Americans do not withdraw from sports; instead they approach them with the vigor and dedication formerly reserved for work.

Play and sports, by definition, are nonproductive, carefree, nonserious activities. But for the professional athlete they are handsomely productive. With fringe benefits such as commercial endorsements, the professional athlete can be generously rewarded in our culture, beyond most other professionals and at least on a par with the executives of big business. Even though only a few athletes attain this pre-eminence it does not mean there is no potential.

One may explain the willingness of fans to pay for their sports events—and they pay handsomely—on the basis of entertainment value received. But does entertainment alone account for spectators who willingly endure inclement weather and personal sacrifice for the sake of a sport, for example, the loyal New York Met fans who steadfastly supported their team in baseball's most miserable showing, or the rioting that accompanies the Stanley Cup competition in ice hockey? Clearly, one must look deeper than casual amusement to understand the fans' loyalty, commitment, and willingness to sacrifice.

Whether for pay or from old school loyalty, modern sports are dominated by the spirit of work; arduous practice, long hours of learning signals and plays, sweating, bruising, bone-breaking practice, all in preparation for the big game. Long hours often with limited reward, absolute obedience to coach or manager—is the word "player" really appropriate for an athlete engaged in such activities?

There is a fascinating illustration of the complete reversal of relationships of work and play. Those sports which began as play, such as ball games, have now lost that playful and lighthearted characteristic, and have assumed instead all the qualities of serious, hard work. Hunting and fishing, in contrast, began as the soul of work, and so they remain for primitives—necessary for survival, serious, and productive. But in our culture, hunting and fishing have assumed the true spirit of play; they are carefree, amateur, diversional recreation. They are, in fact, the main contemporary sports which have these characteristics.

THE PARADOX OF SPORTS AND PHYSICAL FITNESS

If the psychosocial functions of sports are paradoxical, can we at least find clarity and continuity in their physical benefits? Proponents of sports activities equate them with physical fitness and consider this the important justification for their existence. Nothing should take precedence over our nation's health and fitness, it is said. We must do everything possible to insure the fitness and health of our nation's youth. This is a point of view with which few will disagree.

The basic tenet of this position is that sports activity leads to physical fitness. Unfortunately the relationship is not confirmed by close scrutiny. If there is a correlation, it may be more nearly inverse. For example, in a 1962 statement on the nation's physical fitness, President Kennedy referred to studies by Kraus and Weber at Columbia-Presbyterian Hospital over a 15-year period. During a standardized physical fitness test, they tested several thousand children and young adults and compared the results obtained by American and European youths. Their conclusion was a disturbing one: while only 1 percent of the Europeans failed, 35 percent of the Americans were unable to pass the test. Yet, sports are not ordinarily a major or required part of European educational systems.

The decline in fitness of American youth can also be demonstrated within our own borders. At Yale University a physical fitness test administered to incoming freshmen revealed that 51 percent passed in 1951, 43 percent in 1956, 38 percent in 1960, 35 percent in 1965—a 16 percent drop in fourteen years. The test used, it may be added, was not an overly rigorous one.

These discouraging results have occurred despite the growing importance of sports. Thus, the expected relationship between sports and physical fitness cannot be confirmed. It may even be possible to demonstrate that a negative relationship exists.

The picture is even less encouraging for adults; for the fan sitting in the stadium with a hot dog in one hand, a bottle of beer in the other, is hardly contributing to his own fitness or to the nation's. It cannot even be argued that many of our most popular sports are for the physical benefit of the athletes. On the same day in 1961, the outstanding stars of both the National Football League and the American Football League* were classified 4F by their respective draft boards because of chronic injuries. The

---

* Paul Hornung and Jack Kemp, backfield stars for the then league-leading professional football teams, the Green Bay Packers and the San Diego Chargers.

fate of Benny Paret and Davey Moore who died from injuries received in the ring, although they are extreme cases, is only an extension of common long-range effects of boxing on the boxer.*

Even the physical functions of sports, then, are paradoxical. If there really is a logic behind the American sports mania, we are not, apparently, going to find it in any correlation with physical fitness.

OF MEN AND BOYS

In growing up, a boy is provided with many models of adult behavior. Some are explicit and deliberately offered, others only implied. The models come from a variety of sources: parents, teachers, peer groups, movies, television, history books, and novels. A major function of growing up is sorting from the possible roles those that are impossible. Many such models can be rejected with relative ease. At some point, for example, it is useful for a boy to realize that the American cowboy is an anachronism with little or no place among attainable adult activities. In the case of the cowboy a boy is aided by society in his task of role selection. He soon learns that, outside books and movies, he is not likely to encounter a cowboy†—one just does not often see cowboys in the flesh. In addition, the adult world, while patronizingly tolerant a youngster who is playing cowboy, is actively opposed to adults playing cowboy.

How different the situation is in sports! The adult world not only looks with favor on the role of athlete, but deliberately fosters it. American youth is explicitly prepared for the athlete's role in exquisitely accurate miniaturi-

* Sercl and Jaros, European physicians, reported evidence of chronic brain damage in 9 percent of boxers, even among those who had had only a few fights.

† See "Appearance and the Self: Gregory P. Stone in *Human Behavior and Social Processes,* ed. Arnold M. Rose (Boston: Houghton Mifflin Co., 1961), p. 86 for the importance of costume in these models.

zations of the professional team. Little League baseball and Pop Warner football are almost exact duplications of major professional sports. The uniform, the publicity, the arduous practice, the complex plays, and, most of all, the pressure of adult expectation, make the role of professional athlete not only a future possibility, but a present reality.

I once watched the telecast of a football game together with a former professional football player. Anticipating a college or professional game, we sat uneasily for several moments watching, with only a vague realization that there was something different, and not knowing what it was. We then realized that the players were children and that this was a Pop Warner football game. So completely was the adult sports role simulated, even an expert could not tell immediately that they were only boys.

Moreover, this role is thrust upon boys at ever younger ages. A football-shaped rattle for infants is now available to get them started right. Before children can read they wear replicas of sports uniforms. Once they can walk, training begins in earnest.

A boy will have daily encounters with sportsmen at all stages of his development. Older brothers, coaches, fathers, and fans are all eager to show him how it is done. There is probably no adult role in which each stage of development is so omnipresent and clearly visible as the athlete's. In a world filled with social discontinuity, there seems to be a place for everyone in sports.

On the other hand, work roles, in which there seems to be little if any continuity, are in sharp contrast. In our specialized society, a child often has very little first-hand knowledge of his father's work. To begin with, the child never sees him at work. The extent of first-hand knowledge is that the father leaves home at an appointed hour, just as the child goes to school, five days a week. Beyond that, everything is hearsay.

I once witnessed a colleague attempting to explain his work as a psychiatrist to his seven-year-old son. The frustration of the father was exceeded only by the bewilderment of the son, until finally, in desperation, they agreed to go out later and play catch. This, unlike the father's work, was something they could quite conveniently share.

Although the function of a psychiatrist may be especially esoteric, this scene occurs thousands of times to stock brokers, bank tellers, scientists, and factory workers. Even if there is a product involved, there may be little hope of a father's conveying any real understanding of his work to his son. The little boy who says "My daddy makes missiles" would hardly be able to answer a second question. In fact, even his father may have only a hazy notion of how his job fits into the total operation.

At home, on weekends, a boy may see his father at a form of work, but it is strange work, for it may be helping with the housework or gardening, or some of the more nostalgic simulations of work represented by the do-it-yourself movement. Here a son may see his father make things, unusually inferior to the manufactured product and costing a little more.

Of course, there are a few fathers whose jobs, usually remnants of the nineteenth century, can be carried out at home in full view of their families. But such jobs are diminishing in relative numbers and such fathers represent a minority.

Boys are more apt to see their fathers at play or at work simulating play than at the occupation which provides them with a livelihood. This play often takes the form of sports, with parents and children sharing the role of spectator, or with parents as spectators to their children, or with a father instructing his son in athletics. In such circumstances, a boy's interest in sports is carefully nurtured, but we may well ask to what end this preparation is directed.

A CBS television documentary in 1961, "The Secret Life of Sam Huff," depicted the hard life of a professional football player. It was about the daily life of the New York Giants' middle line backer, and detailed the punishing drudgery of the professional athlete. As the program reached its climax, Sam Huff turned dramatically to the television screen and said that pro football "is for men, not boys." If the men are the ones playing football, what are the boys doing?

The present-day ideal for boys is no longer the Horatio Alger success story; the notion, true or not, that every boy can be President is less exciting than it used to be. In place of these traditional models has come a new dream, the dream of Peter Pan, of perpetual youth, with every boy a major leaguer. If a boy learns to play well enough, he may drink from the fountain of youth and continue to play as a professional athlete. For playing, he will be more handsomely rewarded than if he worked.

Unfortunately, even though almost every boy is rigorously prepared for this role as a star athlete, very few can achieve it. But the preparation is continuous through childhood to adult life. Unlike other models, which eventually are discarded as impossible or impractical, the role of sportsman, in some form, is continually and firmly reinforced by society.

There is something, a kind of consolation prize, for those who fail. They can become fans, and most of them do. They continue to follow intensely the progress of athletes and teams. Emotionally, if not physically, they remain ever ready if the call to play should come. Spectators and athletes join hands with entrepreneurs to keep the hopes of all alive. In sports there is indeed, something for everyone.

Although there is something for everyone in sports, it is unfortunately not enough. The spectator's role maintains a continuity of interest in sports, but often at the expense of other activities in which there are opportunities to participate more actively. To the fan, much of life seems insignificant in comparison with the excitement at the stadium. He lives in a sitting position, viewing the action through field glasses from afar.

Even a star professional athlete sometimes recognizes the paradox of his greatness. Roy Campanella, before his nearly fatal automobile accident one of the greatest baseball catchers of all time, noted that there must be a lot of "little boy" in a professional athlete to allow him to play. And, in a more critical tone, Bill Russell, the most valuable player in the National Basketball Association, for many years, described the dilemma this way: "We're a bunch of grown men playing a child's game. It's a child's game we've made into a man's game by complicating it. Silly, isn't it?" Even in greatness, the player's role sometimes seems a form of arrested development and may prove embarrassing.

Whatever their deficiencies, the roles of fan or athlete are more viable and exciting for Americans than most others. Sports occupy a treasured position so cherished and guarded that there is a reluctance to study their real significance. A review of the psychiatric and psychoanalytic literature to 1965 revealed only 20 papers attempting to explore the psychology of sports. In contrast to the psychological literature on sports there is the overwhelming mass of writing which reports the results of contests almost instantaneously. That race to keep up with the results and almost never to look beyond is not without significance, for as Freud long ago observed, people are reluctant to make any penetrating examination of activities which give them pleasure. Even though the activity may have many limitations and even create problems, it is experienced as better than nothing; and a deeper understanding of it is vigorously resisted for fear that the understanding will deprive one of the pleasure.

The psychological literature on the play of children provides a further contrast, representing one of the largest areas for psychological study and serving as a principal vehicle for the study of personality development. Is it not curious that sports—adult play—should be exempt from the same scrutiny? Instead they are treated as facts to be reported and accepted at face value.

Despite this apparent reluctance to find out more about the meaning and motivation of American sports, there are compelling reasons for a search. The United States is the second great nation in history to spend great amounts of time and resources in elaborately producing spectator sports. The first was Rome during the period of its decline. Whether or not the same fate will befall us is a matter for conjecture. Sports are an overwhelming influence in the lives of Americans, and if our society is to progress we must know what we are doing and why. It is to this end that this book has been written.

The concepts of sports and their language are so familiar and pervasive that they are used to clarify by analogy other major aspects of American life. Presidents Eisenhower, Kennedy and Johnson have been referred to in the press as "quarterbacks" or "team captains." Their cabinets have been called the "teams." (I have never heard a quarterback referred to as a president for clarification.) In business, salesmen are told to "keep your eye on the ball" and to have "team spirit." Even theories of human behavior have been viewed as "games people play." But, as we have seen, Americans feel embarrassed about recognizing their importance, for it is contrary to traditional concepts of what should be important. As traditional work becomes less familiar and serious, sports assume the characteristics formerly associated with work. Player and worker become paradoxical terms.

This confusion has its strangest influence on the growing American boy who is seemingly prepared for a life of dedication to sports. Although thoroughly familiar with sports activities at ever-earlier ages, American boys have little first-hand knowledge of modern occupational roles to which they might more reasonably aspire. Most prepare themselves in sports for roles that will never be realized, and as "has beens" by their teens, they join the army of spectators. There they become more fully occupied in watching from afar than in actual activities in which they might find first-hand involvement.

The effect of these paradoxes on the personality development of the individual is that the transition from boy to man becomes a contradictory journey to nowhere.

Play is unquestionably an important aspect of personality development. It is a way of trying out new roles and of symbolically mastering childhood anxieties. The primacy of sports for both American boys and men suggests that new roles are likely to be less significant than those already fully explored in youth.

2 INTRODUCTION TO CASE STUDIES

At one time in all fields of medicine a sharp distinction was drawn between health and illness, but as knowledge increased it became clear that there is an entire spectrum ranging between the concepts of health and illness. The matter is no longer a distinction between black or white, but between shades of gray which fall on a continuum. As one psychiatrist has stated, it is no longer a question of whether an individual is mentally ill, but rather, how much mental illness he has.

This concept has been enhanced by many studies. In one, patients in a general hospital being treated for medical conditions with no psychiatric components were examined for psychiatric symptoms. A surprising amount of psychopathology was revealed. The problems these non-psychiatric patients faced were the same faced by patients considered mentally ill. Studies of populations in which physical illness is not a factor showed similar findings. These and other studies suggest that the same conflicts and biological needs lie beneath the facade of personality in everyone.

The distinction between the healthy person and the sick or deviant one appears, then, not to be a matter of symptoms or problems, but rather the so-called healthy person's ability to find successful ways of coping with discomforts and deviations. Thus, the murderer, the neurotic, and the healthy person all share occasional murderous impulses. The murderer, however, has failed in his attempt at control. The neurotic is tortured by the impulse which becomes disguised in the form of symptoms and obsessive guilt. The relatively healthy person has found a culturally accepted method, not foreign to his personality, of expressing his impulses. For example, Rocky Graziano said of his battles in the prize ring with Tony Zale, that his sole purpose was to try to "kill him," but Graziano made this attempt at mayhem within a socially accepted structure. He was, in fact, cheered and rewarded for his attempts. How different this is from the death row inhabitant who is regarded with revulsion by the public. Aggression thus may lead to success in sports, a successful business career, a one-way trip to San Quentin or frequent trips to a psychiatrist.

Similarly, the scoutmaster's affection for his boys is applauded and admired. A less well-controlled interest in boys may lead to a diagnosis of and conviction for pedophilia with subsequent scorn for the offender. There is also a continuity between the husband stimulated by his wife's nudity, the professional burlesque goer, and the Peeping Tom who is compelled to look into windows.

Modern theories of psychology of the normal individual stemmed from the study of deviants and the mentally ill. They have been confirmed by careful examinations of normal populations, finding that the person who becomes mentally ill is merely exposing his latent problems.

The following are case studies of athletes who sought psychiatric treatment, men whose lives were indistinguishable from those of other successful athletes until they reached a point of breakdown. Their stories provide material from which we can reconstruct portions of the common psychological background of the athlete.

Specifically we will be interested in finding the answers to certain questions relevant to sports. What did sports mean to this individual? What appealed to him about his particular sport? How did he get interested? What is the historical background of his sports interest? How does it relate to his mother, father, brothers, and sisters? What was the psychological function of sports for him? What role did his sports activity play in his psychiatric disorder? How did his psychological makeup affect his competition under pressure? How did he fare in making the transition from boy to man and from play to work?

3 BASKETBALL PLAYER

THE BOY WHO PLAYED THE GAME TOO WELL

One morning several years ago, an overworked colleague complained bitterly to me about the inappropriate use of psychiatric hospitals. His irritation stemmed from an experience the night before when he was called at a late hour to admit a young college athlete referred for psychiatric hospitalization. My colleague insisted there was nothing wrong with him, aside from his having had a disappointing basketball season. He described how this young man had appeared at the hospital and cheerfully requested admission with a letter from his psychiatrist. He continued with the brief history that the youth had been attending a nearby college, was in his senior year, captain of the basketball team, and the star of the previous year's championship team. In his last year, however, amid public expectations of athletic greatness, he had failed even to approach previous performances. He did not reveal much disturbance on admittance to the hospital, and it was easy to understand how my harassed, overworked and tired colleague had little sympathy for someone who looked so cheerful and whose major disappointments were about "play."

The day following this conversation I had occasion to visit this young man on his hospital ward. He was an impressive sight, towering six feet seven inches, his lithe muscular frame topped by a blond crewcut. A handsome

18

youth, almost too handsome, he was a caricature of the all-American boy found on the cover of a fall issue of The Saturday Evening Post. He greeted me with a breezy, "Hi, doc, what can I do for you?" Even to a psychiatrist, blasé from long experience with incongruous behavior, this was startling. Strong, cheerful, seemingly composed, his only expressions of concern were sympathetic remarks about the other patients and his gratuitous offers of help to the professional staff. It was not until we moved into an office, behind closed doors, that his mood seemed to change. "Doc, I let everybody down, especially myself. I don't understand what's happened to me," he began. This was the story he told:

In his college town he was considered potentially the greatest basketball player in the school's history. The coaches and sportswriters who saw him as a freshman, a sophomore, and then a junior, said all he needed was "maturity," which would undoubtedly come the next year when, as captain and leader of the team, he would realize his ability. There was mention of All-American honors. Most of the players were returning for this climactic senior year and it was taken for granted that the team which had had a good previous season was likely to have an even better one, especially when led by their experienced and popular, if sometimes erratic, star.

Although he considered statements about his ability unwarranted, he was nevertheless pleased by them. Personal success, however, was something Cal rarely acknowledged, attributing what came his way to his teammates while underplaying his own role. The fact that he insisted that he was not as capable as everyone seemed to think was accepted as the becoming modesty fans have come to expect of outstanding athletes.

So appealing was his manner that in this fateful senior year he was elected fraternity president. Although he was not the driving organizer usually elected, his "brothers" recognized the prestige he would bring to the house because of his campus and athletic popularity. They arranged his duties so he would not be burdened with the administrative details of office and could devote himself fully to the basketball season. After all, he was their most celebrated member. He seemed pleased with his lot, although he deliberately avoided thinking too much about the coming athletic season.

As it began, the significance began to dawn on him. A single thought haunted him. "This is my senior year, it's the end of the line." After this season he felt there would be nothing ahead—no future. This recurrent thought concerned him so much that he could think of little else.

Although he was never one to discuss his problems with others, he became so preoccupied that he did mention this fear to his buddies. They were quick to point out his potential in professional basketball, business, or in coaching, and dismissed his concern as further evidence of the modesty that made him so popular. They didn't understand, so thereafter he kept his concerns to himself.

He began this most important season amid the fanfare of a campus anticipating a championship. In the past, he had not been an extremely high scorer, only because he was such a dedicated team player. He always led the team in "assists" and had a more-than-presentable 18-point average. He always said he would rather "feed off" than shoot. For, as he saw it, the team was far more important than the individuals on it.

The previous year's chief scorer had graduated, so in the sports chatter and speculation everyone assumed that the burden of this function would be carried by Cal. During practice, much coaching time was spent preparing him for this role. Cal, however, found it difficult and did not shoot any more in the first few games than he had during last season, in spite of his coach's remonstrances. Then, as the season wore on, he took fewer and fewer shots. His performance actually became ludicrous since he would "feed off" even when he had a "setup." Rather than take a "dunk shot" while standing alone under the basket, he would dribble out until he could "feed off." The crowd roared its disapproval at this strange behavior. His game average dropped to ten points and then to five points.

The more pressure he felt, the more he refused to shoot. It was not that he was uncooperative, for he agreed wholeheartedly with the coach's instructions, but with every growing demand he had to be more of a team player, despite the fact that the team wanted him to score. Through it all was the growing, haunting thought, "This is the end of the line; after this season there is nothing."

He believed he could master his growing tension by working out harder. This was the way he had solved problems before. He took extra workouts and practiced fundamentals almost every waking hour. If he had any energy remaining, he would run up and down the empty basketball court. Even now, as he sat sprawled in his chair in a mental hospital ward, he said, "I'm sure if I just could have worked out harder, I could have handled this thing."

As his playing became worse, he began to believe there was a physical basis for his discomfort, perhaps the "flu" or even heart trouble. Each morning he appeared at the college infirmary with a new set of minor physical complaints referrable to every organ system in his body. He said, "If someone just could have told me it was something physical, I would have been the happiest person in the world." But no one did, and he continued to decompensate.

The main solution still seemed to him to be harder workouts. One day, in spite of running and jumping vigorously in practice, he felt no relief. He put more effort into running, but it did not seem fast enough. He felt a rising sense of panic, and ran to his car, got in and drove off as fast as he could. Somehow he felt if he could get going fast enough he would feel better. Out into the country he drove at a furious speed. Then, as his tension turned to confusion, he slowed the car and finally returned to town, to drive aimlessly, slowly, for several more hours.

Finally, stopping at a service station, confused and bewildered, he found the telephone number of a physician who was one of his fans, and called him. The doctor came immediately to see him and sedated him. Lying in the college infirmary in a hazy state, a new solution to his panic emerged. If this were not his senior year, if the end of college and of the team were not in sight because of graduation, then things would be as before.

The next morning he took steps to drop some courses so he would not graduate on schedule. He also made another decision which he said he could not understand at the time. He spoke to his advisor about switching his major from physical education to psychology. Before this, he had scrupulously avoided psychology courses.

This plan was, of course, doomed to fail and now new problems emerged. Dropping courses terminated his sports eligibility, and separated him from the team precipitously, instead of reinstating him. In addition, he had to contend with the basketball coach's outrage and the team's and the fans' perplexity. Now he felt like a freak. Eventually he was referred to the college psychiatric consultant who, in turn, recommended his hospitalization.

What had happened to this collegian, this All-American calibre basketball player, this fraternity president? What had happened to this sought-after man-about-campus, and why had such a promising future turned into no future at all? Why had college, the preparatory phase of his life, turned out to be the end of the line?

As he talked, it became clear that his future seemed completely blank. He had never given more than momentary thought to what he would do after college. In fact, he behaved as if school would never end. Even more curious, it seemed that his past, too, was blank. It became apparent that he had blocked out his past and future with a curtain of sports. He had fantastic detailed information about sports and athletes, and the events of his own sports career were remembered in the tiniest detail. Each morning he "memorized" the sports page. The performances of great athletes were extremely vivid to him, and their records were the vital statistics of his life. With such a preponderance of objective, factual material accumulated, he had no room for thoughts of his or anyone else's personal life outside sports. Thoughts about his parents and his relationship to them were vague, so vague as to seem nonexistent. To questions about his feelings, he usually responded that he did not know. So massive was this wall of repression that only the simplest and the most benign events were available to him.

Those few personal events he did recall resulted in blind alleys. For example, he remembered that when he was eight years old he slept for a time in the same room with his grandmother. One night she became seriously ill, a doctor was called, but after several hours the old woman died. The undertaker came and took her away. He reported he slept undisturbed through this eventful night, and he was surprised the next morning to find her bed empty. The emptiness was like his own past and future. His surprise at hearing the events of that night was like his surprise in realizing school would not go on forever. He was completely unprepared for events outside of the sports realm.

He was known as "Cool Cal," a nickname that followed him through his athletic career. During games he always appeared relaxed and unconcerned. Moreover, he was always reassuring his teammates to "take it easy" or "don't worry." So widely known was this reassurance that his fans used to shout their encouragement by friendly mimicry,

> Take it easy,
> Take it easy,
> Co-o-o-l Cal!

He scrupulously avoided things that were serious, and was known as a clown, for it seemed that the more the tension grew in a situation, the more he joked. He rarely contemplated what was happening, but made light of even serious situations. His actions were almost always interpreted by others as colorful.

Although Cal's early childhood was one of enforced seclusion, imposed by his mother, as he grew older he developed a legion of "buddies" who shared his interest in sports. He was one of a group of inseparable companions, and by the time he reached high school he was an expert athlete and was already well known. He achieved all league honors in high school in three sports: football, basketball, and baseball. Although his sports interests were all consuming, he nevertheless, rather successfully, went through the motions of other student activities. He became president of his student body. He attended school dances and other affairs with a variety of girls but never had a "steady." He avoided any more intense involvement, in spite of the fact that he was sought after, and, at times, literally "chased" by girls, with the excuse that he didn't want anything to interfere with sports and never wanted to let the team down.

His sexual experiences, too, were in the service of "team sports." He was not really very interested, and those few occasions when he did become involved, he did so only to be part of the team. Sometimes after a game, he and his "buddies" might pick up some girls, or, on a few occasions, they even went to houses of prostitution.

Although his interest and proficiency included all sports, his participation was limited to team sports: football, basketball, and baseball. He tried tennis, golf, and track, the individual sports, but found them dull and empty. On one occasion he was enticed by the track coach to run a quarter-mile for practice. In this first and only attempt, Cal ran within two seconds of the school record. The coach's joy turned to frustration, however, when he found Cal had no interest whatever in track. Arguing, pleading, threatening were all to no avail. As Cal put it to the poor, bewildered man, "It's no fun running out there all by yourself."

Even though it was predicted that he could have done equally well in football and baseball, basketball was Cal's choice in college over the less vigorous and sometimes slow deliberateness of baseball and the hostile contact of football. In basketball he felt a strength derived from the closeness to the other members of the team. His most meaningful relationships were with his basketball teammates, who were his "buddies" and with whom he enjoyed the team play on the court. "Feeding off," which was later to reach such compelling proportions, had always been the most fun. Nothing held such satisfaction as weaving skillfully down the court to hand off or to pass to a teammate for a score.

There were some ominous signs pointing toward the tragic conclusion that began this story. They were deeply submerged, however, by the brilliance of Cal's athletic achievements and the superficial characteristics that made him, among his peers a popular, colorful, all-American boy. The most outstanding was his inability to make even simple personal decisions, avoiding them until a decision was forced. When at home, his mother was only too willing to take over, insisting that her decision reflected Cal's desire. In college his "buddies" performed this function.

Now, as his amateur collegiate playing days drew to an end, he was faced with decisions only he could make. In characteristic fashion, though, he blanked these out of his mind and consequently life lost its meaning and he became aimless. He could no longer fill the void between the past he had to forget and the future he feared to approach, with vigorous sports activity. Neither coaching nor professional sports, both of which seemed reasonable fields for an easy transition, held the slightest appeal for him.

Cal's family story seems bizarre because of the extremes, yet it is similar in nature if not in degree to that of many American families. The story begins with dissatisfied parents. His mother was a career woman with a certain bitterness toward the new baby for having interfered with her orderly life. He was an unplanned child and remained an only child. She could not warmly hold, feed, or cuddle the baby yet she did become preoccupied with fears for his safety. Intolerant of her own bitterness to the point that she had to conceal it even from herself, she overcompensated by controlling him and being overprotective. Unable to give warmth and love to him, she willingly assumed the responsibility for restricting him.

His father responded more positively to his new

role. A thread of freedom, warmth, and mutual regulation developed between him and the boy. Perhaps as much out of opposition to his wife as out of affection for the child, he took over many of the traditional mothering functions. (This is the case in many American homes where the mother's working blurs the accepted roles. When both parents work, sharing the traditional paternal functions, both must share in the mothering functions.) Cal's father despised his own work for its tedium and enthusiastically put much of his energies into sports participation. The warmth and companionship between father and son developed against a background of sports.

Our young athlete learned one thing well from his father: how to fill an empty life with sports, a phenomenon not uncommon in American homes. While his mother talked and nagged, his father ignored her and read the sports page. As Cal put it, "There is a lot of not-listening at my house." This fact was amply illustrated when at one point in Cal's therapy, father, mother, and Cal were seen together. Cal sat between them, nearer his father, looking furtively toward his mother from time to time with a perplexed expression. As his mother spoke, his father turned his head away and whistled a silent tune, occasionally interrupting impulsively.

During Cal's growing-up period, his proficiency grew in sports, but his entire activity was limited to the sports stadium. In his relationships with teammates he found something akin to the closeness of mothering, which in his experience was really the fathering experience. It was here that he learned what was to be his greatest joy in basketball, "feeding off" to a teammate.

As was inevitable, though, the golden dream of perpetual youth collapsed—for permanence and growth are mutual contradictions. The transition from boy to man could not be delayed. The signaling experience of impending disaster occurred the summer between his junior and senior year when one of his lifelong friends married. Cal was in the bridal party, and, as he stood beside his friend, he felt a feeling of faintness come over him, and had the thought, "It's all coming to an end right here." This was the clue to what he could not tolerate—the transition into manhood which meant he would have to be responsible for himself, for his pleasure, for his aggression, and could no longer be diffused within the team. He had to stand alone.

Cal played games to perfection: he had skill, sportsmanship, and color. But to him it was really not a game; but all there was. It was not a preparation for his future life, but life itself. Without school sports, life had no meaning. Therein lay the flaw in his character and one of the neurotic problems common in sports.

It was only over the course of his next year in therapy that the deeper meanings of the story behind this cloak of emptiness began to unfold and become understandable. "Cool Cal" was the prototype of the American ideal, a fine athlete who carried sportsmanship and team spirit to an extreme. He was, in short, a boy who played the game too well.

The conflicts which lay behind this all-American boy with the blank past and the void future were anticipated by three dreams. He told the first of these dreams in one of the earliest therapeutic interviews, for it was a vivid dream and he had had it many times. He dreamed that a vicious gray wolf was chasing him; terrified, he ran and ran and ran. With the wolf nipping at him, he had to run faster and faster, but nowhere could he escape his pursuer.* His only hope was to run ever faster. Before a conclusion was ever reached he would awaken, frightened and perspiring. This first dream suggested something of the function of his athletic activity and how Cal, when his breakdown began, hoped that working out and flight might lead to a solution.

The second dream, reported a few weeks later, was described as being like "High Noon," the Western movie in

---

* The wolf has an honored place in writings on dreams. One of the classic cases in psychiatric literature is Freud's "Wolfman," so named because of the patient's dream about wolves.

which a law officer, amid great tension, awaits the return
of vengeful outlaws on the noon train. In the dream, he
and four of his buddies were waiting expectantly in the
upper story of a barn to "gun it out" with an attack which
was expected at four o'clock. He felt confident, but as the
hour approached he became fearful. The tension mounted
until just before four o'clock, when he awakened from the
dream. His gang was clearly the basketball team; four o'clock
was the fourth year of college, his senior year. With the
team he felt potent and confident, but as the fateful hour
approached, his fright grew.

In this dream the frightening object is unknown;
in the first dream it was the wolf. The third dream screamed
the name of the subject he held in terror. In addition to
the content it revealed, the dream shrouded his primitive
fears so poorly that it demonstrated the extreme fragility
of his personality structure and its tenuous protective defenses. It, too, was a dream of flight. He was driving his
car and his father was sitting with him. "I was driving like
hell and had it down to the floorboard, but I was scared
and no matter how fast I drove, I couldn't get away. My
mother, stark naked, was chasing me and she was almost
catching me."*

Cal was an only child. His parents were in their
late thirties when they married and it was almost ten years
later before they had their son. It came as something of a
surprise to them when his mother became pregnant, because both parents had given up their hope for an heir. His
mother, with very little formal education, was a self-taught
bookkeeper, very efficient and proud of her ability. She
was reluctant to give up her job even though she was quite
uncomfortable during the pregnancy. In addition, she was
plagued by the obsessive concern that the child might be
defective. As the time of delivery drew near, her tension

---

* The terror in dreams often represents a twisted wish, here suggesting
the incestuous nature of the problem. This also raises a question about
the seemingly warm relationship of father and son who might be expected to be rivals.

increased. Her labor was difficult, but a healthy child was delivered. From the first, however, his mother would not hold him, for she said she was afraid that she might drop him. She was also too nervous to breast feed him. It is not surprising that as an infant he was fretful and colicky. The mother's tension mounted and her usual control threatened to break down. She was able to regain her composure by returning to work only a few months after the birth of the child.

Although there were relatives and housekeepers, Cal's father willingly took over much of his care. He had worked as a civil servant in the Post Office Department for nearly twenty years and the only promise his job held for him was its potential for retirement. He was disgruntled and often berated himself for not having found a more satisfying occupation. He felt trapped between the job he despised, and a wife with whom he could not cope.

He had found one avenue of escape which was acceptable to both his wife and the community where they lived. He was a sports fan, rarely missing any local sports events, and often travelling to nearby cities to see them. Sports were his main source of satisfaction, and they re-called to him the pleasant days of his own modest athletic career.

In addition to providing his newborn son with some of the routine care babies need, Cal's father was able to combine this with his own pleasure. When Cal was still an infant, he would wrap him in swaddling clothes, take along some baby bottles, and head for the nearest sports event. At home, he held his son in his arms while listening to sports events on the radio. Thus, the father provided many of the traditional mothering functions of feeding and cuddling against the background of an ever present athletic contest. The sounds of sports were soon associated with warmth, tenderness, and comfort, calming the infant.

One area in which Cal's father had no part was controlling his growing son. The mother, an orderly neat woman who "couldn't stand a mess," willingly assumed the responsibility for training functions. Here she was confident, where she had been uncertain and fearful in feeding and holding young Cal. Her strong discipline, however, resulted in the child's sucking and biting objects, even including his crib sidings and clothing. She found this behavior particularly offensive and became even more harsh to the boy.

Her fears that something would happen to him were almost realized when Cal began to walk. One day when she crossed the street to mail a letter, he followed and was almost struck by a car. The mother's fright was quickly mobilized into action as she placed unreasonable controls on him. Cal was literally kept indoors for much of his early life except when he could be accompanied by an adult. He was sickly, and coupled with his mother's intense concern for his safety, he developed into a shy and inhibited child. He spent his time sitting immobilized lest he displease his apprehensive mother, and his movements became awkward, clumsy, and indecisive.

The redeeming factor in Cal's life was his relative freedom in sports. Sports were his father's realm, and by unspoken agreement, his father had complete autonomy here. His mother's concern about safety was peculiarly isolated to exclude sports. Although her obsessive concern for his safety kept him from ever having a bicycle, from the time he started school he was allowed almost complete freedom when playing sports or games. More important even than the excursions Cal took with his father to sporting events, was his freedom to express otherwise constricted physical desires when in his father's company.

At first Cal was awkward and inept as he attempted to learn the intricacies of athletics, but his tentative attempts at playing became gradually freer. He found that it was safe to participate in sports and also that they lacked parental prohibitions. He received approval and encouragement while his father spent long hours patiently instructing him in the proper way to throw a ball or hold a bat. His cautious experimentation grew into exuberant skill, and as his ability and confidence grew, his absorption in sports was nearly complete. Thus the stage was set for the surprising disintegration of a promising life.

Riesman* has described the growth in the number of "other-directed" middle-class people who are guided more by peer groups, associates of the same age and social class, than by desires for achievement, by family, or by traditions. The pressures of these groups are reinforced by television, comics, and other mass media, and by parents whose dearest hopes for their children are for them to be popular.

The disorder which tends to affect such people is role diffusion, for their roles are defined by the group, without whose support they suffer a loss of identity. Erikson† has described as the nuclear problem of adolescence the dilemma between identity and role diffusion. Adolescents characteristically cling together in gangs for identity support, but the difficulty grows if in adult life one relies on the group for role definition and identity. The group cannot always supply this support, and, further, it does not always believe its definitions. If a person relies completely on signals from others for his direction, he is vulnerable if he receives conflicting signals or if he is directed towards a goal which has dangerous personal significance.

For Cal, graduation meant individuation, that is, becoming a unique person responsible for his own pleasures and choices. It meant alienation from his primary nurturing, the team. Seeing his "buddy" make the fateful choice of marriage was the beginning of the end. "Feeding off" was one way of trying to secure "feed back," to insure his place within the team.

His desperate clinging to peer relationships was necessary because of the frustrating failures in infancy and childhood to develop trust, autonomy, and initiative. The

* David Reisman, *The Lonely Crowd,* (abridged edition) D. Riesman, N. Glazer, and R. Denney (Garden City, N. Y.: Doubleday & Company, Inc., 1953), p. 37.

† Erik Erikson, *Childhood and Society* (New York: W. W. Norton & Company, Inc., 1950) p. 307.

major consistent thread of security in his growth and development occurred within the context of team sports: being fed and held by his father at games, and the liberty he was allowed in sports by his mother, and ultimately his identity with the team.

The dynamic forces of his development fitted almost too perfectly into the culture of his peers. He was wafted into a remarkably successful, if temporary, school career. He seemed to accept quite literally the only half-believed expectations of his peers. He was a cartoon caricature of the collegian in appearance, athletic ability, sportsmanship, even sexually.

His success is both tribute and indictment of the institutions which supported him, for while they did not serve him permanently, they did offer something in place of nothing. The tragedy was that the pressure toward sports was so powerful that they replaced all other possibilities.

If Cal had had a modicum of success at other stages of development his regression would not have been so devastating. As it was, he had little in the way of alternative personality skills to employ, even temporarily. The fact that he had no alternatives distinguishes Cal from so many other American boys. His case highlights the problem of giving up some of the satisfactions derived from sports for other opportunities for satisfaction. This is a problem experienced by a great number of youths. It thus serves less to set Cal apart from his peers than to emphasize his similarity to the group.

A FOLLOW-UP NOTE

The person whose pleasures come mainly from action often finds words a weak substitute. Such action-oriented people may initially find psychotherapy of dubious value, since it relies heavily on verbal communication. When a psychological disorder hits a man of this type, he finds himself in a serious dilemma, for although action has failed him, it was also his principal source of gratification. Talking, directed toward the goal of understanding and opening a wider choice of action, is not only alien for such people, but is a threat to their principal protective system. Their past strength came from the instant response of action, and the therapist who asks for thought before action may be striking at the patient's deepest-held fear.

If someone is action-oriented it does not necessarily mean he is impulsive and unable to delay action successfully. The healthy person uses thought or speech as preparation for action and they serve him well when his usual behavior has failed him. His action is deliberate and is directed toward the goal of choice.

Cal learned early in life to distrust words as idle, ineffective chatter. The joint interview with his parents bore witness to how this was learned, for each parent ignored the words of the other. In his experience only action had meaning. When he was unable to cope with a situation, his only quest for solution was physical—through "working out." When this failed, he was certain that his disability was physical.

By the time Cal entered the hospital he had had an unrewarding experience with psychotherapy, equally unsuccessful drug treatment, and electrotherapy. The challenge in treating him was to overcome his mistrust by choosing areas of therapy in which he had strength which would not also threaten his shaky defenses. In talking about sports, he felt on reasonably safe ground, so this became the focus of individual interviews. Often these meetings took the form of discussions of a recent football or baseball game. Superficially this might seem far removed from his problems, but in such discussions the important elements of his difficulties were present—the team, isolation or membership, winning or losing, the coach—all of which symbolized the important issues in his life.

In addition, in his ward treatment community Cal was able to re-establish relationships with a group similar to the team. He received support from his new "teammates" in facing his problems squarely. As could be expected, he was a good "team member." In his job assignment in the hospital recreation department he was able to develop work skills and to face the emptiness he anticipated in work.

After several months he returned to college, graduated successfully, and is now teaching in a junior high school with most of his assignments in physical education. When last seen, his hope was to move into high school physical education and coaching.

When Cal went back to college, plans were made to continue therapy there. However, he failed to follow through, still dubious about the value of talking. I have seen him periodically, usually at my invitation, and although he seems grateful for these occasional visits, he has shown no desire for more intensive therapy.

Although his work performance is reported excellent, he still feels his life is not meaningful. He is keenly aware of his isolation from his buddies, all of whom have married. He dates occasionally but never seriously. Looking back upon his illness he sees it as a "bad dream," and still wishes it had been physical. Nothing in his present life has been able to compare in appeal with his college playing days, so nostalgically recalled.

4 FOOTBALL PLAYER

ROCK'M, SOCK'M JACK

I can't say I had ever had a conversation with Jack, yet I felt I knew him well—in the way one knows an athletic hero. We both attended the same college, and bits of information proclaiming his football abilities would pass along the student grapevine until his comings and goings were as familiar to me as those of a roommate. Such a relationship between students and football star is a strange one. Students greeted him and he returned the greetings perfunctorily; much was known about him yet he knew nothing of his greeters.

I felt a strong kinship with Jack. Even though the college was large, and our sports interests were different, in the gymnasium we shared a fraternal spirit. We spoke little to each other yet each knew who the other was. Our relationship was not personal and did not continue beyond the gymnasium. Thus when his wife (whom I had never seen) called me many years after college, I found it hard to place her. She explained that her husband had been seriously depressed and, too depressed to call himself, had asked her to call me for an appointment. When she said Jack remembered me from "better days," a flood of thoughts rushed to my mind. What did she mean? Whose "better days" was she talking about? Did Jack know I was physically handicapped and in a wheel chair?

Then I began to remember Jack from college. He

had been known as "Rock'm, Sock'm Jack," probably the most spectacular blocking back in the school's history. I could see him making one of his patented leaping moves, which took out two or three key men with a single block. (He was more exciting to watch than the ball carrier.) He was also the defensive spark plug, moving up and down the line, encouraging our boys with words and slaps. He seemed as wide as he was tall, burly and rough on the field, but surprisingly youthful in street clothes.

The anticipation of seeing him filled me with a mixture of feelings—he reminded me of pleasant college days and of the admiration I had had for his athletic ability; I was curious and concerned that someone who seemed an invulnerable specimen could become so depressed.

As he was led into my office by his wife I immediately sensed my professional role. This was not a college reunion but a serious clinical situation. I did not see the "Rock'm, Sock'm Jack" I remembered. Rather, a drawn, thin man led by his wife moved slowly into my office. His short stature was apparent, not his strength. Although the day was hot he was bundled up in a sweater with the collar turned up, and looked as if he were preparing for a freeze. He stared blankly at me for a moment, stood motionless, then forced a weak smile and began to cry softly and tearlessly. The only audible sound was an occasional whimper.

I began to see Jack regularly and his history unfolded slowly. Since college he had played pro football for one short season. He hadn't done well; in a game of giants his short stature and relatively small size had been too much of a handicap. He had a series of minor injuries and his professional career ended. Returning home, he went to work in his father's automobile parts store. Although a failure in pro football he was still a hero to his home town, acclaimed one of the best athletes they had ever produced. Old friendships were renewed and he basked in the recognition of the townspeople. He joined the Chamber of Commerce, the Elks, and led the boosters of the high school

football team. Informally, he helped coach the team, working especially with the blocking backs and the linebackers—
his old positions. He felt like "one of the boys" and they
accepted him as one, calling him by his first name.

The one dark spot in his life was his job—he hated
the work. It was sheer drudgery trying to sell things to
people, and still worse organizing automobile parts. He felt
life would be horrible if work were the only thing to look
forward to. The only saving factor of the job was his enjoyment in talking to the workmen and customers. Otherwise
he performed his job in a perfunctory and listless manner.
As could be expected, tension developed with his father-
employer. His father accused him of being a "playboy,"
but was certain he would grow out of it in a short time.

Jack was one of the town's most eligible bachelors
and made the most of it. His sexual exploits were fabled,
and sometimes bordered on the heroic, with two consecutive dates in one evening. After a couple of years he began
dating one girl steadily. Although he had his pick of the
town's lovelies, he did not choose a pretty girl but, as he
said, "one who wanted me more than any other girl did."
She was always waiting for him, never disagreed with him,
never seemed too upset if he was inattentive. He felt sure
he could trust her. He did not know who proposed to
whom, but, at any rate, they were married in one of the
drunkest, wildest, and most celebrated local events of the
year. Jack, the football hero, was married.

Jack's life continued very much as it had when
he was single. He spent nights out with the boys, went
to poker parties, participated in alumni groups and other
clubs. He found to his pleasure that his popularity was
even more enhanced by his marital state and his faithful
companion. The wild sexual orgies of bachelorhood had
become a strain for him and he was now quite happy to
confine his sexual activities to his wife while still enjoying
the companionship of his friends.

Toward the end of the second year of their marriage, Jack's wife announced there would be an heir to the

family. Jack was wild with joy, let out a whoop which was to lead to a three-day celebration, with mountains of cigars and cases of liquor. He had great, even grandiose plans for his child, whom he saw as a continuation of the family football dynasty.

This was a momentous event for Jack's father, too. He hoped that prospective fatherhood would stimulate the maturity he anticipated in his son. He recognized his own advancing age and looked forward to retirement. The plan which he then initiated was to have far-reaching consequences for his son. Jack was gradually given more and more responsibility in the business, with the idea of his taking it over. This seemed appropriate to Jack and he tried to work hard at fulfilling his job. However, the sense of emptiness within him grew in proportion to his increasing responsibilities. He was now haunted by a repetitive thought that there was "nothing to look forward to but a life of work."

This was an idea he dared not share with anyone. He was able to go through the motions of work with reasonable success, so no one knew of his torment. The once-spontaneous smile was now a forced part of his facade. Jack puzzled about many things. He had once reveled in the adulation and praise he received, but now praise about his work seemed hollow and meaningless, giving him no satisfaction. But to the town and to his family, Jack was progressing as they had expected and everyone was pleased.

When first married, Jack and his wife had moved into his family's home. This seemed a practical idea since all the children were married and the big, old family house was nearly empty. He had been away from home a long time and felt somewhat excited about returning. He was a little surprised at the intensity with which he found himself insisting it was the right thing to do, but once they were settled, the tension seemed to leave. His wife, as always, was agreeable, since this was how Jack wanted it. Sometimes he thought to himself, secretly of course, "This is the life. I have both my mother and my wife." His mother hovered over him, as she had always done before, and continued to be solicitous.

Jack's wife also cherished some private thoughts. She had agreed to this arrangement only because she had wanted to please him. But tension developed between her and Jack's mother since she could not appreciate the mother's ways. Try as she would, her anger increased. With the coming of the baby she talked seriously with Jack about getting a house of their own. Actually, Jack had also thought of their moving out, for he was becoming sensitive to some of the remarks his friends were making. Still, he could not avoid the desperate feeling he sometimes had of wanting to stay at home with his parents. Although he did agree to look for a new house, it was without enthusiasm. Eventually they were able to find their own home in one of the new, upper middle-class areas of town. To Jack, however, it never seemed like home.

With this move, Jack seemed to change. His wife sensed something was wrong. When they were alone, he pouted when he didn't get his way. More disconcerting, his wild enthusiasm for the baby had now turned to disinterest. With the couple's increased responsibilities, his wife expected more from him. She hoped he would do little things around the house and was worried and annoyed that he seemed to resent this. They had harsh words about it.

Jack, too, was self-critical. He was angry at himself for his lack of interest in the home and in his coming heir. When he felt tense or low he would return home to "visit the folks." This generally helped him feel better.

Although both Jack and his wife saw the changes that were taking place, they entered into an unspoken pact to say nothing about it. This did not smother the irritation, however. Although she regretted it many times afterward, she found herself yelling, "What did I marry, a man or a little boy?"

Her remark struck a vulnerable spot in Jack because it expressed his own unspoken concern. He repeatedly told himself to "act like a man," but the more he tried, the worse things became. His few remaining pleasures began to slip away. In his weekly poker parties with the boys, he had always been a fierce competitor and hated to lose. Now he found himself uneasy if he won a big pot. He didn't want to be ahead, and was comfortable only when he just broke even. All joy was taken out of playing, but he still went through the motions. Only his wife knew of his inner anguish.

When his wife went to the hospital to have the baby, Jack was very tense, but was reassured by his friends who told him all expectant fathers worried. He sat out the waiting time with two old high school football teammates and actually began to feel pretty good while waiting, talking over old times with them. When the news came that he was the father of a fine baby boy, he was numb. After whoops of joy one of his friends went to the phone and called Jack's father, giving Jack the phone to make the announcement. In a stunned voice he said, "Dad, we have a little boy." As he listened to himself his voice sounded very distant and strange. The voice on the other end of the line cheered loudly and in his dazed state, he had to hold the receiver away from his ear.

His father's mood changed and the voice at the other end become solemn. He announced the decision he had made several months ago. "Son, I've been waiting for this moment to tell you. I'm going to retire. I'm stepping down in the business. You're in charge now, my boy. It's all yours." Jack didn't comprehend. It all seemed strange, as though it couldn't be happening to him. He held the telephone receiver for a moment that seemed interminable. Finally, he turned mechanically, abruptly said, "Thanks," and hung up.

His two companions became concerned about Jack's strange behavior and the expression of bewilderment on his face. They watched him carefully; then, not knowing what else to do, they shouted more congratulations, and pounded each other on the back, shouting, "Oh, we'll really

tie one on tonight! How about that, Jack, old boy!" But
Jack hardly heard them.

Over the next few weeks Jack's feeling of being
stunned and distant deepened to sadness. His stomach hurt,
he was concerned about his bowel movements, he had
trouble sleeping, and he would awaken very early. He
didn't hear what people were saying to him because he
had become preoccupied with himself. He hated to go to
work, and when he was there his depression was occasionally punctuated by periods of irritability. He was edgy
and kept noticing the astonished looks on people's faces
when he would suddenly burst out with an angry remark.
He couldn't concentrate, he felt as though he had to get
away, but his usual haunts, certain favored bars and clubs,
didn't make him feel any better. The poker parties were
empty, his friends were distant, and even football held no
interest for him. Visiting his mother didn't make him feel
better. He seemed to lose interest in everything, felt use-
less, and castigated himself, saying, "I'm not much of a
man. I wish I were half the man my father is."

Even worse, he was tortured with recurrent and
terrible thoughts about his new child. He would lean over
the crib to look at him and view that innocent face, when
suddenly a picture would flash into his mind of throwing
the child against the fireplace or strangling him. He had the
same kind of thoughts about his wife. When he saw her in
bed or caring for the baby, he would say to himself,
"Don't kill her, don't!" He began to think she was suspicious
of him and that she knew his thoughts. He resented her
attention to his son, was irritated if she slept late, angered
if his meals were delayed or if things weren't exactly in
order when he got home. He hated himself for such ideas.
They seemed completely alien to his image of himself.

His depression deepened. He tried to find solace
by reading his long set-aside Bible. He began attending
church again but found little comfort. In fact, he believed
himself so unworthy he could not continue this and rejected
the pastor's offers of help. It was his family physician who

suggested a psychiatric consultation. Of the names suggested, he seized upon mine, since it triggered some vague, nostalgic "last hope" of someone who would understand his ordeal, having suffered a similar one.

On his first visit, when Jack saw me in the wheelchair he could see that we both had had a similar abrupt halt to our sports participation. It was easy for him to understand the cause of mine with paralysis, but what had been the cause of his experience was beyond his comprehension. My paralysis was a physical expression, an understandable counterpart to his psychological conflict. I had clarity of reasoning and a paralyzed body while he had a paralyzed mind and a strong body.

He asked me over and over how I managed to come to terms with a life devoid of old, meaningful activities. While I tried to keep the focus on his dilemma, I was keenly aware of my own, and our working alliance truly become one of mutual exploration. Jack asked me questions which I had not dared ask myself and touched certain unhealed wounds I had superficially solved. Indeed, how had I managed my own sudden transition from an active physical life to an enforced sedentary one?

I worked with Jack early in my career as a psychotherapist when I believed, as I had been taught, in the importance of the therapist's anonymity to his patient. The therapist should be a blank screen on which conflicts could be projected and objectively examined. But there could be no such anonymity here. He could see that we were both involved in a situation which touched our individual lives deeply. How absurd to use the popular technique of reflecting questions when our encounter had such evident importance in my life as well as his!

I summarized the major events in Jack's life which had precipitated his agony and depression: marriage, the birth of a son, and success in business. His emotional paralysis occurred in the wake of events expected to bring only joy to a man's life. But in the context of his life it meant something quite different: severe depression, thoughts of self-destruction, and frightening homicidal wishes toward those he loved most. This was the beginning of that process of psychotherapy which is filled with vicissitudes and agony, but also with the gratifications of growth.

Certain traditions in Jack's family played a vital role in the formation of his personality as well as the other siblings'. He was the youngest child, with older brothers and one older sister. His brothers, being quite a few years older than he, had clearly set the pace for him. They had been fine football players and had played blocking back as Jack had. They had also attended the same high school and college. Jack did not depart from the path well-worn by his brothers until after college. They had not returned to the family home after college but had moved to other states, were apparently happy, economically successful, and devoted to their families.

Jack's sister, on the other hand, was two years older than he and lived near the family home with her recently acquired husband. As Jack saw it, the family had always been divided into two smaller family groups, each separate. His two older brothers and the father represented one family unit, while the other consisted of himself and his sister with the mother.

While the adults were technically the same in both families, their roles were not. Some differences were subtle, some were not. During the twenties Jack's father had become a very successful business man and had amassed a considerable fortune. He was a dynamic community leader and a patronizing patriarch at home. When the prosperity of the twenties was followed by the depression of the thirties the family fortune was lost, leaving him a broken man. He was shattered and helpless, and for over a year he sat at home just shaking his head in disbelief. Jack's mother moved in to fill the vacuum. She had been a flighty socialite before but now had to assume the responsibility abdicated by her husband. During the darkest period she took in washing to support the family and occasionally worked outside the home during the day.

It was only in recent years that Jack's father had partially regained his former business position. The older boys had grown up under the tutelage of the dynamic, confident, and prosperous father. Jack, who was only two at the time of the financial losses, knew only the indecisive, doubting father who relied completely on the mother. Thus, the two family groups differed in leadership; the older was his father's family and the younger was his mother's.

There appeared to be an unspoken agreement between the parents about this. Jack recalled vividly that when, for example, the family went to an amusement park, he and his sister had to stay with their mother and watch while the older boys and his father went on "dangerous" rides like the roller coaster, the ferris wheel and the whip. To Jack, the older boys and his father were adventurous, with a devil-may-care attitude, but his mother was the hovering, ever-present, worrisome, fretful, concerned woman.

Jack's father was a great sports fan and as a former player, football was his favorite game. He was proud of his boys when they played, and he never missed a game. He had shown the older boys all he could about the fundamentals of the game and had offered steady encouragement to them. When Jack was old enough to begin to play, his father was still suffering disillusionment and so could offer Jack little support. Jack missed this acutely, for he longed for the day when he would be close to his father. His desire to emulate his older brothers was intense since he hoped in this way to win his father's interest. He tried to tag along with the brothers when he could. Although they were rough and sometimes teased him, on other occasions they did encourage him and taught him some fundamentals of the game. This never sufficed, however, to take the place of the father's attention he missed.

Jack's mother never attended an athletic event, for she was afraid the boys would be hurt in football. Although in the family tradition she had to "steel herself" at home while the men were away in danger, she succeeded in

making her suffering clear to all concerned. She was fearful and trembling whenever a game was played, always
anticipating the worst. When one of the boys did have an
injury, minor though it was, she hovered over him and ex-
aggerated its seriousness. Jack clearly recalled the feelings
he had when he was too young to watch his brothers play
football. He had had to stay home and watch his mother
wait and worry. It seemed an injustice that she should suffer
so much while they played.

     As an infant Jack was less robust than his brothers.
He had suffered from severe, recurrent, respiratory ailments,
sometimes hovering on the brink of death. His mother was
very apprehensive that pneumonic disease would some day
take her youngest son. As a result, she always bundled him
up in heavy coats and sweaters to make certain he would
not get a chill. He never left the house without a final
check and approval from her that what he wore was warm
enough. To sneak out without approval usually ended in
his mother's creating an anxious, hand-wringing scene.

     In a way, the crumbling family fortunes had set
the stage for such overconcern, for the loss of plenitude
once held is more devastating than consistent need. Jack's
early feeding experiences were a focus for the family economic struggles. His mother believed she could demonstrate
that they still had plenty by stuffing him just beyond his
capacity. In those depression years the world was a capricious and unfriendly place. Jack's mother wanted to protect her youngest son against its dangers in every way she
could. In her daily warnings to Jack she also tried to make
it clear that although the outside world was filled with
sources of illness, injury, starvation, and freezing, she would
always take care of him. She hoped this would offer him
the sense of security she did not feel herself.

     As he grew older, Jack took over the responsibility
for worrying about his personal safety. He would engage
in a personal dialogue before he went out, asking his own
questions about whether his clothes were warm enough
and whether he had eaten enough. He never liked to cause

his mother undue worry and did his best to heed her warnings about being careful. He knew it would cause her great pain if he were hurt or sick, and it bothered him even more to think how she would care for him tenderly despite her own hurt, if something were to happen to him. Yet this also created a vague appeal for being sick or weak, for it meant his mother would be extrasolicitous.

Jack's fear of, and wish for, injury and weakness created some problems. This tenuous balance was sometimes tipped in one direction or the other. On occasion his fear of injury or illness became the self-fulfilling prophecy of disaster.

In order to fulfill the male expectations in his family, he also had to be a rugged boy. He found he was aggressive and in frequent fights with neighborhood boys. The fights and his occasional injuries became his personal compromise between the two families, representing the pleasures of infancy with his mother and the desire to emulate his older brothers and his father. The sense of being drawn toward both weakness and strength left Jack with a feeling of cleavage in his personality.

Another event gave heightened significance and perhaps more fundamental meaning to Jack's dilemma. His parents were devoutly Catholic and when they determined it would be unwise to have any more children, they agreed to sleep in separate rooms to avoid temptation. Jack's father moved in with the older boys and Jack joined his mother in what had been his parents' room. While sleeping with his mother was the realization of fond hopes, it also filled him with apprehension for he knew he was depriving his father of a valued position. An angry look from his father would freeze him in panic. Although in later years he was to find ways of partially mastering this situation, he always carried a residue of terror and guilt from these events. They set the stage for the tragedy which was to befall Jack as an adult.

One way Jack dealt with having replaced his father

was taking on his father's characteristics—identification—
most obviously by emulating his father's fervor for sports.
Discussions at home centered around football, with the
dinner table often becoming the setting for spirited and
sometimes heated conversations about the relative merits
of teams and players. The living room often served as a
simulated practice field for check blocking and play learning. Jack, his father, and his brothers thus shared this overriding family interest. His mother, though, remained a direct
descendant of the long-suffering women of the world who
fearfully, but pridefully, watched their men go into battle.

It was predestined that Jack would be a football
player and that he would be a blocking back. In this family
this was as much a part of being a male member of the
clan as wearing trousers. Nothing was more important to
the family than his learning football skills. His developmental years became an apprenticeship, his progress in
school measured not by grades or courses completed, but by
the success of the team on which he played. Ordinary events
were relative to the fall football season, spring training, or
the dormant time in between. By the time he reached junior
high school he had mastered many of the game's fundamentals, and was an outstanding player. He progressed
through D, C, B classifications and finally to varsity football. After high school came college and then professional
football.

Jack's attitude toward studies mirrored that of his
brothers. It was necessary to keep a certain scholastic
average to participate in the real business of school, which
was athletics. He was bright enough to keep his grades
passing and to keep himself from becoming too emotionally
involved in his school work. His school performance was
further enhanced by the quiet respect he always showed
to adults. He was not, as so many of his teammates were,
rowdy and discourteous in class. His compliance elevated
his grades so he slid through school without involvement
and it took only a spurt of study in his senior year to get

him into college. He was always well liked by his school-mates and regarded with the respect accorded an all-league star and team captain.

Jack felt at ease in most situations, developed some lasting friendships, and was popular with his peers. However, he felt best on the football field. All else was subordinate to the physical contact he had there. Whether in practice or in a game he sensed a special kind of thrill in executing a perfect block, or hitting a ball carrier low and head-on. He had a feeling of almost orgiastic pleasure when he felt the solid crunch of leather against leather. He was dimly aware that he entered each play with a fear that he would be injured or with the peculiar certainty that this would happen. Then, when he survived, he felt the profound relief of a condemned man who had received a reprieve. To the fan in the stands he was the symbol of rock'm, sock'm football.

During the first few weeks of psychotherapy, Jack talked endlessly about his shortcomings and failures; each hour was filled with self-castigation. He re-evaluated his entire life, making it an object for self-criticism, distorting pleasures and successes so that they would reflect badly on him. Obscure motivations which formed only a minor part of his whole life loomed large and sinister to him. He called himself weak and cowardly, remembering his fear of being hurt while playing football. When reminded of his aggressive play despite his fear, he concluded that he had blocked and tackled hard just because he wanted to hurt the players on the other team. He condemned himself as unprincipled, sadistic, selfish, perverse, and without virtue.

What affected him most deeply were his thoughts of hurting his wife and child. This seemed to be the most dramatic demonstration of his basic evilness. "I'm no man, I'm like a monster. What kind of an animal would want to harm his own family?" He was preoccupied with his failure and that he couldn't take responsibility. He pleaded to be "put away forever" so he could never harm anyone and would not be a burden to his family. He said that if he really had any "guts" he would have done away with himself long ago.

In a profound depressive reaction like Jack's, life memories are sorted out anew with those conforming to an inner sense of evil and worthlessness remembered, while those of any positive value are discarded. While the emphasis is unrealistic, it does reveal some of the ordinarily unspoken or hidden feelings. Although these retrospective accounts are usually unreliable when compared with objectively derived information, they nevertheless reveal ideas and feelings of the utmost importance to the individual. They are the unintegrated troublesome fragments of the personality.

For our understanding of this case it will be of value to synthesize some of its elements. Marriage, involving fatherhood and taking over his father's business, reactivated a whole group of unfinished conflicts in Jack's life. Maturation should naturally have carried him toward independence, success, and self-reliance, but when Jack tasted these he was terrified. This was merely a recapitulation of replacing his father in the parental bedroom, and of feeling that his father was beaten and weak as a result of him, Jack, rather than the reality of financial reversals in the great economic depression. As a child he could turn to his mother for protection from his fears, but as an adult he could not.

His memories focused now on actions he interpreted as homosexual (despite the fact that he had never had any homosexual relations), instead of those as a man, a father, and a husband. This selective remembering served a dual function, the more obvious being to confirm his sense of badness. The second function was to defend himself against the responsibility of displacing his father. If he were to see himself as a homosexual, he could avoid seeing himself as a competitor to his father, the man.

I began my work with Jack over a decade ago. Since then many changes have occurred in American psychiatry, and my own orientation has also become somewhat different. There are now available a group of drugs which are helpful in depressions and contribute to a more rapid recovery. Although electrotherapy was already a serious consideration when I first treated Jack, it was not utilized because of family objections. The most important change, perhaps, would come in my approach to psychotherapy. Today I would be much more active, focusing on the interchanges of the moment between therapist and patient. Thus, although this description of Jack's therapy is faithfully reported from my notes, it is somewhat anachronistic in relation to my present approach to therapy. My interest at the time does provide this specialized information which is useful in understanding the psychodynamics of sports.

Jack gradually developed more trust in me as we met and he dared to talk about things he had shamefully hidden before. His depressive symptoms gradually decreased and his mood slowly began to elevate. One of his fears had been that telling me about his terrible thoughts and evil intentions would have a contagious effect and they would hurt me or make me "sick." He was relieved when this did not happen and was pleased when I understood what was troubling him. Later, however, this praise for my objectivity was to turn to criticism: I was not sufficiently sympathetic and compassionate. At first he saw me as warm and understanding and his family as disinterested; then I changed in his eyes and seemed cold, while he portrayed his family as helpful.

As the depression lifted and he talked more freely, his self-castigation began to be directed outward. His father was the first main target for his anger. Jack criticized him for being both threatening and weak. He said his father was cold, callous, and unconcerned. "He never really gave a damn about me." He revealed the strange belief that he had actually "killed" his father on the day of his own son's birth, when his father announced he was giving the family business to him. When he first experienced anger toward

his father he was stunned and there was a mild recurrence
of his depression. Then gradually he was able to appraise
his feelings more realistically. The shadows of his expectations and disappointments were projected on me and the
relationship between his attitudes toward me and his father
was slowly clarified. However, when he became more at
ease with this image of his father, his mother became the
recipient of his hatred. During the time in therapy, when
he hated his father, he saw his mother as faultless and
spoke of her in idealized terms. He eulogized that it was
only her love that had sustained him through the years,
and only his concern for her had kept him from committing
suicide in his darkest moments. Closeness to her, however,
contained elements of anger for her overprotection. He
gradually began to complain that her concern had kept him
infantilized and fearful. Her long-suffering fearfulness had
caused him to feel guilty for any slight discomfort he may
have caused her. He moaned that she wanted him to feel
guilty, because that was her way of tying him to her.
"That suffering business, that's a way of controlling me."
He recalled that her constant concern for his eating habits,
his bowel movements, and his need for warmth had scared
him. There seemed to be no middle ground. He either had
to completely give in to her and do as she thought best
or get away from her entirely. He said his brothers had
felt similarly bound to his mother and remembered his next
oldest brother saying he had left town to make a "clean
break"; if he had not he could never have had a life of
his own. For a long time Jack vacillated between extreme
opinions about his mother. On one hand she was a dominat-
ing ogre, while on the other she was the gentle, sweet,
devoted parent. Only very slowly was he able to see her
as she really was—a collection of mortal faults and virtues.

Since he was grown now with a family of his
own, his dependence upon his parents was emotional rather
than physical. This made them relatively safe objects to
be angry with and to examine. Their images could be de-

stroyed by his words with relative freedom since they were no longer the only persons in his life. Once destroyed, they could be reconstructed more realistically.

His resentment toward his wife, however, was more immediate and therefore more threatening. Anger toward his child seemed so reprehensible and irrational it was impossible to even talk about it. Any criticism of his wife or child was immediately followed by symptoms of guilt and depression. He was gradually able to understand that he had expected and demanded the same smothering relationship with his wife as he had with his mother. He feared this and yet was drawn to it, but his wife's failure to comply with his efforts and reconstruct the mother-son relationship with her led to his anger. When his own son was born, it became even more difficult to act as a child to his wife. These disappointments led to murderous thoughts of doing away with both of them.

Transference of attitudes and feelings for significant figures in the past to the therapist is vital for the progress of therapy. The therapist slowly clarifies the distorted impressions until the patient at last sees him realistically. Jack's transference of unrealistic attitudes to me was altered somewhat by the reality of my disability and my need for a wheelchair. This disability had helped in the formation of an early rapport, as he believed I could understand his problem better. I also appeared less threatening to him. Later, he was concerned about me because I seemed more vulnerable to attack. At first, Jack saw me as the understanding, all-giving, idealized recapitulation of his mother; at another stage I represented the cold and disinterested father whose favor he sought, but who had always been somewhat distant. Later still, he projected upon me the image of the "smothering" parent who prohibited him from taking risks and from enjoying himself. During this period he saw me as restricting even his sexual pleasures, and as trying to make him feel guilty and indebted to me.

Therapy continued for almost two years, initially

in the hospital, thereafter on visits to my office. After several months, Jack was able to return to work but this old problem of work became the central issue of his later therapy. With all his good intentions of returning to a responsible role as father and husband he continued to despise work. The best he could muster was, "This must be my cross to bear." He contrasted himself to his father, who had developed a successful business, while Jack was a freeloader without drive. During his hospitalization and subsequent therapy, his father had returned to head the family business. When Jack went back to work, he was again working for his father. Now, however, he began to recognize that it had only been in his declining years that his father had developed any satisfaction from his work. The fact that his father had experienced similar problems and had resolved them, was encouraging to Jack. Heretofore he had been unwilling to examine his father's work attitudes. A turning point came when his father, due to failing health, definitely decided that he had to step down from the business. If Jack could not take over, he would sell out. Jack decided he would like to take over the business, but on the same basis as anyone else. He drew up a contract with his father arranging to buy him out over a period of years, during which his father would step down gradually. The gradual changeover, its mutually agreeable businesslike nature, and the fact that Jack was in control of the transition, made it possible for him to complete the task. His therapy was complete when he was in full charge of his business. Work was never truly satisfying for him, but he was able to see himself as he was, disliking the routine managerial aspects of his work, but enjoying his contacts with people. His greatest satisfactions came from his family, lodge activities, and once again, poker parties.

Jack maintained a vital interest in sports, but with some significant modification. Formerly, football had been all-consuming in its importance. He had never missed a game, and, in a vain attempt to recapture his lost playing days, he had spent considerable time working out with the high school football team. Now, with the growth of his responsibilities at home and with the business there was a growing distance and objectivity toward football. He was still a student of the game and an active alumnus of his college, but other interests seemed to develop priority. Football and other sports became, appropriately, recreation and leisure rather than life's major activity.

I occasionally hear from Jack, usually at Christmastime. The last time I received a note from him, he had been asked to talk to the high school football team about "school spirit." His theme was to be, "Don't forget, boys, it's a great game, but it's only a preparation for living."

In each stage in each individual's life, different problems and satisfactions are available. If one is unwilling or unable to meet the challenges of a new stage he tries to make it into an old one that he formerly managed more adequately. Sometimes the new stage can be remolded in the image of the old, but often the people involved are unwilling to be molded, so the situation precludes too many changes. Then the individual begins to descend his personal developmental scale in a quest for peace, attempting to find some stage where he is comfortable. This was our football player's experience. Well adapted to playing football, he was unable to face the problems of middle adult life. He stood on the childhood side of a great gulf separating him from the satisfactions and responsibilities of parenthood and work. To bridge this he had to encounter an awesome but vulnerable father toward whom he held murderous wishes. At the same time, he felt pulled backward in time to being his mother's child again. His wife and baby were unsuitable and unwilling subjects to be made into the images of the past and, as interferers with his quest for comfort, he grew furious with them. Because it hardly seemed right to express his rage to them, he turned it on himself. Although his forward motion was temporarily suspended and he seemed to move backward in time, he had a strong need and desire to overcome his conflict. This desire was the motivating force making eventual progress possible. Bridging the gap between boyhood and manhood was finally accomplished by a controlled and mutually agreeable arrangement with his father. His goal, not unlike that of any young man, was to take over his father's business but before he made the step he carefully examined it with me, wanting to avoid any impulsive act.

During the course of his measured steps, he looked at the experiences leading to his present predicament, using the microscope of psychotherapy. This searching revealed much that was hidden. One contradiction of American life is that the only situation in the athletic stadium and gymnasium where overt expressions of physical affection between men are publicly tolerated, is the same one where the castigation of homosexuality would be greatest. When seminude men gather in a gym they desperately need to deny the positive feelings for one another and displace the restrictions of conscience to projected objects of scorn. Jack had experienced great sensual pleasure from hugging and being hugged by his teammates in the enthusiasm of victory. As a defensive linebacker he derived similar pleasures from patting them on their squatted buttocks and their backs. These pleasurable sensual feelings were acceptable within the framework of the game and to the thousands of spectators who watched him, but outside the sports arena with heightened needs for such pleasures, he critically and derisively re-evaluated his feelings. In the service of his depressive symptoms his actions became demonstrations of his perversity. He believed he must be "queer"—perhaps the most derogatory term among athletes.

Another significant pleasure came for Jack when he was playing, driving hard into an opponent while tackling or blocking. He then had intense feelings of satisfaction and a vague sensation that he had won; he felt strong for "taking his man out." In this situation alone he could engage in aggressive competition and remain free of guilt. It was actually a safe realization of his fearsome competition and murderous wishes toward his father and brothers. The adulation of the crowd encouraged him in his violent aggressiveness and helped absolve him of guilt. It was guilt which was to arise anew while working with his father, since in this situation his conscience could not be ignored. Not only did he fear his fantasies of doing away with his father, but he magically feared the expected retaliation. In his psychotic state when his father turned over the business to him he felt that his fantasy had been realized and that he had actually killed his father. The very psychological qualities which had made him a successful rock'm, sock'm football player spelled disaster when the rules of football became the rules of work and parenthood.

Jack had to be a football player to assume the expected role of the man in the eyes of his parents and siblings. So strong were these expectations that they even determined the position he was to play on the football team. However, he had no such clear guideline for his role as a father and a worker. There was a discrepancy between the words he had heard spoken about responsibility and success and the behavior he had seen in his models. He was confused by his father's impotence and withdrawal from financial reversals and his brothers' fleeing from home. His sexual identification with the masculine members of the family was weakened in his developmental years by the division of the family into two groups based on age: his sister and mother forming one unit, while the masculine unit was made up of his father and older brothers.

Jack eventually found a suitable identity of his own, which was not as stereotyped as the models he had to follow. His innate strength and purposefulness coupled with the psychotherapeutic experience allowed him to become nearly a whole person. He could meet the demands of his conscience and yet experience the satisfactions available. This was accomplished largely by being able to leave the past behind him.

5 GOLFER

A CASE OF STRENGTH THROUGH SPORTS

Jerry was a golfer, a very good one in fact. A young married man, 33 years old, he found himself in our clinic under the coercion of the probation department. His feelings about coming to the clinic were very mixed; he was angry with the police for forcing him to come, but yet sensed desperately that something had to be done. The relationship between his sport and coming to a clinic for psychiatric aid was not obvious at first, but the important function golf served in his life was to become apparent during his psychotherapy. This man was the patient of one of my psychiatric residents-in-training and although I never saw him personally I heard about the case regularly in my weekly supervisory sessions. The clarity and perceptiveness in the analysis of this case then are tributes to my colleague's astuteness.

Jerry's present predicament had a long background, starting on a rain-slicked, crowded freeway, driving home from work. He was in a hurry to get home so he drove fast even though he had a premonition that an accident might occur. And just that did happen; he saw a gasoline tanker swerve and overturn. Skillfully he moved into another lane to pass the truck safely, but just as he came abreast, it burst into flame, showering its fire across several lanes of traffic, including his lane and his car. His arms, face, and a good part of the rest of his body were severely burned before his clothing could be extinguished.

Hospitalization, which lasted almost three months, was a horrible experience for him. Movement was almost totally restricted and he was faced with the terrible threat of permanent scarring and disability. In this condition his tension rose to terrible proportions. Yet, in this situation as in all uncomfortable periods in his life, from marital discord to losing a sale in his work, he found comfort and consolation in thinking about golf. He engaged in meticulous fantasies of playing the various courses he knew, hole by hole. He would visualize himself standing on the tee, surveying the terrain, considering the distances and traps, weighing the advantages of various clubs, finally making the selection and then swinging. He felt the whole process and showed remarkable facility for visual recall of the courses he played. These were not idle fantasies, for at each hole he challenged himself to make the ideal play. Practicing and reviewing his plays served the same purpose as actually playing the course. This is how he dealt with unpleasantness.

When at last he was released from the hospital, he had almost completely recovered from his burns, but despite the reassurance by his doctors that he would completely recover without incapacity, he had doubts. He was certain his wrists would be too weak to play and he would be too frail to compete. Now that golf was actually available to him again, he was afraid to play. He could not turn into actuality the fantasies of practice which had sustained him through his difficult period of hospitalization. Eventually, the prospect of failure and of possible unpleasant consequences of playing were so frightening that his fantasies became blocked as well.

In the meantime, the family income had ceased due to his illness, and his wife was forced to work for the first time in their married life. She worked as a cocktail waitress in a local bar and restaurant, and made good money. Now that thoughts of golf were no longer satisfying and he strongly doubted his ability in anything, his disturbed thoughts became focused on his wife. He began to believe she was going out with the male employees at the bar and providing sexual favors for them and/or for the customers.

In attempting to deal with these thoughts he made renewed conscious efforts to play his golf courses in fantasy and to achieve some mastery over them. But he could never proceed very far because now there was the imminent reality that he would be put to the test. If he actually played again he might find out what he feared, that is, that he had lost his ability. Fantasies of golf became entirely replaced by fantasies of his wife's sexual promiscuity. He was consumed by these feelings and began following her to work to spy upon her. Doubts about his own sexual adequacy were now projected on her. He was sure she considered him weak, scarred, and damaged and so preferred other stronger men. He began to accuse her openly and they argued and bickered constantly. She reciprocated with retorts which hit his vulnerable spot, making implications about his worth. Eventually she could stand it no longer and suggested separation. This was only further evidence to Jerry that she did prefer other men. He was damaged. He was worthless. Again they quarreled and this time, in more positive tones, she spoke of divorce.

In his desperation he decided to commit suicide. Searching for a way, he found a bottle of sleeping pills and took all of them. His wife had been increasingly concerned about his behavior and unexpectedly returned home to discover him semiconscious. An ambulance was immediately called and he was taken to a hospital, where emergency measures saved his life. But now his weakened ego was further disturbed by the toxic drug effects and he became overtly psychotic, shouting, raving, alternately angry and fearful, and panic-stricken. "They" were trying to get him, to immobilize him and to put him at their mercy. "They" were his enemies; "they" were the Jews, the doctors, and the police. He was so wild and disturbed that physical restraints were used to try to quiet him. This did not work and he leaped from his bed, forcing aside the attendants, and clad only in his hospital night shirt, ran out of the hospital into the street. Frantically he began looking for his own car which, of course, was nowhere near. A crowd began to collect, adding to his panic. To him the people seemed like a lynch mob. As he passed a car he saw a gun lying on the back seat; he seized it and brandished it at the growing crowd; their laughter only served to infuriate him. It was many minutes before he realized that it was only a toy gun, and he threw it aside in disgust. The police had been called and now arrived on motorcycles. In his psychotic state he did not feel worthless, as before, but grandiose. He was certain he could outrun the motorcycles, but in case he could not, he formulated a weird plan: he would let a policeman grab him, then he would seize the man's gun and shoot him. A policeman soon caught up with him and started to grab him. He reached for the officer's gun but was quickly subdued. Wild with fury that he could not carry out his plan, he was taken to the psychiatric facility to be committed to a mental hospital. The effects of the sleeping pills he had taken diminished, and he rather quickly reconstituted after about three days. Seeming well enough to be released, he was allowed to return home.

At home relative calm prevailed for several weeks since he was still stunned by his experience. However, jealousy over his wife began to grow again, and the cycle of rage at her, her supposed lovers, and his own self-destruction resumed. He accused her of being a "whore" and they quarrelled violently. His jealousy reached a climax one evening when, with a couple of drinks, the last vestiges of his self-control were released. He dramatically announced to his wife, "You like Alfred Hitchock finishes, don't you? Well, I'll make a fascinating one for you!" He poured kerosene over himself, dowsing his clothing, then threatened to set fire to himself. His wife was able to get away to call the police, who soon arrived. Jerry's first sight of them filled him with uncontrollable rage. As he said later, "Cops always make me see red." He tried to attack them with a baseball bat, but again was quickly subdued and arrested. This time he was taken to jail where again he recovered quickly and was released on probation. A condition of his probation, wisely, was that he seek psychiatric assistance. And so he came to the clinic and my colleague began therapy with him.

Jerry was born in the Charlestown section adjacent to Boston, far away from California and even farther from a golf course. His particular neighborhood, a slum area, was known as the roughest in the city. Both of his parents were born in Ireland and had come to the United States as young adults, each having left home because of disagreements with parents. Immigration westward to what seemed like an adventurous frontier was merely the climax of years of opposition to and stubborn resistance against parental autocracy. When they first met, they felt a rapport of common experiences. But as is the case with those who bring unresolved problems into a marriage, who seek a partner who can supply understanding that will undo all the past wrongs, the old problems rose anew. The geographical distance between them and their families in Ireland was no barrier to their primary conflicts. They carried these conflicts with them like traditions, from the old world to the new. The question of who was in command became the subject of their own marital discord. In fact, Jerry's father became the very father he had tried to leave—the hardworking laborer who prided himself on his strength and honesty, whose hard labor was interrupted by church on Sunday and too much to drink several times a week. He was a shadowy figure to his children and after the day's work, took little part in the family activities. Similarly, his wife took on the characteristics of her mother. She was a formidable woman, a nagging shrew, and literally threw the father out of the house when he was drinking. The battle raged, with sufficient truces to conceive four children, of whom Jerry was the youngest. By the time Jerry was eight years old, his father had been thrown out of the house for the last time. His eviction, however, did not mean any improvement in the household or any greater tranquility for now the mother threatened the boys. Although their offenses varied, the threat was always the same, "I'll throw you out just like your father," or "I'll send you to an orphanage." To Jerry this was a fearful threat. He remembered sitting for hours at the window waiting for his mother to return from work, fearing she might not come back or might send him away.

With the father gone the oldest brother was in command in his mother's absence. He was known as the family sadist. One of his "games" was to whirl Jerry, then the most sensitive and vulnerable, around his head and then let him fly into the wall. He also insisted on Spartan-like behavior from his younger brothers, sometimes forcing them to sit for hours with heads bowed while the family pet, a parrot, dug its claws into their scalps. Despite this brutality Jerry recognized nothing but admiration for his brother. He talked of his great physique and strength, and was impressed by the fact that he had posed for pictures as Atlas holding up the world. An exceptional athlete, this brother had specialized in baseball. At home his directions were followed instantly. It is of no casual significance that this brother became a policeman. Only while Jerry was in his psychotic state could the rage and fright associated with his brother be overcome and expressed by displacement to any policemen around him. It was no meaningless statement when he said, "Cops make me see red."

Physical competition among the brothers was encouraged. They fought constantly, and when one was reluctant to fight he was provoked. Jerry was constantly teased, abused and "tortured" until he could stand it no longer and would break down and cry. When he cried he was further demeaned by being called girls' names and "sissy." He despised his weakness and identified himself, as best he could, with the aggressive role of his brothers, the role expected within the family.

He attended parochial school as was expected in his family, was compliant, and caused no trouble. In fact, he was a good student. When he was about 15 his behavior changed and he rebelled against the nuns who were his teachers. This rebellion reached such proportions that he was finally dismissed from school. His previous good record, however, allowed reinstatement, but shortly thereafter he lied about his age and joined the Navy. One driving force behind his enlistment was the idea that he was outdoing his brothers, especially the oldest one since none were yet in the service. After a few months, however, his age was discovered and he was discharged. In the meantime, his eldest brother had joined the paratroopers. Jerry was seized with a compelling desire to do the same, but eventually went into the Marine Corps, where he felt pride in being a member of that "tough" organization. He felt at home with the rough training, rigid standards, and firm discipline although the Marine Corps did stir up some of his sexual anxieties. He had a distinct fear of being approached by a homosexual, and carefully avoided any possibility of such contacts while in the Corps. Heterosexual activities out of wedlock were seriously frowned upon by the family, so he restricted himself to fantasies of glorious sexual victories. His many doubts about himself, however, led him into a moderately active series of unspectacular sex experiences, the principal feature of which was an intense desire to satisfy the girl.

The Marine Corps gave some direction to his life, but this disappeared after his discharge. His hatred of the authoritarianism of the Corps precluded his re-enlisting. In his aimlessness he often thought of finding his father, and eventually he did set out to do this. The compelling motivation to find him was a desire to prove his mother's accusations false and his father right. A long, tortuous search ensued which ended in momentary elation for Jerry when they met in Chicago. Jerry persuaded his father to come home with him, hoping to achieve a reconciliation and have him reinstated. None of the other family members showed any interest in the father, however, and Jerry's hopes were shattered. The father soon left, and the following year became ill and required emergency surgery. Since no other member of the family had any interest in him, Jerry willingly signed for the surgery. As a result of the operation his father died, leaving him with an enormous sense of guilt and a feeling of being responsible for the death. Giving consent for the needed surgery now seemed to him to have been a deliberately hostile act rather than an act of mercy.

A few months after his father's death Jerry attended a party and was immediately smitten by a girl he met there. He had never felt such passion for a girl before, and was spurred to heroic efforts to win her. Engaged at the time, she was attending the party with her fiance, but he talked so hard and fast and so persuasively that she allowed him to take her home. His competition for her was fanatical, and his romantic fervor, professed love and devotion apparently had great appeal for her, and the whirlwind romance was consummated a few months later in marriage. Throughout the courtship he had proceeded with an almost religious dedication with the single purpose of winning her.

With victory claimed, new problems arose. He began to doubt his capacity to keep her and feared she might find someone else more satisfying. He became jealous of her past loves and interrogated her endlessly about them. He was never satisfied with her responses—if she denied something, he doubted her, but if she admitted anything, he was in a rage. When his fear of losing her and his doubts about himself increased he tried to win her favor in a way quite different from his courting tactics. In contrast to his previous aggressive ardor, he now tried to win her by being submissive, passive, and curiously compliant. He voluntarily helped her and even took over many of the functions of a housewife, doing housecleaning, dishwashing, cooking, and laundry. In these areas he considered himself more capable than she, and was quite content to demonstrate it. Throughout all of this, however surprising, their sexual relations remained fairly satisfactory, for he was always eager to please her. Even in their darkest periods she would say, "You may not be too much good in other ways, but you're sure good in bed."

Before his marriage Jerry had accepted, at least on the surface, his family's standards: the ideals of hard manual labor, scrupulous cleanliness and honesty, devout religious adherence, pride in getting pay for hard physical work. Drunkenness was a part of virility and was proven, almost ritualistically, on weekends. His wife's family, on the other hand, tended to live by their wits and contemptuously looked down on hard manual work. They idolized cleverness, especially in making money, and their motto seemed to be, "Anything goes, as long as you don't get caught." One of the brothers had had several brushes with the law. They maintained no religious affiliation and had little interest in such activities as housekeeping.

When he married, Jerry exchanged his family's standards for those of his wife's, with little apparent conflict. He quit his hard furniture-moving job and looked for something easier, misrepresenting himself to get an insurance selling job, and then moving into a door-to-door sales operation on the fringe of legality. Perhaps some inner turmoil was reflected in the fact that he flaunted his change in behavior in front of his brothers, trying to demonstrate his "superiority" to them. He missed no opportunity to tell them how late he slept, that he could make more money lying in bed using the telephone in one hour than they could make working hard all day. His arrogance, of course, angered his brothers, who countered with physical attack and moralistic scorn.

Although he had assumed the superficial facade of his wife's family, the change was not entirely successful. He started to feel guilty about cheating the people to whom he sold his goods. His elaborate rationalizations did not completely work. He began to worry about his two children, having thoughts that they might be injured by an irate customer. This, plus uneasy doubts about his wife's fidelity, made him feel compelled to return home frequently to check on the family. The question of birth control also became an issue. Although both he and his wife wanted no more children, the inner voice of Catholic conscience prohibited him from using contraceptives. As time passed, it became more apparent that Jerry's "transformation" to his wife's way of life was just in the visible, superficial aspects, and that he was in increasing conflict with the occupational, religious, and socioeconomic standards of his own family.

Jerry's new role involved another significant change. In his family, he and his brothers had been baseball players and fans. His father had been a professional player for a time and had achieved a considerable reputation as a long ball hitter, until his drinking affected his playing. Two brothers, following in the father's footsteps, had played semi-professional baseball. Jerry had gone through the motions of playing baseball with a modicum of success but the game had never meant very much to him.

With his new social status he took up golf, more suitable to his new superficial exterior, but a game which, to his family, was for "sissies" and old men. In golf there was no hard physical activity, but there were opportunities to bet and make a fast dollar, and opportunities for business contacts. But something was happening to Jerry. What was at first only a superficial attempt to find an image, rapidly seemed to become a meaningful life in itself. His interest in golf was almost immediate and thorough, and his progress in the game was so rapid that he arranged his weekly sales schedule to include many golfing hours. The game took hold of him and proved to be an activity providing him with an outlet for aggression and opportunities for gratification hitherto unknown to him. When he was anxious or upset, a round of golf always made him feel better and if an actual game were impossible his fantasies of playing were almost as satisfying. As he improved he considered becoming a professional and his rapidly developing proficiency made this a possibility. He and his wife decided to move to California so he could play golf the year round. He had found a personal identity in this segment of his life. Golf was not a superficial imitation or a coerced activity as most of his other activities had been.

The most important part of the game for Jerry seemed to be the competition and his intense desire to win. He was extraordinarily successful, although in other sports he had been a rather timorous competitor. His goal was to win the "rabbit" which was the ante each player put in for the winner's prize. The distinction of this game from the overt physical competition with which he had grown up appeared to supply him with the necessary psychological distance to allow all-out vigorous competition. This prize, "the rabbit," could be sought without fear of retaliation or abandonment.

He liked to play in foursomes and felt a special sense of satisfaction when he won in such a group. These foursomes had the same basic structure as his family competitive unit, but without the sadism and frustrations of boyhood competition with his brothers. He could now compete successfully with his chosen "brothers" and freely express rage, frustration, or contentment. He developed a good reputation at the clubs where he played, and in a modest way augmented his income through his winnings. In one important way he was different than most of his companions: he had magical beliefs about his golfing abilities, feeling that he really did not need to practice outside of his fantasies. He considered himself to have an innate ability setting him apart from other players.

When playing well and successfully and when he won the "rabbit," he felt confident, worthwhile, and found his jealousy for his wife disappeared. His psychiatric disorder developed at the time of his injury, when playing golf was precluded and when golf in fantasy became blocked. This is dramatic indication of the important role golf had in keeping him intact.

Jerry was a nice-looking, engagingly pleasant young

man. He was generally cheerful and outgoing with his
doctor and always eager to please. In fact, he often spent
part of his treatment time attempting to entertain his therapist with the latest jokes. He perceived his doctor as being
in an authoritarian position and was almost ritualistic in
his compliance. His apparent gregariousness was a thinly
veiled attempt to conceal the persecutory fantasies which
lay just below the surface. Under stress, he had become dis-
organized and paranoid. Golf, which had become a coa-
lescing force for his personality, had now been disrupted
as a result of his injury. One of the tasks of therapy was
to assist him in re-establishing himself in his sport.

Before this could be accomplished, however, it was
necessary for him to learn that his therapist was someone
he could trust. From the first he was suspicious of his
doctor's motives and continually tested the relationship to
its limits. He attempted to identify his therapist with the
hated police authority and kept testing to see if he would
be informed upon or "turned in." When he was able to
separate his therapist from the authority of his probation
officer, the first stage of therapy was complete.

This accomplished, Jerry was supported and encouraged to try out his golf again. After tenuous and fearful beginnings he discovered that he was physically able
to play. In spite of the doubts, confidence gradually began to
emerge again and he was willing to risk competition. He
needed considerable support during this initial period when
he was shakily trying out his skills. Gradually integrity
and a feeling of identity returned, and with this his jealous
paranoia retreated from sight. Golf again provided him with
confidence and opportunities to release the otherwise destructive aggression. As this occurred he was able to return
to the approximate level of psychological adjustment he had
before his accident. A relative truce prevailed at home and
he returned to work. At his insistence his wife stopped working, eliminating one source of his concern. When his doctor
moved to a new facility they agreed together to terminate
treatment. The last information received about him was

that he was getting along satisfactorily and was once again planning to take a professional job in golf. A position had been offered to him at one of the local clubs. Of course he was in no sense cured, but he was restored to a functional level of adjustment. Beneath his adjustment there always lay a deep mistrust of himself and others, the shaky foundation on which all of his development had been based. Any slight rebuff or damage to his fragile self-esteem signaled the appearance of jealous paranoid ideas and feelings of worthlessness. They were quickly concealed, however, either through playing "his game" or through elaborate fantasies about golf. For him golf was always there as a source of strength.

DISCUSSION

Golf has a very special public image of plush greens and tweediness. It is associated with wealth and status, the "upper crust" society. Advertising men who wish to suggest that their products are "exclusive" show them with a background of a golf or country club. Golf also carries the connotation of unhurried leisure, of methodical walking in solitude over green turf, with an obedient caddy carrying clubs. Perhaps the caddy is important in the symbolism of golf: the relationship represents an island of feudalism with a master and a servant, the servant assisting his master in seeking pleasure. Although the caddy is giving way to the golf cart, and the game is being played by an increasingly wide spectrum of socioeconomic groups, it has not lost its image, but remains a game of presidents and millionaires. Its greater availability, in fact, has enhanced its prestige value for the hungry status seeker.

For Jerry, golf represented important in his search for a new identity in money and leisure: a mimicry of the ideals of his wife's family and a stubborn reaction against those of his own family who knew little of country clubs and despised elegance. It was a symbol to him of his own

change in status, similar to the dream of a caddy who does
not share all the same privileges as the club member but
may traverse the same ground. As at the Roman feast of
Saturnalia when slave became master, on certain special
occasions the caddy can assume the master's role and use
the club's facilities and golf course. He may also aspire to
membership if he plays well or works well. This status
change was what appealed to our patient.

The other more important appeal of golf was not
entirely evident to him. This was the driving force which
made him feel "This is my game," a sense of wholesome-
ness, confidence, and comfort he had never felt before. Golf
was uniquely suited as a vehicle for the release of many of
the frustrations Jerry had felt throughout his life.

In his family, fierce physical competition in fighting
and baseball was actually fostered between the brothers.
Jerry had as much aggressive competitive drive as his three
older brothers, but he was bottom man in the sadistic peck-
ing order. His aggressiveness was stimulated by provocation,
but expression was blocked by the retaliative threat. In
addition, he felt a primitive fear that if he was too aggressive and displeased his mother she might throw him out
of the house and abandon him as she had his father. He
was, as a result, an erratic, fearful competitor.

In contrast to the frightening, naked physical
aggressiveness with his brothers, the competition in golf
is abstract. In golf there is no physical contact between
players, neither is there any opposing stance between competitors as in tennis or volley ball. The competition is in
parallel and is evident only by comparing the relative
scores of the participants. Thus the competition is mainly
symbolic, with players close to each other only at the
beginning and end of a hole. In the rest of the game on the
fairway the player can withdraw from his competitors and
be aggressive and competitive through fantasy, obtaining a
psychological rather than a physical release. For the individual whose aggression requires proximity to others but
solitude and distance from them as well, golf has many

advantages. In addition, the physical activity is not vigorous and the "club atmosphere" serves to mute the possibility of violence.

These qualities of the game provided the psychological distance and safety necessary for Jerry. Distance
allowed him to realize, without the fear of retaliation and
abandonment, the latent aggression and competition that
had been blocked. He reconstructed in his golf foursome
the relationship with his three older brothers, but now the
rules were different and forbade reprisals when he won.

This young man had stumbled through life in danger of falling at any moment. His identity was diffused into
unintegrated fragments gathered from the attitudes of his
own family and his wife's family. Was he a woman who
did housework or a man who did labor? He struggled between feelings of worthlessness and delusions of power,
desperately trying on the modes of life which appeared to
be successful to others as if they were his own. In golf
he found a coalition of these diffused identities which was
his own; he could be genuine and totally involved. Golf
became the glue which held him together and hid the underlying paranoid schizophrenia.

Because of the shaky foundation of Jerry's personality and its potential for disorganization, it is academic
to discuss where things went wrong in his growth from
boyhood to manhood. His development had not proceeded
in an orderly manner allowing one to distinguish the point
where it had been arrested. Perhaps one could say the flaw
was at the beginning. The unstable foundation of his personality made subsequent development "patchwork." Golf
for him was not regression into the play of childhood, re-
tarding the assumption of adult responsibility, but rather
his principal source of strength, the main unifying force of
his personality.

His feminine characteristics should be seen in the
same light. His fear of submission to authority was not a
discrete issue as in the previous cases discussed. It was,
rather, one of the many fragmented identities with which

he lived. For him a unique, saving feature of golf lay in his being able to sample the pleasures of male companionship without getting too close. He could be with his competitive friends on the tees and greens, but at a safe distance most of the time while on the fairways.

As with Rock'm, Sock'm Jack, Jerry's sports enthusiasm was related to his older brothers. Jack identified solidly with the other male members of his family and had an intense desire to play football just as they did. With Jerry, the competitive struggle and frustration with his brothers was also there, but he was frustrated in playing their game by their rules. Taking up golf was a spiteful reaction against them and one way of winning and breaking family ties. In contrast, Jack had always been, and wanted to remain, a member of his family. Selecting football as his sport kept him in the family group.

Jerry broke away from the family just as his parents had done when they left Ireland for America. In another era and under other social circumstances he might have moved westward in keeping with the pioneer spirit. Breaking ties and heading for the frontier is the time-honored way a youth escapes family traditions. The present-day American carries many of the frontier attitudes into sports: the physical competition, the hard life, and in some sports, the danger that characterized the westward movement. Winning or losing simulates the survival or death of the pioneers. It was fortunate for our golfer that he did find a sport which met his needs. Only on one other occasion, in the zealous competition for his wife, had his competitive aggression been fulfilled.

Jerry might never have become a patient had it not been for an accidental series of events. Golf had provided substance to an otherwise aimless existence. With the accident, burns, and prolonged hospitalization his dread of being damaged and abandoned was reactivated. Further regression occurred in his delusion that his wife saw him as damaged and preferred other men. His paranoid jealousy was punctuated by two overt episodes of psychotic behavior in which he tried to kill his rival. The fantasies of playing golf which had carried him through other difficult situations might have sustained him this time as well, had they not been blocked. He realized they were only fantasies and it was up to him to try out his golf to determine whether he was capable again. Unwilling to take the risk, he could only try to forget the whole thing. One of the principal functions of therapy was to help him re-establish his much-needed sublimation in golf. Eventually his previous level of adjustment was regained.

6 TENNIS PLAYER

THE KILLER

Although the origins of tennis are obscure, it is known to have been played in many ancient lands with somewhat differing rules. It was played in the ancient court of Persia, in the dry moats of castles in the Middle Ages and in nineteenth century England on Major Wingfield's patented hour-glass shaped court. In all of these different settings there was one note of social continuity: tennis has been a game of the aristocracy, and was even called "The Royal Game." It was popular among European kings and their courts and it is recorded that Louis X of France died from a chill contracted after playing tennis.

Just before the turn of the century, Major Wingfield's form of the game was transported to America by way of Bermuda. In the new world it continued to be associated with the "upper classes." Tennis clubs sprang up wherever the wealthy congregated and even today the principal American tournaments are played in exclusive clubs in cities and vacation resorts where the wealthy congregate, such as Newport, Southampton, the New Jersey shore, and Palm Beach.

Although tennis courts are now available to nearly all Americans, the game still carries the connotation of the social classes of its origins, and retains a certain snob appeal. The public setting and availability of courts has given those who choose to play the game a peculiar sense of social elevation* rather than transforming the image to a more popular one.

Wherever aristocracy or pseudo-aristocracy exists, so too, are found those pretenders, the "social climbers." The first inroads into the exclusivity of tennis were made by a group of modern-day courtiers, the "tennis bums." They were men and women of modest means and modest social position who coveted the status and the material benefits of wealth. The nature of their seeking also implied a preference for reaching the prized position by receiving personal favors or by the condescension of the privileged, rather than by their own work.

The historical relationship of the game to the aristocracy, the muted applause which substitutes for cheering, and the meticulous white attire which is the standard uniform have provided tennis with the additional connotation of being a "sissy's game." Yet, like any of the major sports, if played well, it is physically demanding and requires great stamina and technical excellence. In fact, there is probably no more gruelling athletic activity than a five-set tennis match. So, although it is a tough competitive sport available to masses of people, it has, paradoxically, maintained a close relationship to leisure and wealth.

The social mythology of a sport is a major factor in its being selected for participation. The pool hall, the football field, the bullfight arena, the baseball stadium, and skiing slopes have unique appeals based on their social environments and the images of their contestants. A sport may symbolize the personal psychology and the social striving of the individual who selects it. And this holds true of the tennis player also.

When Ken came to my office seeking psychiatric help he had been experiencing anxiety and tension for

---

* Many players and fans of tennis have been working towards popularizing the game. Their efforts have been to improve professional tennis, initiate "open" tournaments, and encourage baseball-type cheering. But enormous resistance is met from those who wish to maintain the aristocratic image of the game, and progress to date has been slow.

several months. It had developed when he had, according to plan, entered his brother's business. He was tall and tanned, with handsome features. His tailored sport coat, covering a tieless shirt, gave the impression of meticulous disarray. Although he undoubtedly had come to me with a burning purpose, his manner was a veneer of studied casualness; he found it difficult to get to the point. The psychiatrist becomes accustomed to this in patients so I listened to his warm-up talk of tennis, of recent and up-coming tournaments, of how he had heard that I was a psychiatrist, and of a number of mutual friends.

Ken was not a complete stranger. I had seen him play several times in tournaments and could recall him on the court. The similar meticulous dress, seemingly casual attitude, powerfully aggressive game with its booming service and hard-hit volleys were impressive. But I was struck also with the worried look on his face while he played. As I turned my attention to him now, I could see the deep furrows in his brow, now relaxed, which helped me to realize that he was the same "Killer Ken." So worried at play, so casual in a psychiatrist's office!

As if on cue from me, the furrows appeared, the worried look came over him, and he began his narrative. Now in his late twenties, he had ranked high among the nation's tennis players for several years, winning a number of national titles. About a year ago he married, and a few months later entered his brother's advertising business. Although on the surface he seemed unchanged, he began to feel constricted and tense, longing for his tennis-playing days.

Most disturbing of all was a change in his relationship with his brother John, seven years older, with whom he had always been very close. Their relationship, especially after their father died, was more like father and son. They had planned since childhood to go into business together. Now that the dream was a reality, it turned out to be a nightmare for Ken instead of a happy culmination. He became increasingly tense with his brother, sometimes feeling he was being picked on. Such thoughts he quickly dismissed, though, because there was no factual evidence. He was "touchy" and had even "blown up" several times. This was foreign to him, since in his recollection he had never lost his temper before. His brother, somewhat bewildered by this behavior, tried to talk to Ken but was rebuffed and avoided. Ken harbored a secret fear, he revealed later, that in some way he might be provoked by his brother and inadvertently harm him. This seemed quite incongruous to him since he was really very fond of John.

The boys had grown up in a small town north of Los Angeles. Here they had been confronted with two very different worlds—a rich one and an austere one. Ken's father worked as caretaker on a wealthy man's estate. Their family home was modest to the point of austerity, although it was set in the center of a broader world of luxury and wealth. The "Boss," in a moment of democratic magnanimity, had decreed that "Charlie's kids" could do anything his "kids" could do. So Ken and his brother were allowed to move freely between the two worlds, seemingly accepted by both. To casual observation, this order was followed to the letter, but for Ken and John, there was never any doubt about the real situation. At home, before they went into the Boss's world, they were always cautioned to behave, not to offend, and to act like gentlemen. They had a vague realization when they played with the Boss's children, that they had to be careful, for in some way their family's survival depended upon their good deportment. They were models of good behavior.

The Boss was genuinely fond of these boys, for they were handsome, well-mannered, alert, and good athletes—all he admired and wanted in his own children. As a result, he often held "Charlie's kids" up as models to them. As could be expected they did not take kindly to these unfavorable comparisons, and the seething anger which developed in them became the price exacted for the freedom allowed "Charlie's kids." But in any conflict between the "Boss's kids" and "Charlie's kids" the former had the ultimate weapon—they belonged there.

When he was five years old, Ken, bewildered and ashamed, not quite understanding, came to his mother with tears in his eyes and asked what a "servant" was. His playmate, the Boss's son, had scornfully put him in his place with this word. The Boss would never have tolerated such an overt display of snobbery, but in their conspiracy of silence Charlie's family would never have reported any interfamily conflicts for fear of offending. In later years as the children of the two families grew up, their differing social roles were maintained by innuendo rather than by such direct pronouncements. Clearly implied differences always lurked beneath the Boss's egalitarian decree.

The smiling facade Charlie's family showed the Boss did not reveal the intense competition between the families. Charlie's family was very close and united in mutual support, and seemingly stuck together on all issues. But this in itself produced many tensions within the home. The closeness of the family and its code which prevented any expression of discord to the outside world forced them to handle problems within the home. There were thus few opportunities for the dissipation of tensions outside of the family.

Charlie was a good-natured fellow who easily accepted his subservient role; for him the most important thing was peace. He wanted peace in his own family and between his family and the Boss's. He approached his existence with an air of calm. Charlie's wife, although warm, encouraging, and protective of her brood was more ambitious, and envious of the benefits of wealth and position which she saw. The family often spoke of how fortunate they were in their circumstances, but there was never any question that the men in the family, Charlie and his two boys, could please her by seeing to it that she had more of the good things of life. Nothing was more important to the members of this small family than gaining Mother's favor. Charlie, for example, bought her gifts which were beyond his financial ability. Although these tokens were promptly returned to the store, there was little question of her secret pleasure from these gestures which told her that, if he were able, Charlie would provide her with a life of luxury. This was their little game of make-believe. It was through the boys that she entertained her greatest hope of some day realizing her ambitions. Charlie's wishes for the success of his boys were mixed with his own feeling of envy for the favors his wife gave them.

There was no place in this family for spankings or other severe punishment. Any overt competition outside the home was restricted because of the need to maintain the family's "proper place." Yet at home the rivalry for mother's favors was intense. One way the men of the family dissipated their tensions was through mock wrestling contests. As fathers will do, Charlie engaged in friendly contests with his boys. He was actually stocky and powerful and had to mute his own efforts to make the competition more nearly equal. Ken's brother John always seemed aware of his father's latent strength and never really entered enthusiastically into these wrestling matches. But Ken's efforts were undiminished by the reality of the situation. In fact, although he was small, his enthusiasm was so great that sometimes he actually was able to get the advantage of his father. He could get a strangle hold which caused Charlie to gasp for breath, and, half playfully, admonish Ken, "You're a real killer, Ken. You're dangerous." Ken experienced his father's comments with a vaguely formed mixture of emotions: guilt over possibly hurting the father he loved, and pride in his own strength.

In school, Ken and John tried to conform to the apparently inconsistent standards set by their parents in the home. They wanted to be "popular," in keeping with their father's values, but they also strove for the more material successes for which their mother yearned. Ken learned from his brother some of the techniques to accomplish these seemingly incompatible goals. Though he was an excellent and industrious student, he made a considerable display of disinterest in school work and grades for the benefit of his classmates. Meanwhile he was very enthusiastic about sports. In their school, the "in" group of boys felt to be "a grind" was subhuman, and althletes who were poor students were of the highest social order. Thus the sometimes paradoxical standards of the family were matched by an equally contradictory set of standards at school. Ken and John found satisfactory solutions, however. They were good athletes and members of the "in" group, while they overtly scorned scholarship, but studied secretly. They were careful never to be seen carrying books home and always disclaimed any responsibility for their high grades. If confronted, they would reply with measured casualness that they could not help it if they were lucky.

On the estate, too, as they grew older, they developed some opportunities for achievement without incurring the wrath of the Boss's family. The Boss loved sports and insisted that his brood, which included Ken and his brother, participate vigorously. It was the only opportunity on the estate outside of the family circle for the open expression of the competition which burned so strongly. Tennis was the big sport.

Each week a tennis professional came to teach the Boss's kids. Ken and John were allowed to watch and later to practice with their privileged playmates. The caretaker's children maintained a respectful distance from the lessons, but they were always present and they observed carefully. They caught on quickly and practiced hard. Both Ken and his brother improved more rapidly than the Boss's children. Ken was especially precocious. His brother, just as in the wrestling with his father, seemed less determined and more willing to accept second place.

Ken became so expert he began entering tournaments at the Boss's insistent sponsorship. Of course, when first encouraged he modestly insisted he wasn't good enough. Privately, he could barely contain his enthusiasm at the prospect. One of the contingencies was that he play doubles with the Boss's son, but this was a small price to pay.

He began playing local tournaments with immediate success. Bursting with pride, he would bring home a medal or a small trophy signifying victory and give it to his mother. He could always anticipate her expressions of joy, as she experienced his success as if it were her own.

Ken's brother was also quite willing to sacrifice his own tennis ambitions to be Ken's sparring partner and advisor. The competition between the two boys was only occasionally obvious. Then, in moments of anger, they played against each other furiously. It was at these times that the tensions arising from the closeness of the family bonds became fully apparent.

In the beginning of his fifteenth year, two very important events occurred in Ken's life. He realized his dreams of success when he became tennis champion of his age division through a sparkling series of outstanding victories and was heralded as a future tennis great. But victory for Ken meant defeat for someone close to him: his father developed tuberculosis. His father's illness seemed to realize his worst fears of the consequences of his success. Ordinarily even the events of early childhood were clear and distinct in Ken's memory, but these two events had become so confused in his mind that he was not certain which had taken place first. The extent of his father's illness was minimized by everyone at first. But over the next few years the telltale signs and their ultimate conclusion became clear.

Ken saw his formerly robust father shrink in size and wither away. He was now away for extended periods in the sanitarium. Ken was stunned and nearly overcome when he saw his father and the tragic changes which resulted from the illness.

The Boss was sympathetic, and even though Ken's father was no longer able to work, he allowed the family to stay on in the caretaker's cottage. But now they had to subsist on the rapidly diminishing family savings. His mother went to work; fortunately Ken's brother was now nearly finished with college.

When old Charlie was finally laid to rest, it was a great relief for everyone. Seeing him suffer and wither away had been agonizing and his slow lingering death left a deep scar on the tight family group. Ken seemed more affected than the others.

Times were good, however, and as soon as John finished college he was able to assume the burden of the family's financial problems. He did this so successfully that his mother was able to stop work, and Ken was once again free to pursue his academic and tennis careers.

But a strange thing occurred in the way Ken now approached tennis. He had always been a tenacious, steady player who won primarily because he outlasted his opponents. Now, however, he could not stand long drawn-out matches. Either he won quickly and decisively or he did not win at all. He began to play the serve-and-volley game. In his matches points were decided by a stroke or two. If he got into a long drawn-out match it was an agonizing experience for him and he could think of nothing except ending it.

This change in the way he played caused Ken's star to fade for a couple of seasons. He became known as a teenage "has been" whose principal assets were a bludgeon-like serve and a hard volley. He went "all out" on each point, hitting for the winner. The point was practically always decided without a rally.

He had lost his confidence, too, and questioned his own ability, something that had never happened before. Inevitably his hard, reckless play produced some sensational victories. If he was "on," he seemed to be able to beat almost anyone. His confidence gradually began to return after he defeated world class players easily on several occasions. However, he was just as apt to lose to a mediocre player if he happened to get into a long match. As he put it, "Long matches just didn't seem humane." Although he was very strong, when he found himself in a tight struggle on the court he became concerned about his health and sometimes even about the health of his opponent. He often found himself short of breath.

Ken utilized well the social skills he had acquired in childhood on the estate, and became one of the most popular players in the game, with both fans and players. His mannerly casualness did not betray the intensity of his competitive spirit. His tournament record continued to be spotty, however. There were dramatic decisive victories over outstanding players, but also seemingly inexplicable losses to inferior players. His nemesis remained that not being able to win, and seeming not to want to win long, agonizing matches.

Ken got along well with both boys and girls, and developed quite a following with girls. At the tournaments where he played there was always a ready band of admirers to greet him when he came off the court. They provided him with a plethora of sexual opportunities. Although his fellow players took advantage of such opportunities, Ken was different. He was chivalrous and protective of women and he preferred long-term stable relationships. As a result, he tended to avoid many of the available opportunities. He felt uneasy if he satisfied himself sexually and not his partner, and bitterly resented other players who "took advantage" of girls. He was always cautious lest he hurt someone.

In his mid-twenties he met an attractive girl at a tournament and a serious romance bloomed. She was the daughter of a wealthy industrialist and an ardent tennis fan. Their courtship extended for many months and eventually they were married. She was a warm and intelligent girl and deeply loved her husband. Ken had not been unaware of the material advantages of this marriage. Although he was genuinely fond of his wife, he found himself obsessed, first with the desire for material advantages which could come to him from their marriage, and then with self-castigation over taking advantage of the situation.

After a tennis honeymoon, the young couple settled

in an apartment in her family's home. From the beginning, Ken felt ill at ease there, as though he did not belong. He could not "let down," even though his wife encouraged him to do so. In her parents' home he felt like an outsider, in the same way he had felt ill at ease entering the big house on the Boss's estate in California. As a result, the young couple developed some strange habits, spending a good deal of time in hotels and motels where Ken did feel comfortable.

Although he had dreamed of a life of leisure, when it became available to him he could not accept it. The solution seemed easy, and he decided now to go to work in brother John's advertising business, as had been their plan for years. They had always said they would one day work together and when they finally made the decision, both looked forward eagerly to it. Ken's wife was pleased, too, because she thought at last he would be happy.

Ken's life showed a pattern of extreme social mobility with his ascent occurring largely through tennis playing. Sponsored by the Boss as a boy, he achieved recognition, and then married into wealth all mainly because of his ability to play tennis. His upward mobility was the result not of work, but of play.* Moving from servant to leisure class left him with the anxiety of not feeling at home anywhere.

And now here he was in my office. His appearance did not betray the extent of the turmoil he felt within, for he had learned early in life to show on the outside only what he wanted to be seen. But he experienced great tension, and anxiety beyond anything that he had ever felt before. He reported that since entering his brother's business he slept very little and when he did, he had a recurrent dream which troubled him.

---

* Jan Huizinga notes that play is unreal and not serious. It is the introduction of reality into a player's life which so often leads to difficulty, for he becomes responsible for his actions and their consequences. Old conflicts, which could be denied as unreal in play, are reactivated and must be dealt with anew.

He said he wasn't sure, but believed he had had
the dream from time to time since childhood. Now, whenever sleep did come, he dreamt this:

He was climbing a steep mountain with another man.
It was dusty, rocky terrain. They climbed together.
Then he could see an avalanche coming. By running
up ahead at an angle he avoided the avalanche,
which passed just behind him, but in so doing it
carried his fellow climber down to his death. He
stood on the mountain motionless and became aware
of eyes in the front and in the back of his head. With
the front eyes, he looked up the rest of the mountain
where he wished to go, while with his rear eyes he
looked back with regret to where his companion
had been. He would then awaken.

Ken's story was that of a boy who had grown up
in a specialized social milieu of wealth and luxury. The
main people he knew outside his immediate family, the
estate owners, impressed him as having a different set of
concerns from his, and he looked to their lives as an
ideal to be sought. They were unconcerned about the mun-
dane activities of survival which occupied his own family,
and were interested primarily in living a good and meaningful life. He was impressed with the disparity between himself and his playmates and he surreptitiously coveted what
they were born with.

Ken and his family were like an isolated minority
on the estate. They remained there by virtue of the Boss's
grace. Although they were allowed privileges, it was always
apparent that these could be revoked at any time. Ken was
always aware of the differences between his position and
that of his playmates, and between his family and the Boss's.
In some respects it was like living in a medieval feudal
society.

But there were important differences between Ken's
society and the feudal one. The clarity of roles between
servant and master was blurred by other factors which
allowed him to hope he could have what belonged to the

Boss. The Boss decreed that there was equality among all of the estate children and encouraged competition among them. Ken excelled and could win over all of them. As he moved into the world beyond the estate, he became further aware that it was possible for him to change his social position. His appetite for success had also been whetted long before.

His own family relationships had already prepared him for his view of the world in which he lived. His family was a microcosm of the way he saw himself in the world. In the immediate family the males, Ken, John, and his father, were competitors for the favors of his mother. The disparity between his social role on the estate and that of the Boss's family was no greater than that between himself and his father and brother in the home. They were Goliaths and Ken was David. In the home, just as on the estate, there was an egalitarian decree. There were mock wrestling matches in which his father and brother pretended they were no more than equal to Ken. Ken's brother never took the pretense seriously and recognized full well the relative differences in size and strength between himself and his father. But Ken did take this seriously and believed he could win. His enthusiasm, if not his strength, led to occasional, apparent victory when wrestling with his father, who then dubbed him the "killer."

Other factors amplified the tensions of competition: the code that one had to be careful not to offend, that one must not complain. This confined the expression of the tensions within the family, since when one was outside the home one always had to be on good behavior.

As Ken grew older, another opportunity to express his desire for competition outside the home developed. The game of tennis became almost the perfect expression. On the court, so long as he kept his sportsmanlike demeanor, Ken could compete furiously. There he could truly be equal or superior, with the one restriction of appearing modest and polite. As his proficiency in the game increased, other advantages accrued. He was able to live among the wealthy, and eventually join them permanently by his marriage. His

mother, whose favor he sought, was delighted by his progress, especially in the social advances which accompanied
it. Ken had become a successful social climber.

In his successes, however, Ken experienced a vague
sense of regret, as though he had achieved something he
should not have. This had also been the case in the family
wrestling matches, and now it happened when he played
tennis. A vague concern for the regretful consequences of
victory grew and finally came to fruition as the realization
of his worst fears. His father became ill and eventually
wasted away to death. Ken felt unconsciously responsible,
for, after all, had his father not designated him "the killer"?

Although much of what had taken place was beyond Ken's awareness, it nevertheless had a profound effect
on his tennis. His competitiveness was impaired. Whenever
a match triggered a dim reminder of his father's slowly
deteriorating health he grew panicky and, not caring whether
he won or lost, wanted only to end the match. In matches
like this he found himself worried about his opponent's
ability to survive and about his own health as well. He
confused his long past competition with his father and its
tragic ending with his tennis battles. He could allow himself to win only if the victory was quick and merciful.

In aiming to satisfy the dictates of his conscience
to be merciful, he ironically regained his nickname. To win
quickly, he hit terrifically hard. So devasting was his game
because of his attempts to win quickly, that he began to
be called "Killer Ken of the Courts." As it had done long
before, the nickname caused him a mixture of pride and
regret.

In spite of his conflict about winning, he had much
success. He met all problems, on and off the court, with
the same immediate, decisive action designed to finish the
situation at once. Sometimes, of course, in his eagerness
for an ending, his actions were ill-considered and impulsive.
Most of the time, however, his decisiveness served him well.

A series of events intervened, however, to block
the immediate resolution of some conflicts. First there was
his marriage, the realization of a courtier's dream. He

married a wealthy girl and could really have joined the coveted world of the Boss, but the dictates of his conscience forbade this, and he experienced his success as a feeling of "not being at home."

In a desperate effort at solution, he ran headlong into another recapitulation of the same problem. As is so often the case, the object from which one flees is the very one found in the new location. Ken's entrance into business with his brother immediately precipitated a psychoneurotic reaction. He feared something would happen to his brother, who was now in the familial position of his father and akin to the social position of the Boss. He feared he would be the cause of his brother's downfall, as he unconsciously believed he had been in the case of his father. He avoided his brother as much as he could, but the tension mounted.

The dream which now plagued him was a metaphor of his psychosocial dilemma. He had not given up the competition with his father for his mother's favor, although these events were long past, and he found in his present situation with his brother and with his wife a symbolic representation of this unfinished situation. His social and psychological problems mimicked each other. He stood on the mountain looking toward his advance in the family and in social class, but a second set of eyes forced him to look backward at the evil consequences of his ambition.

At a deeper level, there was the issue of his sexual identification. His mother, in her quiet way, had been the dominant figure in the home, and in accepting her standards, he partially identified with her. The split in his identifications required strange behavior in school. He hid his scholastic ambitions and studying—his female identification—while he displayed his male identification in seeking popularity and competing in sports. Tennis represented a suitable solution to this dilemma for, although it was a vigorous sport allowing him the masculine role, it carried feminine connotations as a "sissy game." Sportsmanship, the counterpart of popularity, was the perfect subterfuge to hide his intense ambition.

In infancy the excessive protective concern of his

mother, the bountiful giver, had laid the groundwork for Ken's future hope that the world could be his. The inevitable disturbance in this union between mother and son led to the doubts and the guilt which later, when reactivated, pervaded Ken's life.

*   *   *

The formulation of a case from historical information may serve as a basis for therapy, but it is not therapeutic in itself. The experienced therapist knows that the problems he works with may be solved in many ways, and it is not necessary to explore every hidden recess of a patient's life. Formulating the factors which lead to neurosis is an important scientific exercise providing a preliminary understanding of what should be handled and what should be left alone. However, the patient needs help with what bothers him at the moment and a complete exploration of his life may be not only unnecessary but not even in his best interests.

Ken had always solved problems by action. He was not, as is the case with many athletes, one to contemplate or to see much virtue in understanding. His smooth social veneer gave way to a vitriolic attack against me for my inability to "do something" immediately to change him. In his scorn for the impotence of my words he relived the wrestling matches with his father. He could only admire someone who could overpower him. In therapy, he was not rewarded for his vehemence, nor could he find any objective evidence that he had hurt me. As a result, he began to feel there was enough power in talking, and, perhaps even in me, to be useful. Having, for the moment, found some peace in this relationship, there was a resurgence of feelings directly related to his father. In our interviews Ken spent much time in talking to his father as though he were actually in the room.

He began to see this unfinished situation as distorting his present relationships with his brother and his wife. At various times he treated me with the deference reserved for the Boss, and competed with me ambitiously to have anything that I had, while feeling regret for his desires. At other times he tried to curry my favor as he had his mother's.

Although his relationship with his brother improved greatly, he made a decision not to continue in business with John. Eventually he entered a related business in which his tennis contacts were advantageous. He thus successfully made a place for himself on his own and even felt more "at home" in his own home with his wife.

From the standpoint of his tennis, a fascinating change did occur. Ken had become mainly a weekend player and entered only a few tournaments each year. He had maintained his old reputation as a court "killer." One day he could upset almost anyone, but just as easily at another time he could lose to a mediocre player. During therapy, the significance of his horror at winning a long, drawn-out match became clear. The guilt-producing unfinished competition which had caused him to view any long tennis match as an agonizing re-enactment of the muted battles with his father and which had led to his father's slow, painful, tubercular death was largely completed. A tennis match, long or short, was now only a tennis match. Freed from the compulsion to lose long matches, his tournament record actually improved. In the few top tournaments he played in each year, he was often the winner and only playing the small number of tournaments he played in kept him from being ranked highly. Although certain tennis officials encouraged him to play in more tournaments, some of Ken's intense interest was gone. He now had other interests: a growing family, and his occupation. These seemed more urgent.

Ken showed clearly how personal conflict can influence the way an athlete plays the game. There are front runners, strong finishers, faders, clutch players, chokers, and an infinite number of other types. There are power players, beguiling players, offensive players, and defensive players. The choice of which mode an athlete uses is based not only on his physical attributes, but also on the psychological meaning with which he invests the competition.

7 THE CHAMP

A WAY OF BECOMING SOMEBODY

Almost every mental hospital has among its long-term inhabitants a formerly prominent boxer. His badges of courage—scarred and thickened ridges over the eyes and a vacuous stare mirroring dulled wits—are easily recognized; his is the shell of a once proud, powerful figure who danced about the ring to cheers of fans. He served them well. But the human skull, admirably designed to house the vital and vulnerable brain which makes its possessor human, can protect only to a point. Inevitably the pain of the blows is dulled, pummelling of the skull becomes increasingly vague, cheers of the crowd more distant. Eventually the brain is irreversibly damaged by the blows, the seemingly-limitless earnings are plundered by the payoffs, and the fighter stands alone, a hollow hulk. In the end, there is the institution, erected by those who cheered, where their discarded creation can be hidden. The damage is done, the brain cannot be restored, and the only issue is custody. Perhaps the Roman crowd which turned thumbs down on a maimed gladiator was more merciful.

Not only is the boxer's danger great, but his rewards are small and fleeting, with the barriers against achieving even these almost insurmountable. Kirson Weinberg, studying 127 fighters, found that only 7.1 percent achieved national recognition. The financial gains, sought at such great risk, are reduced by training expenses and taxes, managers, and silent underworld partners. What the fighter actually receives he usually squanders recklessly.

And what after the boxing days are over? The career is brief, for only the youngest and healthiest can stand the physical punishment. The tragic specter of a Sugar Ray Robinson, perhaps the greatest and smartest fighter ever, and well past his prime, still fighting in relatively unimportant events in a vain attempt to maintain the living standard of the golden years, portends the fate of every boxer. Once his ring career is over, the boxer is ill-equipped to carry on in business and society. He can shine shoes like former champion Beau Jack or sell ties like Kingfish Levinsky. The story of Gene Tunney is the great exception. He retired at his peak, his mind and body intact, and went on to new successes in the business world. But most boxers undergo a sharp decline in status after retirement.

An examination of 90 former champions and leadings contenders, each of whom had earned over $100,000 during his ring career, showed the following occupations upon retirement.*

26 work in taverns	3 bookies
18 trainers	3 race track workers
or trainer-managers	2 wrestlers
18 unskilled jobs	2 liquor salesmen
6 work in movies	2 gas station attendants
3 cab drivers	2 janitors
3 newsstand vendors	2 in business

The boxer's lot is not a happy one and his future is almost always dim.

What makes a man enter a profession that holds such a questionable future? Why does a man subject himself to beatings, fleeting fame, almost certain failure? The dull hulks of former boxers who are custodial patients in hos-

---

* Gregory P. Stone, "American Sports: Play and Dis-Play," *Mass Leisure,* eds. Eric Larrabee and Rolf Meyersohn (Glencoe, Illinois: The Free Press, 1958), p. 255, quoting S. Kirson Weinberg and Henry Arond, "The Occupational Culture of the Boxer," *American Journal of Sociology,* LVII (March 1952), p. 469.

pitals are unable to supply the answers. Their desires, their motivations, their memories, like their money, have long since disappeared. Only a still-alert boxer could supply such information.

I have known several of these ghostlike figures who were once great boxers, but the Champ was the first former fighter I met who retained the alert awareness to provide information about his past and his motivations. Unlike his more deteriorated colleagues, the Champ's profession was not apparent from his appearance. He was of medium height, not overly stocky, and he had a regal bearing. His most characteristic mannerism was the slightly disdainful look he wore, looking through or past those to whom he spoke. It was a pugnacious, challenging stare which suddenly, without apparent reason, would change to anger in response to some hidden association with the past. Just as quickly he could change to laughter, and with a twinkle in his eye, make feinting, bobbing steps backward, as if in the ring. Conversation with him was like being in the ring. He first moved relentlessly in on his opponent, then, just when least expected, he would back off with some fancy verbal footwork, keeping his antagonist slightly off balance.

He spoke in a slightly hoarse, high-pitched voice and the words he used did not seem like his own. He referred to the hospital as "this worthy establishment," and to me as "my friend, the good doctor." He never missed an opportunity to use one of his practiced cliches, even if it had little to do with the conversation of the moment. Whenever I talked with him, he would say at least once, in stylized fashion, "May the better man emerge victorious." This was almost a trademark and sometimes, if there were no other opportunity, he used it in place of "Hello" or "Goodbye." Most of the time his enunciation was clipped, his accent a peculiar mixture of North and South, but when he grew excited, he lapsed into the drawl he had learned as a boy—and then he seemed more genuine. For the most part, though, there was an unreal quality to his speech and he seemed very distant.

At the time I first saw him, it had been nearly five years since his last fight, with the last few years of his ring career spent in relative obscurity. As an amateur in the Golden Gloves he had been champion, but as a professional he had never been more than a leading contender.

He was seething with anger. When examined by a hospital doctor, he responded to an innocuous request for place of birth with great irritation. "Of course I'm from the South, Birmingham, but I'm proud of it; some Negroes are ashamed of coming from the South, but I have no bitterness." His answer was like the angry response of a man who had just been attacked.

Even though he had been a promising fighter as a boy, he could not compete in his home state but first fought professionally in New Orleans where his manager passed him off as Mexican, giving him the name of Raoul Dominguez. His strict instructions to speak to no one lest he reveal the secret of his origin proved to be no small task, since it resulted in unforeseen reactions. He won his first fight in impressive style but when the press requested an interview he fled to his dressing room and locked the door, confused, frightened, and disappointed. The occasion which might have been expected to be greatly satisfying turned into one of the most painful experiences of his life. His confusion turned to anger, and his anger to fury. He hated everyone, his manager the most. He couldn't be himself; he didn't know who he was supposed to be; he couldn't even talk. Under the bare bulb in his dressing room he made some vows. He would leave the South and never return; he would become somebody and never be muzzled again.

His manager pounding on the door made him feel trapped. He didn't know how to be a Mexican, he wasn't white, and he couldn't return to being an obedient colored boy, so he solved the problem by leaving through the dressing-room window.

He now began an agonizing journey, hitchhiking and walking, to Detroit, the only Northern city he had ever heard about, because he knew that he had an "auntie" there. During the trip he was near starvation and his physical discomfort helped nurse his bitterness, but it was not at all clear to him against whom his anger was directed. Was it the whites for their discrimination or the Negroes for their complicity? He was angry at anyone who reminded him of his humiliation and confusion.

In southern Illinois he was offered food, his first in several days, in a railroad hobo jungle. He felt uneasy but grateful to the men who had invited him to share their food. In a clumsy attempt at friendship, one of his hosts said to him, "Another darkie boy trying to escape up North." In a burst of rage he leaped to his feet and pummeled his host. The man dropped to the ground with a dull groan and the others jumped up to drive him off. As he ran, he glanced back through the trees and saw them leaning over the prostrate form he left behind. He felt no remorse, only a rhythmic rise and fall in rage. Yet he was puzzled. What had triggered this attack? Was it because he had been called a "darkie boy" or because the man had suggested he was trying to escape? As he trudged along, he kept reassuring himself, "I don't run from nobody."

Arriving in Detroit, half-starved, he found his way to a Salvation Army mission where he spent several days regaining his strength. A kindly member of the staff tried to offer him spiritual and practical guidance, and talked about finding him a job. The rage and fear still boiling inside the young Negro made it impossible for them to communicate, and the offer of help only seemed to irritate him. His would-be helper finally told him that he was just like a porcupine and that he had better pull in his stickers if he were going to get anywhere. This confrontation had the desired effect and he began to talk about himself. He explained that he was a boxer and what he really wanted to do was to get himself a fight. His counselor, after trying to persuade him to find a "regular job," at length helped him find the nearest boxing gym.

He arrived at the gym and tried to discover how to get into a professional fight. After a brief workout, even in his weakened condition, his natural ability stood out, and he found a manager with whom he signed a contract that same day. He knew nothing of the terms and was not interested; all he wanted was to "get a fight." He told his manager that he was going to "be somebody" and was convinced that as long as he had enough to eat and could work out and fight, he'd be satisfied. He wanted to earn a "name" for himself, to be recognized.

The young man considered his speech to be the most shameful aspect of his origin, so he began a serious effort to learn to speak like people in the North. He attended a few sessions of night school, but around other people, he was embarrassed and quickly gave that up. It was through his own efforts, imitating, and using a dictionary, that he did change his speech. His imitation was very deliberate. When he heard someone who sounded "elegant," he would try to talk the same way, copying the tone of voice and the phrases used. Once, for example, he heard a well-dressed man at a fight speak of "utter nonchalance;" after a trip to the dictionary, he found "utter nonchalance" in nearly everything he did. Many of the words and phrases lifted out of context were used inappropriately. Often he had a special word or phrase, recently acquired, which he would use over and over again at the gym. The results were sometimes ludicrous, but those who frequented the gym soon learned that to laugh meant a challenge, and his growing reputation as a boxer made this unwise. Those who ridiculed him learned to do so outside his hearing.

His boxing career progressed according to plan. He chose a new name, emulating one of his idols. With this name he felt an identity he never felt with his other one. His prestige was enhanced, and he progressed through club fighting, preliminaries, and finally went on to main events. Within a few years he was a feared contender who had developed a "name."

He liked to think of himself as a scientific boxer, but his reputation was that of a relentless attacker whose assaults were punctuated by seemingly lighthearted, taunting,

back-peddling. He had his share of defeats, but they were
mainly from being overmatched early in his career. His ring
future appeared very promising.

His image was now crystallized: the disdainful look,
the relentless attack, the stilted speech. It was almost entirely a synthetic front presented to the white man's world.
He still had moments when he responded in a more natural
manner, consistent with his childhood—some of uproarious
abandon and joy, and others of tenderness when he was
with people who shared common experiences, common origins, and common suffering. But these friends satisfied his
drive to be "somebody" less and less. It was not with them
that his battle raged, it was with the others, those who had
made him suffer. The battle became so important to him
that the times when he was his old self became fewer and
fewer. The look of disdain was with him almost constantly,
as was the rest of his armor. Always ready for battle, he kept
his guard up.

As his boxing improved and his reputation grew,
his desire to become "somebody" increased. A little success
only made him more demanding. His contract and his manager, once acceptable on any terms, now were constant irri-
tants, mere impediments to his progress. He had no idea
how the fight money was distributed; all he knew was that
he was getting very little for his fighting and did not live in
the style expected of him.

His dissatisfaction reached its climax one day when
arguing with his manager about money matters. Telling him
the "facts of life," that phrase so universally used to describe
falsities one fears to change, his manager explained that it
was essential to pay the right people to protect his boxing
career, but that they had to remain anonymous. This explanation meant nothing to the Champ; all he knew was that
someone in his position should have more money. Finally, in
the frustration of not being able to comprehend this injustice,
he flailed out against his manager, dropping him with two
rapid punches. When the police arrived, he was booked for
assault with a deadly weapon, the usual charge against a

boxer who uses his fists. Once again, the skill he hoped would secure his place in the world had instead brought him punishment.

After a single night in jail, he was released when his manager (who was able to swallow his pride in the interest of his pocketbook) refused to press charges, fabricating a story which exonerated them both. This was not the Champ's first brush with the police, for there had been several arrests before, on charges ranging from assault to petty theft. The penalties had always been mitigated by his manager, and the Champ was left with a fine, a night or two in jail, and then release.

After this outburst, the manager did make some adjustments in the money the Champ got for his fights, but the basic inequities were still there. Although he was now a headliner and considered one of the best men in his division, he had not had a championship fight. The problem of a championship fight was simple: before he could fight the reigning champion, he had to agree to lose the first time in order to get a return bout in which he would have a chance to prove himself legitimately. To lose a fight intentionally, to give up, would mean that he would have to endure the same kind of humiliation that had caused him to flee from the South: that of not being himself. He absolutely refused. For the Champ, this had nothing to do with morality; it was entirely a matter of pride. With the championship or even the chance at the championship blocked by his stubbornness, he could go only one way, and that was down. His fame began to fade, and it was harder and harder to get fights. His manager, who had been willing to endure a good deal, saw the future fade—and dropped him. There followed a series of managerial changes, but to no avail. His hopes of ever becoming champion were gone and he became apathetic about boxing.

In the meantime, he had married a quiet, undemanding girl who loved him deeply. They lived quietly and, despite the modesty of his winnings, his wife, a better-than-average financial manager, had saved most of the money. Seeing the decline in his status and the impossibility of a future as a boxer, she finally persuaded him to quit fighting. It was becoming more and more difficult for him to get a good fight, and although she did not use it as part of the argument, she was aware of the increasingly severe beatings he was taking and was concerned about their effect on him.

He went to work for a construction company and was a good worker. His domestic life was tranquil, and he adequately cared for his family, which now included three children. However, he felt his shrinking fame as though it were a physical pain. To compensate for his loss of prestige, he began bragging. He declared first that he should have been champion, and after some months he insisted that he actually had been. Sometimes he would simply say that he was the uncrowned champion because he never got the fight, but at other times there was a formed delusion that he really was champion of his division. What he had not been able to achieve in the ring, the tricks of his own mind now gave him.

The patently false character of his claims resulted in skepticism on the part of his fellow workers. Finally, the knowing looks and jeering smiles when his back was turned became open derision. He no longer seemed so frightening to the men, and they were willing to take a chance and needle him. There were several episodes when he threatened his detractors. At last he could contain himself no longer and lashed out, severely injuring one of his fellow workers. Another arrest followed. This time the charges were pressed and a jail sentence resulted; no fast-talking manager was there to get him off. Although the charges were reduced because of the circumstances and he was released within three months, he was not the same. There had never been a question of his work ability, but now no employer would take the risk of hiring him because of his impetuous outbursts.

After he got out of jail, surly and bitter, he spent all of his time around the house. Nothing seemed to comfort him; he grew more distant from his family and became so easily irritated that after a while his wife, too, gave up any attempts to help, and withdrew. He spent this silent time going over in his mind the injustices that had been done to him in his life. Hate was all he had and he nursed it carefully, but his self-enforced seclusion gave him no object to spend it on. Deprived of boxing, which had once given him an acceptable way of striking back at injustices, his anger ached like an inner wound until his hold on reality was nearly gone.

He began to hear voices yelling "Kill, kill, kill him!" —the voices of the fight fans—and he was back in the ring, savagely attacking an opponent. One evening while he was watching the fights on TV, his wife came to sit beside him, silently sharing in one of the few things they could still share. The fight was exciting, and the Champ began to feel himself drawn into it. The voices—which in his fantasy had become the fans cheering him—were louder than usual. He was in the ring, on his feet throwing punches, bobbing and weaving, the fight the only reality. When his wife stood up to calm him, touching him on the shoulder, he whirled and struck her in the abdomen. She crumpled to the floor.

He was stunned by what he had done. The anguish at having struck and seriously hurt the one person who loved him and had stuck by him shocked him back to reality. He awkwardly comforted her until he was sure that she would be all right. Then, without a word, he left in search of a "crazy house," an action which he had been contemplating for many weeks.

At his own request he was admitted to the hospital. The admitting doctor's note said:

> This 34-year-old unemployed former boxer seeks voluntary admission after striking his wife. He is agitated, anxious, withdrawn. Auditory hallucinations are present saying, "kill, kill, kill." He is irritable, guarded and suspicious. The affect is flat and there are loose associations. Diagnostic impression is Schizophrenic Reaction, Paranoid Type.

Because of his history as a boxer, further examinations were made to rule out brain damage. Although there were some questionable findings in the electroencephalogram, neurologic and psychiatric examinations and a battery of psychological tests failed to find any evidence of injury.

When I talked with the Champ a few days later, he was less agitated. He started by telling me the details of his ring career, this introduction being necessary to establish that he was "somebody." Hospitalization removes any person from his usual environment and separates him from the accustomed symbols of identity. A strange place, different clothing, very limited private space, and distance from familiar people and things—all make it difficult to remind oneself of who one is. For the Champ the problem was even more acute, but once his "name" was established with me, he felt more relaxed, and over the next several weeks he became increasingly confidential. It was from these later interviews that I learned the details of his life that I have already given. His natural intelligence and sharp memory made him a good informant. Considering his brief education and his lifelong pattern of acting rather than talking, he had remarkable insight into his life.

As the descendant of slaves, he knew nothing of his background beyond the rural plantation environment from which the family came. His grandfather had been a slave, later freed, but freedom had changed neither the geographical location of the family nor the social nexus in which they lived.

His mother died when he was an infant, and the women in his childhood had been a series of aunts, sisters, and other relatives, generally kind and gentle, as he recalls, but in his memory lacking individuality, fused in a rather amorphous maternal image of kind, sweet devotion with an elusive quality of "here today, gone tomorrow." For him, mother, mother substitutes, and, later, all women, had this same quality, they gave the promise of pleasure, kindness, and warmth, but there was little that was enduring. Women were objects to be sought and held as long as possible, but the threat of their imminent departure was always there.

His father had no such tenuous quality; he was described as a solitary, unique figure. His mother had been his father's second wife, and there was another wife after her. He had something like 20 brothers, sisters, step-siblings, and half-siblings and became quite confused when he tried to enumerate them. The Champ himself was somewhere in the middle. He had kept in touch with only one member of the family, an older brother. His father, known as "Big Frank," was a feared member of the community and commanded considerable respect. He was quick-tempered and, at times, brutally beat his children or his wife. At other times he was lighthearted and easygoing. Because of his quick-changing moods most people kept their distance from him, not knowing what to expect next. He also had a considerable reputation for sexual prowess.

The Champ regarded him with a mixture of admiration and contempt. He was impressed by the deference with which his father was treated and by the stories of his fighting and sexual adventures. Among his paramours, it was said, were several white women. But in the white man's world Big Frank wasn't so big. He bowed and smiled and said "yassuh" and "nosuh."

There were also vivid memories of the beatings he received from his father. Big Frank, when in foul mood, would taunt and tease his children. The Champ recalled bitterly seeing his older sister taunted relentlessly until she would cry. Even more vivid was an occasion when, in her frustration, she made an attempt to strike back and was brutally beaten. On this occasion the Champ tried to defend her and received a beating himself. Similar punishment continued until his early teens. He recalled these assaults angrily, not because of the physical punishment but because of the humiliation that he felt. After such occasions, he would vow revenge against his father.

In his neighborhood, he was known as a tough kid and was often in fights. As his confidence grew, his opposition to his father became more open. The climax came when he was about 15 and his father nearly 60. During what his father undoubtedly expected to be a routine beating of his son, the Champ fought back savagely and a stalemate was reached. Thereafter they had little to do with one another, and within a few weeks the Champ left home and went to the city to live with relatives. He never saw his father again.

In all that he said he seemed very alert, stated that he had had six years of schooling, and considered himself to have been the smartest boy in school, which he probably was. Psychological examination showed his intelligence to be well above average.

In the city he was a laborer, with a reputation for being a hard worker. His quick temper and ready fists found plenty of activity in street fighting. His boss, unusually tolerant because he was such a good worker, saw him fight on several occasions. One day he told him he ought to be a boxer and arranged for to him to work out in a local gym for Negroes. He also introduced him to the man who was later to become his first manager.

It is difficult for a Negro to tell a Caucasian frankly how he feels about segregation, particularly if he has grown up in the South where the code of conduct between races is very strict. Attitudes of deference necessary for protection are deeply ingrained. Although during the time I worked with the Champ, he became relatively free to talk about many deeply personal things, he was never free enough to explain how he felt about being a Negro and what it had meant to him during his formative years. What I know about his feelings in this respect was gained mainly by inference. Once he asked me if I had ever been in the South. When I told him that I had spent a year in New Orleans, he immediately clammed up and talked very little for the next several sessions. He later told me that it had made him very uneasy, but he did not reveal the full force of his concern.

Although the bitterness he felt had deep roots in his relationship with his father, the major target was society —the white man's world. His feelings toward segregation and discrimination crystallized while he was in the Army. Whether his hatred for his father was displaced onto the social immorality of segregation or whether it was the other way around it is impossible to say. Perhaps for him the real battle was against the attitude of white supremacy and only in retrospect his father symbolized this injustice. He felt the humiliation of segregation as he did the childhood humiliation at the hands of his father.

In the rural environment of his childhood everyone suppressed the frustration of the social hierarchy. In the city and later in the Army he first tasted the potential of equality and became unwilling to settle for less. Yet when he first met men who offered him equality in friendship, he mistrusted them and tested the relationship until he destroyed it.

In his sexual life, which had been very active since puberty, he had emulated his father. His relationships tended to be lengthy, and even as a youth he often went with one girl for years at a time. He considered himself to be, and generally was, considerate of girls, and many of his street fights were in the service of protecting or avenging them. This was not a fleeting stage, since his relationship with his wife was similar to these youthful romances. He was an ardent lover and protector. Knowing that this was his image of himself made it easier to understand why his anguish was so great when he struck his wife just before coming to the hospital. It was an experience alien to his concept of himself and one which made him feel certain that he was "crazy."

By the time he left the hospital, the Champ's personality was reconstituted and he had a good idea of what he wanted to do. He continued to be suspicious and disdainful, but the crisis was over. He had no desire to go any further with psychotherapy beyond solving the practical issues of employment and his avocational interests, which he could see as the source of his salvation. Psychotropic drugs played an important role in his improvement. He was able to use me successfully to clarify some of his problems, but there was always a barrier of mistrust. He returned home, went back to a construction job, and a year later, the last I heard of him, was getting along well. His devoted wife was his greatest asset. He had also found a modest way of returning to boxing, as a volunteer instructor at a boys' club. As a teacher he vicariously lived through his pupils' struggles to achieve mastery over themselves and their aggression. He also gained respect from the boys, and this was satisfying to him.

*   *   *

I knew the Champ in 1959, well before the birth of the civil rights movement of the 1960's. In rereading his case, I am impressed with the social changes which have already taken place. My discussion of him largely reflects the situation as it was when I worked with him, but I believe that if I were to see him now, I would understand his predicament far better. The new confidence experienced by many Negroes today might also make it possible for him to use me more successfully at this time.

The American Negro has occupied a uniquely problematical social position in the United States. In many sections of the country his social mobility has been sharply limited. There have been limitations also on where he could live and what he could do for work. The appeal of forbidden fruit is always great, and the Negro who has once tasted privileges is justifiably eager to make them his own. The slow opening of opportunities only stimulates his hunger for social equality.

It has been said that the successful boxer must be a "hungry" man. During the depression this meant literal hunger for food. But there are other forms of hunger, for example, for social position, which can motivate a person just as strongly to seek his fortune in boxing.

In this country, achievement in sports has been one of the major ways for a disadvantaged person to improve his social position. Even though business, professional, housing, and avocational fields are blocked, the road to social ascent may be open in athletics. Members of groups which are demeaned and excluded from activities of high prestige and economic reward often see the light of opportunity first on the playing field.

Spectator sports offer the most opportunities, since the crowd seeks ever more able and colorful performances and the promoters try to satisfy them. If prejudice is partly a matter of closeness, those who watch from a distance are not so concerned about ethnic background as are neighbors; on the field the fans will tolerate good athletes who differ from themselves.

In sports with great mass appeal—football, baseball, boxing—minority groups have thus had a special place, and the individual's efforts have served not only his own social progress but that of his whole group. When, for example, baseball star Willie Mays was not able to buy a home because he was a Negro, the event received wide publicity, and a storm of public indignation led to a loosening of such restrictions. When former Olympic diving champion Sammy Lee had a similar housing problem because of his Korean ancestry, a special appeal was made by the then Vice-President of the United States.

The evolution of the American Negro toward cultural integration has been signalled by integration in sports. The order in which sports would be desegregated could be predicted on the basis of the breadth of their appeal to the public: first boxing, baseball, basketball, and football, with the largest followings; later tennis and golf, with smaller numbers of fans. The difficult experiences of the athletes who made the inroads, Jack Johnson, Jackie Robinson, Althea Gibson, and Charlie Sifford, were preliminaries to the desegregation experiences of Southern Negro school children.

Although the Negro is the most prominent current minority group to find his major opportunities on the playing field, others preceded him. The progress of the various groups making up our nation is suggested by the names of All-American football players. In 1889, all but one, Heffelfinger, had Anglo-Saxon names. The next non-Anglo-Saxon name was Murphy, in 1895. Then Irish names became very common on the team. Next came the Jews, the Poles, and today a mixture representing the spectrum of ethnic origins, including Negroes.*

More than any other sport, boxing has drawn its contestants from hungry, lower-class groups. Education and previous experience are not required, only strength, courage, and a willingness to follow instructions. For the boxer's effort, there is the possibility of fame and money. However slim, the opportunity is there, and where no other opportunities exist the appeal of such opportunity is great.

The Irish were the first great wave of American immigrants to be discriminated against. "No Irish need apply" signs were prominent in the nineteenth century. The heroic figure of John L. Sullivan, the first heavyweight champion of the modern era of boxing, symbolized the Irish struggle for cultural integration in his day. Against a background of discrimination, the great John L. proclaimed, "I can lick any man alive." The ranks of champion boxers succeeding him have been dominated by Italian, Jewish, and Negro athletes.

When Jack Johnson captured the world heavyweight championship, the first of his race to achieve such prominence in this country, he became the hope and promise of the Negro Americans looking toward social equality. His success was among the most significant social advances for the Negro since the Civil War. His championship became the second national battleground on which the forces of freedom fought the forces of bondage; but although a number of "white hopes" were developed to "prove" Johnson's inferiority, they generally failed.

Many years later, on the world scene, there was a similar focus on the boxing arena for a clash between significant social forces: the world championship fight between Joe Louis, a Negro, and Max Schmeling, the alleged Nazi superman, a contest symbolic of the great sociopolitical issue

---

* David Riesman, *Football in America: A Study on Cultural Diffusion, Individualism Reconsidered* (New York: The Free Press of Glencoe, 1954), p. 242.

of the day. Nazi doctrine, threatening all Europe and potentially the world, proclaimed the Aryan master race superior to all others. The myth of their invincibility was shattered
when Louis knocked out Schmeling in the first few minutes
of the fight. So humiliating was the defeat to the Nazis that
they could only raise a patently false cry of "Foul!"

Success in sports does not travel a smooth course
for either the spectators or the minority. Many fans eagerly
look for behavior that will confirm their stereotypes of Italians, Irish, Jews, or Negroes, and once such signs appear,
they afford evidence for saying, "See! You've got to keep
them in their place." The athlete himself may create difficulties. Sudden success may lead to exuberant and perhaps
inappropriate exploits as he seeks to establish the boundaries
of his newfound prominence.

When Jackie Robinson became the first Negro allowed to play major league baseball, he had to endure bitter
derision. During his "probation period" he uttered not a
word of protest even under the most severe provocation. It
is small wonder that when he was firmly established as a
major leaguer he released some of his pent-up anger. In
tennis, Althea Gibson was the first Negro to play in major
tournaments. At first, she was frightened and terribly conscious of her manners on the court, but later, when she became the best woman player in the world, she went through
a period of bitter self-assertion.

But it was boxing that first reluctantly opened its
gates to a Negro, in the person of Jack Johnson, who became
heavyweight champion of the world. His wild exploits attest
to the conflict he suffered in achieving his title. As he attempted a personal integration campaign through his marital
activities, he was subjected to the most vitriolic abuse.

The Negro who achieves success in the white community experiences a profound identity crisis. He is caught
between two worlds, in neither of which he really belongs.
His success in the white community separates him somewhat
from his origins; yet, no matter how great his achievement,
he is still black. He feels both relief and guilt for his ma-

terial rewards, like a soldier who is permitted to go home on leave while his buddies continue to fight. He is black, but he relies on the white world for his position. He lives in a limbo of agonizing ambiguity.

The Negro athlete who achieves prominence, however, is only a special instance of the identity dilemma of all American Negroes. The two adult identities, between which black Americans walk a tight rope, have been described by Erik Erikson as "light-clean-clever-white and dark-dirty-dumb-Nigger." The former is "good" and can never be achieved; the latter is "evil" and can never be renounced. The Black Muslim religious movement seeks to offer an alternative identity which includes "black-clean-proud." The appeal of such a movement to a people faced with impossible choices is obvious. Unfortunately, however, it accomplishes its purpose by further dividing whites and Negroes.

Negro children are bright, tender, and expressive, as bright as other children and perhaps even more tender and expressive, but there comes a time when they enter an adult world which offers little continuity of identity. Erikson* has described a poignant example of this difficulty: "I know a colored boy, who like our boys, listens every night to Red Rider. Then he sits up in bed, imagining that he is Red Rider. But the moment comes when he sees himself galloping after some masked offenders and suddenly notices that in his fancy Red Rider is a colored man. He stops his fantasy."

*   *   *

The Champ's identities were isolated fragments. With his wife and family he usually displayed characteristics of the tender, expressive child. In his interviews with me he was sometimes relaxed and spontaneous, too. On those occasions his speech temporarily lost its stilted quality and

* Erik Erikson, *Childhood and Society* (New York: W. W. Norton & Company, Inc., 1950) p. 213.

was as he had originally learned it. He would, as in the ring, back away with a light smile and fancy footwork resembling the jazz steps of his youth.

Much of the time, however, odd mixtures of adult white and Negro identities predominated: the frozen smile, half derision and half pleasure, the stilted speech imitating the white man's but incompletely, and his movements alternately stiff and formal or relaxed and genuine. In the ring, his facade was white: the scientific boxer, but punctuated by moments of elemental assault. No image could be found to fit adequately. It was when he did not know who he was that he lashed out in murderous violence.

The Champ sought to "become somebody," and for him seeking a "name" was indicative of this goal. He wanted a name acceptable to him and known to others. Like many people with identity problems, he hoped that if he could find the right name for himself, he would find a solution. At the insistence of his first manager, he discarded the name which established him as a Negro in a white society in exchange for one which seemed halfway between black and white—a Mexican name. Later he renounced this and chose the name of a famous old-time Negro boxer. Most of all he preferred to be known as "Champ." But none of these names ever suited him adequately. They could not, for a name can only identify a person, and the Champ had difficulty in knowing who he was.

It might be expected that if a man could establish his place in the world he would solve the problem of who he is. But the strange case of Cassius Clay bears witness to the fact that even this is not enough for the Negro living in this ambiguous society. The name Cassius Marcellus Clay was made world famous when its flamboyant owner became heavyweight champion of the boxing world. At the very moment, however, that he solidified his fame, he discarded this most important symbol of identity, his name. Although it had been with him all his life and had served him well, it did not fit a Negro in a white man's world. He next tried Cassius X, emulating his advisor, Malcolm X. But this was not right for him, either, and he settled on Muhammed Ali.

So clouded and ambiguous is the American Negro's identity that he looks to other "dark" or marginal groups for kinship. Cassius Clay settled on an American version of Islam, just as during World War II Negro soldiers often said they were American Indians and the Champ tried unsuccessfully to be a Mexican. Taking a name from other groups helps only temporarily, for one can still only be what one is. Until being a Negro has a dignified and acceptable place of its own in our society, no black American can feel like a complete person. The tragic heritage which fragments his identity is dramatically expressed in the title of James Baldwin's book, "Nobody Knows My Name."

The torment in the disadvantaged person whose identity is fragmented and whose social progress is blocked often explodes in violence. Crime and sports are the most accessible institutions for the expression of this angry retaliation. Only in these fields can a Negro both express his bitterness and get some reward for it. The criminal and the boxer both give direct expression to their aggressions, but the boxer is sponsored and applauded by society. Where else can a Negro beat up another man, perhaps even a white man, and be cheered for it?

There can be little argument that if the choice is between crime and boxing, the latter is preferable. However unrewarding and brutal it is as a sport, its effects both on the individual and on society are more admirable than crime. There seems little doubt that boxing has enabled many disadvantaged Americans to renounce criminal careers.

The Champ's psychiatric illness occurred when he was no longer able to maintain his most substantial identity, that of a loving husband. When he could not find any place for himself outside his home, his warm relationships there became contaminated by his bitterness. His hate appeared in the alien form of the hallucinatory voices that shouted, "Kill, kill, kill!" Most psychological symptoms, as in this case, occur when there is insufficient opportunity for expression of a part of the personality that is repressed. When repression fails, the alienated part returns to consciousness, usually in some disguised form—the symptoms.

When the Champ's boxing career came to an end, he tried to maintain his self-esteem with the delusion that he actually was champion. But he was ridiculed for his boasting and felt the familiar sting of humiliation he had so often known before—with his father, in his first fights in a segregated army, and in being deprived of a championship fight.

Boxing is perhaps the only sport available to the poor, educationally deprived, southern Negro for a great leap in social position. However dangerous the consequences, it holds for him the hope if not the reality of finding a successful identity.

8 WEIGHT LIFTER

"I'M STRONG AND I CAN PROVE IT"

One morning as I approached the University psychiatric clinic where I worked for a time I found the clinic social worker waiting anxiously for me. "I wanted to catch you before your first appointment to see if you could see a case for me today." There was a sense of urgency in her voice as she continued with the details.

The day before, she had received a referral slip from the University urology clinic with a scrawled message, "No GU pathology; recommend psychiatric evaluation." The procedure for such referrals required a preliminary interview with the social worker.

She found the subject of the referral to be a young male student. When ushered into her office, he stood at the doorway, seemingly paralyzed with fright as she greeted him. Invited to sit down, he flushed and remained crimson throughout the interview. He continually looked furtively about, as if seeking an escape, and never once glanced at his strikingly attractive interviewer. She asked the series of routine and innocuous questions to which he responded by squirming in his chair, glancing toward the door, stammering and stumbling, unable to formulate a complete answer. As the interview proceeded his frustration became contagious, making his interviewer uncomfortable also. She finally suggested, in desperation, that he come back the next day to see one of the psychiatrists, since he and she didn't seem to be getting anywhere. He was hesitant and noncommittal, but she insisted that he come back. The interview was over.

She related to me that she had become increasingly concerned about him after he left and wondered if he were grossly psychotic or perhaps contemplating something "drastic."

My curiosity aroused, both by the patient and the effect he and the social worker had had on each other, I was able to rearrange my appointments so that I could see him later that same day. The moment he entered the office, the situation was considerably clarified for me. He was a handsome young man, clad in tight Levis and an even tighter T-shirt. Bulging beneath this attire were enormously developed muscles which strained at the thin clothing, giving the impression of nakedness. He probably had the most striking physique I had ever seen, but it was almost grotesque. It was no wonder that his demure young interviewer had been unnerved.

On meeting me, he was rather tense and stiff but much less so than I had been led to expect by my informant. In contrast to his interview with the social worker he did not stammer at all, but spoke rather in a low-pitched, measured voice that revealed a Midwestern twang. He made no mention of his unsuccessful interview of the day before and began talking about himself. Evidently the difference in sex of his two interviewers explained the dissimilarity.

In his conversation with me, he said that he had wanted to see a psychiatrist for some time but really didn't believe he could be helped. He had always been nervous and had "an inferiority complex." He talked of his discomfort in crowds, in school and at work, and described symptoms of sweaty palms, headaches, a "queasy stomach," and tension. After a while I asked him why he had first gone to the urology clinic. He glanced quickly at me like a child caught with jam on his face, paused a moment, and then said quickly, "I can't get a hard on."

So the most potent-appearing specimen I had ever

seen was actually impotent! As if on cue he began de-
scribing his body-building and weight-lifting activities. Since
his middle teens he had been a weight lifter, spending many
hours each day working out, gradually becoming very strong
and proficient. When he was about 19 he placed second
in his regional weight-lifting championships. Body building
soon became an obsession. He felt he could really make
something of himself and set goals for himself which he
reached on schedule or even ahead of time. However, this
program did not do for him what he had expected, and
he changed emphasis somewhat. He began to believe that
weight-lifting competition was insincere, impractical, and
maybe even harmful. Perhaps the real thing for him would
be body development, so he changed his goals from the
amount of weight that he could lift, to the development,
appearance, and health "of the whole body."

In this program, too, he regulated himself rigidly.
He worked out a meticulous development program, with
weights and exercises, for each group of muscles, ate only
organically grown raw vegetables, wheat germ, and no meat.
He slept 10 hours a night and carefully watched and regulated his bowel movements.

This way of life gave him a feeling of control and
strength, since he knew "just what was coming in and what
was going out." He felt that if his body were sound, his
mind too would be sound and he would be able to beat
any situation at work, school, or on dates—all places where
he often felt awkward and out of place. He obtained considerable reassurance by playing his "comparing game":
"Steve may have more money, girls, education, friends than
I have, but I have a better build." One of the most reassuring things was to see others look at him in admiration
and surprise. He always wore thin, tight-fitting clothing because of the startling appearance that it created. It felt
good to be "noticed."

He had considered entering the Mr. America contest which he believed he had a good chance of winning,
but he regarded such official accolades cynically, insisting

that the real importance and meaning of his activity lay in what it did for him personally and how it affected his "human relations."

Despite his readiness to tell me about himself, he kept saying he didn't know whether he wanted to talk to a psychiatrist. I explained to him that he did not have to commit himself, and since I could see him only a few times anyway, he would be assigned to someone else if he decided to go further. This appeared to relieve him somewhat, and he was willing to return for the limited number of times I was able to see him. Evidently he feared relinquishing his control to the clinic or to me.

Mike was born in Assembly, Kansas, a small rural town with just under a thousand people. He pictured it as a very proper, orderly place with pious and righteous inhabitants who made him feel like an outsider. His mother was the "only divorced woman in the town," and as he saw it her status was viewed as scandalous. He was subject to the unique cruelty of which children are capable as spokesmen for their parents. He was teased with innuendos about himself and his parents, and taunted, chased, and threatened during recess and on his trips to and from school. He was the smallest boy, not only in his grade, but in the entire rural school he attended, and he was acutely conscious of his size and weakness. In order to compensate for feelings of complete inadequacy in the community he entertained a special fantasy whenever he suffered insult and abuse from his peers. One day he would return to his home town, burst in on his tormentors who would be planning to "get him," and stand like a colossus in front of them, confidently, disdainfully. They would stare at him in amazement and awe, see his tremendous build, and realize his extraordinary strength. In the fantasy one of them would start to smile, but with a ripple of his muscles that smile would quickly disappear. His peers would cower at his motionless stare. In reality Mike feared violence and always fled from a fight. But in this fantasy there was never a fight nor any need to overpower his opponents; his presence alone overwhelmed them.

In my office I saw a muscular, powerful-looking young man who was, in physique, the man of these fantasies. In his thoughts about himself, however, he was still the small weakling. He related a recent situation in which he and his college roommate had entered into a heated discussion about the equitable distribution of cleaning activities in their quarters. The argument reached a pitch at which it seemed that a physical fight would ensue. Despite his much greater size and strength, Mike fled from the room, with the same feelings he had had in childhood. Telling me the story, he said that as the pitch of the argument rose he felt as though he were shrinking in size, and at the moment he fled it was as though he were still the scrawny little boy in Kansas. Despite the physical change that had taken place in the intervening years and the fact that his formidable appearance made it unlikely that anyone would ever attack him, he saw himself as the weak, frightened child of the past. His own words were, "It's a crazy thing. I look at myself in the mirror and I can see that I am really tremendous, but I turn away and all of a sudden I'm nothing again—I'm just a scared little kid." As long as the mirror reflected his size and strength or as long as he could see the look of admiration and wonder in the faces of those he was with, he felt strong and confident. Without signs of reassurance he was left with the uncorrected image of himself as a helpless and vulnerable child.

At the present time he not only avoided any possible physical contact with men and fled from fights but also was frightened of physical contact or friendly relations with girls. As he put it, "I built myself up into something now, and I just can't afford to lose anything. If I get in a fight I might get hurt and lose a lot of ground. Girls can ruin a guy. I've seen it happen; they'll suck you dry, they'll sap your strength until you are just nothing."

According to the plan we had agreed on, after

several interviews Mike had to decide whether or not to continue treatment with another therapist. He insisted that he was now getting along much better and felt no need to continue. Although there had been considerable symptomatic improvement in the brief contact we had had, this was probably not the major reason for his wanting to discontinue. Rather this was an example of the well-known "flight into health" to avoid dealing more deeply with problems. The necessity of committing himself to the clinic for a term of treatment and especially to someone he had not met was out of the question for him. He could not trust someone he knew, much less someone he didn't know at all. Nevertheless he felt better, and the door was left open for future help if he should wish it. He did not reapply to the clinic.

Because of the rather short period of time during which he was seen, much of the information about his family and early development could not be verified; thus, his case study leaves a good deal to be desired. Although I recognized this deficiency in this case, it nonetheless appeared to me worthwhile to include it.

Some suggestions regarding the origin of his present situation can be made with confidence. I have already mentioned that his mother was divorced from his father when he was three years old. He described his mother as very good-looking and as having had many dates when he was young. During his mother's excursions his care was generally entrusted to friends, relatives, or even sometimes to his sister who was five years older than he. He recalled one occasion when his mother was going out on a date and had no place to leave him; she was forced to take him along on the date. He was instructed not to call her "Mother," and she told her escort that he was the youngster of a friend whom she was caring for. He was told to lie down in the back of the car and not to bother them any further.

Despite this rather uncharacteristic relationship between mother and son, she was all he had and the only one who stood by him, so he steadfastly defended her during the interviews. He hardly knew his father, and this relationship with his mother led to a deep mistrust of people.

His sister shared his misfortune, but not his sorrow. They bickered and fought constantly; she, being the elder, was usually triumphant.

All of his subsequent relationships with girls were tinged with an overwhelming sense of embarrassment so that his experience with the social worker at the clinic was not a unique one. He blushed and stammered almost any time he was with a girl of his own age and even found it difficult to order in a restaurant if the waitress was attractive. He was physically attractive, and he could have developed a relationship with a number of girls. But he generally considered them untrustworthy, and his relationships were passive and primarily those of a person who receives favors, money, food, and sex. The last-mentioned, however, presented considerable difficulties for him.

He had a rather evangelistic attitude toward the girls he went out with. He would not kiss a girl who had been smoking, and he crusaded against drinking, two activities which had been of great importance to his mother. Girls who smoked made him feel disgusted and contaminated.

His father, whom he barely knew, was an irresponsible person and his main asset, according to Mike, was a handsome appearance. Mike described his father as a lady killer, a term which he also applied to himself and to which he gave a literal connotation. He believed, and perhaps correctly, that he had lethal charms for the female sex which made him sought after. He saw his path through life as strewn with broken hearts. "I can't help myself," he said. "Girls go for me, but I have a way of hurting them in spite of myself. Even if I don't want to, I seem to say things or do things that tear them up. I'm a heel with girls."

There was one group of people with whom he felt comfortable—the weak. He felt warmly toward old people and the handicapped. He often volunteered to help the physically frail and weak, and from this activity he gained considerable satisfaction.

DISCUSSION

Whether weight lifting and body building should be considered an athletic activity may be subject to question. It is, however, an individual sport, perhaps the most individual. Mike's situation has been included here, in spite of the holes in the case history, because it illustrates several points which have relevance to other sports.

To appear strong had profound psychological meaning for this young man. It was clearly an effort to compensate, or rather to overcompensate, for his image of himself as small, weak, vulnerable, and attacked. The discrepancy between his actual physical power and appearance of confidence and the psychological image he had of himself and of his sexual impotence was most striking. It was indeed a remarakable paradox that one who appeared so powerful should feel so weak.

The concept of the mechanism of defense is one of the cornerstones of dynamic psychiatry and psychology. These mechanisms are the psychological tricks we play on ourselves or others and are more or less outside of awareness, serving as the syntax of the ego. Through these methods we defend ourselves against wishes, impulses, or images which are unacceptable to us or to others. Defense mechanisms help hide weakness, deny anger, displace sexual feelings, attribute evil motives to others, and perform many other functions in an effort to maintain a synthetic image of the self and to conceal that which is forbidden or unwanted. Mike attempted to conceal and deny his feeling of weakness by making himself physically strong. However, this worked only as long as he had demonstrable visual proof from seeing his muscles in the mirror or reading admiration and awe in the faces of others. For him, "seeing was believing." When he had to depend on his own inner feelings about himself he was still the puny child.

Mike's story is not unique. All men try to strengthen any overwhelming weakness they may have. Dramatic, well-publicized examples are present on the daily sports pages. Frank Budd, once the world's fastest man, still carried the remnant of his battle against poliomyelitis which afflicted him as a child. His calf muscle was severely atrophied. Through practice and indomitable courage he developed from a boy who could not walk into the world's fastest runner. Wilma Rudolph, his counterpart among woman athletes fought a similar battle with a childhood illness which retarded her walking for many years. Harold Connolly, the great Olympic hammer throw champion, is another dramatic example of how a person can compensate for disability. But perhaps the best known example is Glen Cunningham, the greatest miler of the 1930's, who as a boy had his legs burned so severely that he was told that he would never walk again. Despite this, through heroic training and practice, he became an almost legendary runner.

Although a weakness may be overcome, there is always a certain lag in keeping the self-concept up-to-date. Most adults do not see parts of themselves as they are at that moment but rather as they were some time before. The turmoil of adolescence and the fragmentation of psychosis are both testimonies to this. Similarly the aging person who lives with old attitudes of himself despises his age and can only look wistfully back. The child reaching adulthood may be stronger and smarter than his parent, but both find it difficult to approach a more equal relationship appropriate to the young adult's new skills.

Mike was frightened of women, whether they were social workers, waitresses, or dates. The source of this was the conviction that "a woman can ruin you." He was like Samson, strong and muscular, but the mere fact that he was strong meant that he had something to lose and was thus more vulnerable. Each female, for him, was a possible Delilah scheming to rob him of his tenuously held power.

To further compensate for his dread of emasculation he carefully controlled all intake and outflow of his body. Only carefully examined foods were allowed to enter, and the accounts were balanced daily by the amount that he expelled. Close contact with anyone was equated with the danger of surrendering some of his control. He feared that if he left himself "open" the delicate balance between what he received and what he put out might be disturbed. His tenuous relationship with the succoring mother made him skeptical of all people's ability to give to him. He feared that he might be called upon to give up more than he could spare and thus empty his reservoir. His faddist activities provided him with a degree of control of input and output.

The influence of his family relationships can be speculated upon. His mother was tantalizing; he recognized her attractive, appealing potential for satisfaction, but she never delivered the goods. However, he had no one else, and despite his frustration with her he saw her as the only one who "stuck by" him, which she had done in a begrudging way. Although his words denied the actual situation with his mother, he felt strongly the bitterness born of deprivation. His anger with her became transparent in the only feature which he believed he shared with his father—they were both lady killers.

His father had never been more than a story to him, and his principal male identification was his fantasy of a strong powerful figure, the sight of whom terrified his childhood tormentors.

Sexual relations were next to impossible for him. Here again his major conflict loomed large—he had to give of himself to a partner, with the possibility that he would not be given enough in return. Also, any closeness with women was tinged with the fear that, as he was a lady killer, he might hurt women.

The safest and most comfortable relationships he had were with those who were weak and helpless, the old

and the crippled. He could try to help them without fear
of being drained of his strength, since they, too, were
powerless.

It is easy to see, then, why Mike chose an activity
in which there was no peer-group competition, cooperation,
or closeness as there is in team sports. Weight-lifting competition and comparison of strength between himself and
others initially had some appeal but soon became hollow
and unsatisfying. The real issue with him was not to prove
that he was stronger but simply to make his appearance
so imposing that it would overwhelm and awe those about
him. Physical competition thus gave way to the more passive
relationship of being seen as strong.

He sought treatment only as the culmination of
this lifelong series of events. Despite his great physical
physique, his impotence was a constant reminder and demonstration of his weakness, and this in turn was only a
reflection of his image of himself as a weak, frightened
child. Sports never carried the usual implication of play;
for him they were more on the order of "a play." It was
a play in which he was the only actor, and the world was a
spectator watching him take the part of Superman of his
boyhood fantasy. He never faced the problem of a transition from play to work as did other athletes. For him his
activity was always in dead earnest.

9 MEMBERSHIP IN THE TRIBE

THE SPECTATOR AND HIS CITY

There are men to whom it is a delight to collect the Olympic dust of the course.

... Horace

In a special sense, the emphasis of this chapter
is a psychosocial one, drawing on both psychology and
sociology. The spectator—the wild-eyed, cheering sports fan
who fills the stadiums and field houses—is as significant to
the psychology of sports as is the athlete on the field, but
he exists in relation to a particular community. Since the
community in this case—Los Angeles—is a modern American city with its own special characteristics, at once a
sociologist's laboratory and nightmare, it deserves a close
look before we examine its effects on one small, displaced
baseball fan among its inhabitants.

Every city in the world has its own personality,
but the image that Los Angeles presents to the world is
especially multifaceted. To a San Franciscan, it is the hated
rival, the place where the barbarians live. To the movie
fan, it is the metropolis surrounding the mecca, Hollywood.
To a majority of residents, it has meant simply sunshine,
jobs, a good place to live. As a result, Los Angeles has

become the fastest growing major city in the United States, a city where it is extremely difficult to find a native or even a long-time resident.

Los Angeles is a melting pot of Philadelphians, New Yorkers, and Chicagoans, of "Okies" and "Arkies," of Rebels and Yankees. These transplanted residents usually continue to consider themselves a part of the cities from which they came, as though they were just visiting. (They resemble the Greek and Italian immigrants of an earlier day who came to this country in the hope of making their fortune and going home and who, as exploiters rather than homeseekers, resisted assimilation and cultivated old ties and native customs.) Even some who have lived in Los Angeles for a decade or more never feel at home in Southern California. Thousands who neither knew nor cared about each other while they were living in their native states now anxiously await Iowa picnics or Nebraska parties, where they can feel at home. They do so, perhaps, because in Los Angeles it is not easy to feel that you belong. It is the only city in the world in which a small district, Hollywood, is better known than the city itself.

Los Angeles is like a great sprawling ameba which extends its pseudopodia from time to time to incorporate a new area, seemingly for no other reason than to satisfy its undisciplined appetite for growth. It has been called a group of suburbs looking for a city. A thousand people a day come to live in Southern California, a majority of them in Los Angeles. The city is spread so widely and in so amorphous a way that it is the largest city in the world in area even though, in population, it is exceeded by many others —so diffuse that one is hard put to tell where the center of the city is or how the parts fit together. The tentacles of communication and transportation spread in every direction, but they don't seem to lead anywhere. Travel on one of the giant freeways at one edge of the city leads but to the other edge. On such a trip one passes the endless series of look-alike houses which comprise the suburbs, clustered into a city planner's bad dream.

Cities of 50 or 100 thousand are distinguishable by their road signs, but in other respects they blend into one another without obvious differences. In these suburbs one cannot find a center of town or a business district. Occasional shopping centers have been developed without regard to city boundaries. People do not work in relation to where they live. Many travel an hour or more on the freeway to some other part of the city to get to work, passing an equal number of others traveling in the opposite direction on the way to their jobs. Homes are no more than sleeping quarters adjacent to the freeway. The towns themselves are analogous to bedrooms in houses that have no living rooms. City planners cry out in protest, but as if with a mind of its own, the city relentlessly advances. It is small wonder that the citizens cling tenaciously to any identification with former cities, for these cities, at least, are identifiable.*

It is not surprising that within this fluid, centerless mass the citizens seek, sometimes desperately, groups with which they can identify, so as to feel that they belong. Los Angeles has become the center of quackery and cultism, of evangelism and prejudice, and of political extremism, both right and left; in these spurious ways, at least, its citizens can feel that they belong to something. Sports appear to have something of the same social function.

Los Angeles is described by local sportscasters and sportswriters as the sports capital of the world. Listeners to radio and television sportscasts hear this description daily. The residents of Los Angeles support their teams with a fervor probably greater than that in any other city. Los Angeles is a city of sports fans. In a single year, 1960, the

---

* The problem is not solely due to the amorphous character of Los Angeles. A newcomer to any city clings to and cherishes memories of his home. And like home cooking or the good old days, it seems better and better with time and distance. Much eulogizing of the cities from which Los Angeles residents came is only fantasy. Yet although similar growth problems have affected most major cities in this era of population explosion, Los Angeles has the characteristics more strongly than other cities, and newcomers' problems are thereby compounded.

city acquired a major professional football team, a major professional basketball team, professional ice hockey, and a major-league baseball team. These were in addition to the already existing professional football team, major-league baseball team, and very popular college sports. In their first year of major-league baseball in Los Angeles, the Dodgers, finishing next to last, set new attendance records.

An explanation of the above is that some of the citizens of Los Angeles needed the Dodgers. They needed something concrete around which to rally, something familiar, yet unique, to provide identity. For many residents, the addition of a major-league baseball team gave the city more substance. It helped to be able to say, "We are Dodger fans," and for those residents for whom baseball was important, the team provided a clearer picture of the place where they lived. Now they had an opportunity to belong to a strong clan, a major-league baseball team, without being branded as cultists or fanatics. As baseball fans they could, with no misgivings, be as avid as they wished, for nothing is more American, less deviant, than baseball. Many who came to Los Angeles from cities that had major-league teams could transfer some of the meaning from the cities they had left to the city in which they now lived. They felt a new pride in living in Los Angeles and being Dodger fans. Separated from their families in distant cities, they found a new family. The Dodger management was quick to capitalize on this emotion. For a small price one could buy a Dodger family portrait or a Dodger family album or even the kind of cap worn by the members of the team. Thus, at last, the new fans could truly belong, truly identify themselves with a family, a team, and a city. They could carry pennants which described clearly and dramatically who they were: Los Angeles Dodgers.*

* Psychologically, the primary sources of identification are parents, family, school, church, ethnic group, neighborhood group, and so on. The city is not the only identification model, nor even the most important. But these primary sources, too, have undergone some dissolution, and when the community fails, many people are left with a void.

In today's complex society, family ties have become attenuated and clan ties have all but disappeared. Grown children rarely continue to live in the same town as their parents. Often they leave the social class in which they were born. Leaving behind one's roots makes it difficult to have a clear picture of one's place in the present and its relationship to past and future. When mobility has carried one to a city which in itself has little identity and whose citizens have all come from some place else, the problem is even greater, for few supports remain for an already weakened identity. The greater the disruption, the greater becomes the individual's need for something with which to identify.*

The Dodgers first achieved notoriety and loyal support in Brooklyn, one of the first of the great American melting pots. Immigrants from Europe had separated themselves from their families and cultural ties by coming to America. They felt a hunger to belong to something, but it had to be something uniquely American, something rich with personal meaning. Baseball was American and easily understood; the image of the Brooklyn team—those motley, often downtrodden Bums—was ideal for the purpose. After serving Brooklyn well for many years, the Dodgers moved to Los Angeles, where they were needed even more. Although the move was made for economic reasons, the great new melting pot was hungry for them, and they were embraced with loyalty and enthusiasm.†

Everyone needs to feel that he has ties with others. With the dispersal of the traditional extended family, the clan, and the tribe, this need to be identified with a group

---

* After World War I, many Germans, through defeat and the Treaty of Versailles, felt a similar loss of identification. This was at least one of the forces which led to the ready acceptance of Nazism; for it did promise identity. Few will disagree that the Dodgers are a preferable identity model.

† In Japan, once a classic example of the extended family system and its attendant social stability, the mania for sports has today grown to American proportions as the traditional social forms and values have been worn away.

of some kind has become more intense. The sports fan
has a readily available group to satisfy this need, at least
in part. He has a meeting place, the stadium, where he is
needed to support the team. He can gather with others, don
his Dodger cap or some other identification badge, and yell
at the top of his lungs for his team. He can memorize the
batting averages, pitching records, and life histories of the
team members, and the standings of the teams, so that he
gets to know the team as well as he knows his own family.
In effect, by doing all this, he becomes a member of a
larger, stronger, family group, a collective entity compa-
rable in some sense to the tribe or the clan.

There is a further value. Everyone needs to be able
to share strong feelings with others. On the other hand,
the typical small American family of one or two generations promotes such intense relationships that the family
members are bound in a kind of unspoken truce to restrain
their strongest feelings, and usually only impulsive moments
of rage or grief break through to be expressed. In contrast,
in the family with several generations under the same roof,
when there were conflicts one could always find allies.
Thus, if a child and a parent were locked in painful hostility, there was someone else to turn to, a grandmother
or grandfather, perhaps, or an understanding uncle. In the
relatively small family of today, no such neutral figure is
available.

The members of the present-day family must get
along with one another or else. In a community which is
new to such a family, where neighborhood ties are difficult
to form, official groups—welfare agencies, churches, schools
—have assumed the function of the extended family.

Official agencies often do not serve as well as
those which develop spontaneously in response to a cultural
need, and of the latter the athletic team, which has developed many of the characteristics of the extended family
and the tribal society, is an impressive example. The fan in
relationship to his team is like the member of a family or
a tribe. He can share intense feelings in victory and defeat.

He partakes of the secrets of the tribe—statistics and team information—and he can exhibit tangible evidence of belonging. He dons his tribal headdress, his Dodger cap, and joins in the ceremonies at the stadium to support the members of the tribe as they do battle. He can complain bitterly to an understanding crowd of the fallacious decision of the chief—the manager. He can complain about the errors of some team members to other tribesmen who, like him, understand.

The fan is united with other fans in his hatred of rival teams. Where else is an American encouraged to leap to his feet, at one with a sympathetic crowd, and vehemently shout, "Kill the bums!" He knows that he does not stand alone in his intense feelings—that, such feelings are shared with a host of others. Anyone who objects must take on all of them. In victory there is a boundless sharing of the joy which the fan experiences personally and collectively.

*   *   *

Keeping in mind the special function of sports in a city like Los Angeles, we turn now to a young man, aged 25, whose case illustrates the psychosocial generalizations that we have been developing. We'll call him Benny.

I first met Benny when his doctor referred him to the outpatient department of a large state hospital. Now, after four months of hospitalization, he was ready to leave, his doctor hopeful that he would make at least a marginal adjustment to life outside if he continued his treatment in the outpatient department.

That first day, although he had had only two blocks to come, Benny arrived for his appointment three quarters of an hour late. He had lost his way. As he sat in his chair, almost motionless, the expression on his face was vacant, and he talked in a monotone. Why had he come to the clinic? His doctor had told him to. He didn't see much point in it, himself. He didn't know just what he wanted to do. His behavior was that of an automaton, but

after we had talked for a time, he expressed one desire—
for the only thing, apparently, that meant anything to him.
Leaning forward in his chair, he said earnestly, "I want to
go home. To St. Louis." He said it softly several times. "I
want to go home. I want to go home."

Little by little, the story came out. I learned that
Benny had been in Los Angeles for three years. He had
come there with his parents from St. Louis where he had
lived all of his life. Both Benny and his father had had
trouble finding jobs in the Midwest, and the promise of
employment in the defense industries of Southern California
had drawn them there. But even though he found the work
he had hoped for, things never seemed right to Benny in
California. He felt alone and lost. He longed for St. Louis—
for the familiar street, the familiar house, his relatives and
friends.

It was hard for him to make friends in the suburb
just off the freeway where the family now lived. He looked
in vain for places where he could re-establish himself. There
wasn't even a corner drug store. To go to a movie—and in
the past he had often met friends at movie houses—he had
to drive for half an hour on the freeway, and even when
he got there it would be a drive-in where he couldn't mix
with the people.

In St. Louis, Benny had been a baseball fan who
went regularly to Busch Stadium to watch the Cardinals.
In California when he arrived there was only minor-league
baseball, and it was no fun for him to go to a small baseball
park where he knew neither the teams nor the fans. It
seemed to him that even the other fans weren't very interested. He tried football, the biggest spectator sport in Los
Angeles at the time, but he had no interest in it. The first
two times that he went to football games, he got lost trying
to find the Coliseum. Somehow he never seemed to be able
to get into the right lane for the parking lots. When he finally
did enter the stadium, the sight as he came out of the tunnel,
of that great gaping hole filled with 100,000 people roused
him to panic, and he ran back down the tunnel and didn't

even stay for the game. A thought formed in his mind: "All those people in that enormous place; I don't know any one of them and they don't know me." He was alone and lost in a sea of faceless people.

In St. Louis when he and his father worked in the same plant, they used to ride the streetcar together back and forth to work. In Los Angeles, on the other hand, he and his father left home at about the same time, but they went in different directions, and Benny never knew exactly where his father worked. At his job he tried to strike up acquaintances with the other employees, but he found that he had nothing to talk about—in St. Louis there had been baseball or the movies or things that went on in the neighborhood. He was naturally shy and sensitive, and a couple of rebuffs discouraged him from further attempts at making friends.

Benny tried to explain his predicament. "I didn't know where I fit," he said. "Sometimes I felt like I must be somebody else or maybe I wasn't anybody at all. I felt like I was beginning to come apart." He was alone in a world of strangers, his real home far away. True, he still lived with his family, his mother, father, and sister. But they seemed different, too, and the house they lived in didn't seem like a house at all, with all that glass, that flat roof that looked like no roof at all, every other house in the block looking just like it. Several times, coming home from work after dark, he got confused and, for a moment, didn't know which house was his.

He began writing letters to a girl he had known only slightly in St. Louis. After two or three letters, he asked her to marry him, believing that this was one way to get back to St. Louis. The girl didn't answer, but her father wrote indignantly to Benny's father, who reprimanded him for his impulsive proposal and left it at that. The next day Benny was picked up by the police, driving his car in the wrong direction on the freeway. He had been on his way to work when the feeling came over him that he was

being swept along with all the other cars and had lost
control over where he was going. Like a lemming, he was
part of a mad, suicidal dash to the ocean. Taking the next
off ramp, he decided that he had to go back the way he
had come. He turned back into the off ramp, ignoring the
Do Not Enter sign. A car that had slowed to turn off the
freeway sideswiped him, forcing him into a fence, miracu-
lously without physical injury to anyone. When the police
arrived, he demanded that they let him keep driving because he had to get home. He mumbled incoherently about
being controlled and several times tried to break away to
run onto the freeway in order to get home.

Just as Benny had lost his way to the hospital
outpatient department, he had lost his way in life. His
environment seemed unreal and unfamiliar, the people
around him strangers. The others on whom he had depended
for knowledge of who he was and where he was going
had failed him. He had managed to survive the rigors of
being in the army where there was no dearth of people to
tell him what to do, but he had lost the nameless battle in
Los Angeles.

A schizophrenic reaction is an awesome thing.
Estrangement and loneliness, depersonalization and loss of
identity—it is a profound personality disorganization with
bizarre attempts to bring order from chaos. Benny's psychiatric disorder did not begin with the move from St.
Louis to Los Angeles; the move, however, was the factor
that precipitated it. Schizophrenia is the end product of a
series of partial failures in personality development.

The failures are not easy to identify with certainty.
There is evidence to indicate that schizophrenia is the final
product of certain social, psychological, biological and bio-
chemical processes. While the proponents of each field
emphasize their findings as the primary ones, the disorder is
probably the result of a complex group of interrelationships
among these different spheres. Benny's case history revealed
the likelihood of genetic determination, psychological depri-

vation in his family life, and social ambiguity, all of which are consistent with factors reported in the development of the schizophrenic syndrome.

There were histories of hospitalization for mental disorders in relatives on both sides of Benny's family, and, indeed, his early environment left much to be desired. He was born to his teenage mother before marriage, and his father evidently had consented to marry under duress. To his struggling parents, their child was forever the symbol of unhappy beginnings. Although they were never overtly cruel, they tried to make believe that Benny did not exist.

The first source of identification for a growing boy is his family, but it was difficult for Benny to feel a part of a family which wished he were not there. In his earliest years, his mother performed her maternal tasks in a dutiful, if perfunctory, manner, while his father who was gregarious with others, did his best to ignore his son. When Benny's sister was born five years later, his parents had achieved a kind of equilibrium; by that time they were free to express a more normal parental affection toward their daughter. Benny no doubt suffered from this, too, but suffering which goes unrecognized eventually goes underground.

By the time Benny reached his teens, his parents had become actively concerned about the anxious, withdrawn, friendless boy in their midst, but their remedial attention was only partially effective. Moreover, there were few others with whom he could identify; his teachers were not encouraged by his withdrawal and he failed to make friends among his peers. Identification with a religion was complicated by the mixed faiths of his parents, although periodically he became an ardent churchgoer.

The family regularly attended St. Louis Cardinal baseball games. It was here that Benny made his major social progress. In the stadium, he could join the family, especially his father, in expressions of favor and dissatisfaction. He became quite knowledgeable about the team, enhancing, in turn, his position in the family. Baseball thus improved Benny's tenuous relationship with the family, and he managed to find some relationships outside the home. Although still shy, withdrawn, and uncertain, he was able to survive the rigors of the army, for they were of a kind which provided direction. He had fleeting thoughts of an army career, but he missed his home, and when his service was completed, he returned to St. Louis.

It was only a short time after Benny's return to St. Louis that his parents, lured by the warm climate and the prospect of more money, decided to move to California. Benny passively joined them.

*   *   *

After the first interview, Benny and I planned his return to his family and agreed to meet regularly in the outpatient department. Over the course of the next year there were a few evidences of improvement. Although at first his mother had to drive him to the hospital, he began driving himself; occasionally now he would venture out of the house; his medication could be cut to a lower dosage. But he was still vacant and alone. He had no interests, and the only time there appeared to be any life or enthusiasm in his sad eyes was when his psychotic thinking took over and he would say, "I want to go home to St. Louis." Even though it was also the location of his childhood deprivation, he clung to it as the best place he had known. As he became more aware of his surroundings, the delusion of timeless security in St. Louis faded.

Psychotherapy was directed at supporting him and helping him to have a better picture of himself, but progress was slow. The slowness of his recovery and his inability to find meaningful relationships or activities did not make for a promising future. A year after his first acute disturbance, there seemed little hope of his being able to reach his previous level of adjustment. His parents had all but given up on him. They were willing to provide him with a home but were unable to give him much more.

When the Dodgers moved to Los Angeles, Benny's father called me to ask if I thought it would all right if

Benny went to a game. The father was rightfully concerned about Benny's going back to the Coliseum, that gigantic football stadium which had now been transformed into a baseball park, for it was there that Benny had experienced his first panic. I suggested that he leave the matter up to Benny, who could, if he wished, talk it over with me at our next visit. Although he did not discuss it with me, Benny decided not to go.

But one day, some time later, the whole family decided to go to a Dodger game. Benny, left with the unhappy choice of either staying home by himself or going with his family to the game, chose to go. When he entered the stadium he experienced none of the panic that he had felt before. The protective coat of apathy had anesthetized him. His parents noticed that he seemed to show no enthusiasm for what was going on, but they were pleased that he had come with them. Not the least of their pleasure was that it had made it possible for all of them to go to the game, since no one had to stay at home with Benny.

The therapeutic effect of his attending a baseball game had not impressed me except as a way of getting him out of the house to join in a family activity, and so I was not surprised by his parents' report of his apparent disinterest in the game. To me he said not a word about the baseball game he had attended.

About a month after his first game, however, Benny arrived for his therapy hour wearing a baseball cap with "L.A." emblazoned on it. I asked him about his cap, but all he said was that he had bought it at a game. He apparently did not wish to discuss it. I viewed his wearing the cap with concern, for peculiarities of dress often accompany a deterioration in schizophrenic patients. In spite of this, there were no other ominous signs, and, in fact, there was evidence of slow but steady progress.

It would be easy to ascribe Benny's improvement solely to the effects of psychotherapy. Indeed, a transformation had already begun with his failure to provoke in me the kind of hostility that he associated with his father.

Secretly, he believed that I, and everyone else, must wish that he had never been born, and anything I could say to the contrary merely illustrated my deceit. He made every effort to prove me a liar.

Whether Benny's interest in the Dodgers started before or after he began to notice me as a person without ill will toward him, I cannot say; the two things seemed to occur at about the same time. It cannot be determined that one was cause and the other effect, for it is likely that each of us, the Dodgers and I, facilitated the other's relationship with Benny. The Dodgers symbolized a less forbidding society, while I represented the individuals in such a society who were turning out to be not so threatening after all.

Benny now wanted to tell me about his experiences. He reported that the first time he went to a game he was afraid, but he was even more afraid of staying home. He found each game he went to after that less frightening. Eventually he began to look forward to the games.

Next, he began attending games alone. He now liked being in the large crowd. He liked the idea that no one knew him and yet that he belonged there as much as anyone else. He felt "just like everybody else."

That year the Dodgers finished seventh in an eight-team league. Benny felt a kinship with the underdog team. He became interested in the players and began memorizing batting averages. One day when the crowd rose to cheer a game-winning run, Benny realized that he too had risen and was cheering. This was an event of great significance to him. He was at once frightened by his own public display of emotion and reassured that no one seemed surprised or concerned about it. He puzzled about this for days. At the next game he quite deliberately cheered his favorites, cursed the umpire, and shouted advice to the manager. It was his team and he was their fan.

His next steps toward rehumanization were taken in an interesting fusion of his two new relationships, one with the team and the other with his psychiatrist. As the reader of the preface knows, I am confined to a wheelchair. Benny began sitting near the wheelchair section at the games. He felt more comfortable there because of his own feeling of identification with the maimed underdog—like himself, like the Dodgers, like his psychiatrist. From passively sitting near the amputees and paraplegics, he began helping them by bringing refreshments. He said that when he did he felt that he was paying me back for helping him and that it made us "more even."

Finally, he began to talk to the other fans, hesitantly at first, but gradually with more confidence. Although he always liked to drop by the wheelchair section, he began sitting where the view was better.

Benny was beginning to find some order in Los Angeles. When he first arrived and got lost on the freeways, he could not understand their purpose. Their aimless, tortuous paths seemed to lead nowhere. When he became interested in baseball and considered the Coliseum the center of the city, he began to see a pattern and purpose in the freeways as they crisscrossed the megalopolis. He even learned alternate routes to reach the stadium. His mastery of the freeways became symbolic of the new control that he was gaining over himself.

Benny eventually was able to go back to work. At the end of the baseball season, he experienced a mild return of his symptoms—aimlessness, not knowing what to do with his time—but he managed to get through the year. The next season the Dodgers came back and won the pennant. Benny's progress, although less spectacular, paralleled the team's. His life has continued to be constricted; he does not have close friends nor has he ever married, but he is fairly content with his life and has not had any recurrence of his illness. He works regularly, lives in his own apartment, and has many hobbies.

As Benny's need of me diminished, I saw him less frequently. He occasionally calls me and I always receive a card from him at Christmas time. The last time I saw him,

he seemed certain enough of the Dodgers (and me) that
he didn't have to worry if they would be there when next
season came around. He talked in an animated way about
the Dodgers' chances and about their new stadium. He complained about the freeways, but it was in the same way
that other Californians complain—they take too long.

*   *   *

The fan is an athlete once removed, an athlete in
spirit if not in fact. Through lack of physical capacity or
psychological desire, he is a competitor without the necessity of facing the dangers of competition. He is aggressive
without threat of injury either to his body or his pride.
Although his competition is vicarious, he can enjoy the
pleasures of victory, the sorrow of defeat, the tension of
the climactic moment. Moreover, he can, if he wishes, express his emotions verbally and even physically without fear
of censure. The fan enjoys a peculiarly luxurious position
between the camaraderie and the anonymity of the crowd.
He can share intense feeling with strangers who understand.

There are, within the population, only a small
number of persons who can become star athletes, but no
matter when one ceases to participate on the field one can
continue in the stadium. Some may never have engaged in
the actual combat, others may have been near-greats, but
as fans all may share the elemental experiences of sports.

The pleasures of the spectator are more passive
than active, and they are derived mainly through the organs
of sensation rather than by means of the action of the
musculature. In spite of limitations in physical prowess
due to age or innate lack, the fan can experience the emotions of the contest. He knows what it is like on the battlefield without going into combat.

The spectator's passive sensory experiences may
begin with only a single sense—auditory, for example, if he
listens to the radio. Even in television viewing and listening,
he is far removed from the actual scene and experiences.

The newspapers or magazines provide him with only visual stimuli. Those elements of the experience which are lacking can be fabricated in the mind through fantasy, and it takes very little to set in motion a train of visual pictures or other associations that complete the experience. The spectator can be far removed from the field of action in the stadium— to the grandstand, beyond the dangers on the field, or to his own living room where even his relationship to the crowd is largely fantasy.

It is the team or the player that counts. In fantasy, the fan can take any part that suits his psychic need. He may be the haughty favorite or the downtrodden underdog, the aggressor or the defense man. He can project onto the players the whole gamut of his emotions as they enact the competitive drama; in sports, unlike the theater, all things are possible in any role with which the spectator may identify, for there is no script. The outcome is always in doubt; as long as it continues, the game can still be won.

The team supports the player; the crowd the team. All are there for a common purpose. As in representative government, the interests of the masses are centered on the field of action, but with the distinct advantage that the crowd can see the proceedings as they occur and make its favor or disfavor directly felt. The team influences the crowd, and the crowd influences the team, in symbiotic fashion. They belong to each other and rely on one another for their vitality.

The experience itself is elemental in a way that has been ascribed only to sex, crime, and sports. For modern man, social custom and the necessity of living close together preclude very much expression of primitive emotions. Regression, the return to simpler and more elemental stages of adjustment, is acceptable within the matrix of sports watching. Grown men carry banners or wear hats denoting their favorites, in the same way that youngsters emulate their idols. Like alumni returning to a class reunion, they act in the stadium in ways different from the way they are free to act in the work world but similar to their behavior in nostalgic, bygone days. Regression, if controlled, tends to refurbish the individual for return to the monotony of his daily life.

All of these elements associated with sports watching were important in establishing and preserving the integrity of Benny's personality. They helped him make order out of chaos in Los Angeles, and thereby to bring order in himself. Baseball served as the medium of exchange in human transaction with fellow workers, spectators, and the city. Baseball had even made it possible for Benny to relate himself to the members of his own family. It is strange, indeed, that it should take a game to allow human beings to feel related to one another.

10 CASES IN REVIEW

The case histories which have been described up to this point are of athletes or participants representing the gamut of sporting activities, from the most vigorous contact sports, such as boxing and football, to the most sedentary, a spectator. The athletes described came from a range of social classes and had widely different natural athletic ability and personality makeup. The psychiatric disorders from which they suffered ranged from a mild neurotic reaction of short duration to chronic psychosis of long duration. No attempt was made to obtain a representative sample of cases, and, of necessity, those selected were chosen on the basis of their availability to me; they were persons who had come to me for treatment and whose stories I have been able to report in disguised form. The main criterion of selection was their value in illustrating the psychological aspects of sports. Conflicts and problems as seen in the psychiatric patient are generally only exaggerations of the kind of experiences that every person has, leading to the observation that mental disorder is a matter of magnitude and quantity rather than quality. In sports, as in any other discipline or interest, a cross section of the various degrees of mental health and disorder can be found. It might appear that athletes, actors, and showmen are more susceptible to emotional disorders than are other groups of people. It should be recognized, however, that when someone in the public eye shows signs of disturbance his behavior receives wide publicity, thus fostering the erroneous impression that his group tends to be more disturbed than other groups. It is not my aim to uphold or dispel ideas about the amount of health or disorder among athletes or fans, but to comment on the psychosocial uses made of sports.

The cases described were athletes in basketball, football, tennis, golf, boxing, weight lifting, and a baseball spectator. Why did each of these persons select his particular sport? In each case, the answer is not simple but probably includes a combination of factors, physical, social, and psychological.

The physical requirements of a particular sport may be highly specialized. Certainly in the case of Cal, the basketball player, his height was a determining factor. If he had been five feet seven inches instead of six feet seven inches tall, his choice of a sport would probably have been different. Similarly, one finds certain unique physical requirements in all sports. Thus, football players must be strong and rugged, with the ability to withstand hard physical contact. Linemen are generally bulky, while backfield men have to be more agile. In track, runners must be lean and shot-putters strong and hefty. But within most sports, fortunately, there is a place for athletes of all sizes and nearly all physical differences. We usually take particular notice of the athlete who does not seem to fit his sport, such as a 150-pound football player, a short basketball player, or a fat tennis player. With exceptions such as these, it can be assumed that the factors which determined the selection of a particular sport were more psychosocial than physical.

Each sport also has its own special social connotation. Among the cases presented, the tennis player and the golfer were influenced by the possibility of elevating their social positions through the sport. So too, was the boxer, but it was the only sport available to him as a Negro in the geographical area where he lived. With the choice, he had to take on the sport's unsavory reputation. Jack, the football player, also had little choice in his selection, for it was expected that the male members of his family would be football players, even more specifically, blocking backs. In contrast, Jerry, the golfer, did not select his sport to conform to the social standards of his family, but rather to be in opposition to them. The baseball fan was perhaps the most vulnerable of all to social influence in his selection of a sport. He was dependent upon the community where he lived for a constant set of instructions as to how to live. His breakdown came when be became confused by the instructions. His recovery occurred when with the aid of local baseball he was able to find some consistency in his society. For him baseball was the only means by which he could relate to others.

Neither social expectation nor physical character- istics alone are enough to explain all choices in sports. It was a personal decision of intrapsychic functioning which led Rock'm, Sock'm Jack to accept the family sport and led Jerry the golfer, to reject baseball and wrestling, which were associated with his family. Mike, the weight lifter and body builder, made himself look strong in order to compensate for his psychological concept of himself as small and weak. Each athlete who gains real satisfaction from his sport finds a particular constellation of maneuvers and activities which are meaningful to him. Whether the psycho- logical meaning of the sport determines the athlete's selec- tion of it or whether such meaning develops secondarily after the selection is usually not as clear as it was in the case of the weight lifter. Each sport probably provides enough latitude for an athlete to re-enact his special unre- solved situations.

Athletic competition often recapitulates earlier un- finished competitions. With reference to the cases discussed, it is to be noted that the first drama within the family years is often re-enacted later, on the athletic field. The golfer continued a psychological struggle with his brothers on the golf course; the tennis player, in a sense, was in competition with his father and brother on the tennis court; the boxer stalked his elusive identities in the ring; Cal relived in basketball the comfort and closeness he had as a child as- sociated with his father; the weight lifter continually tried to make up for his unforgotten experiences as a weak and vulnerable child.

In the novel, "Appointment in Samarra," the principal character, on being faced with death in his own city, flees to another city, which as it turns out, is the very place toward which death is hurrying to meet an appointment. Similarly, though one may flee from the location of an unresolved conflict, it is very likely that the same problem will arise in the new location. A familiar instance is the teenager who finds life in the family intolerable and seeks a solution in marriage, only to find similar conflicts arising there. Perhaps, in the continual testing to see if the problem still exists, it may be re-created. On the other hand, there are undoubtedly times when running away, putting potentially destructive energies into an area that is socially sanctioned, can be constructive in handling conflicts. The case of the boxer illustrates this point. His anger and frustration, which led him into socially disapproved activities and might have led to much more serious ones, actually helped him become a good boxer.

Athletes have different ways of competing or inhibiting competition. There are front runners and strong finishers, clutch players and chokers, defensive players and offensive players. Some athletes prefer team sports where their efforts are subordinate to those of the group; others enjoy the solitary competition of individual sports. All these characteristics seem to be associated with psychological events of the person's past, so much so that it would be possible to formulate the determining psychological events from how an athlete plays and what he plays. The basketball player had to subordinate his own efforts to the team, "feeding off" rather than scoring himself. Early in life he had learned that individual sports held little meaning for him. The golfer, on the other hand, needed a sport which was highly individual. His paranoid sensitivity would allow him to compete only when he was able to maintain distance from his opponents. Some athletes show reckless aggressive abandon when they have the support of a team, while in individual sports they are self-conscious and inhibited. Others find team sports meaningless or fraught with petty intrateam competitions which preclude their effective participation.

The circumstances which led to psychiatric dysfunction in the cases discussed are worth considering. In six of the seven cases the apparent precipitating event for the emotional breakdown was an interruption in the patient's relationship to his sport. In four, the disorder occurred almost immediately after interruption, and in the other two the effects, though delayed, were unmistakable.

It may be correctly argued that the interruption which precipitated the emotional disorders also disrupted other aspects of the athlete's life. Graduation from college, entering business, a disabling accident, moving from one city to another, marriage—all cause changes in every aspect of any person's life. In focusing attention on sports, there has been no intention to underestimate the importance of other aspects of life. It was felt, though, that in these cases sports were given overriding importance by the patient, and it appeared that the thread of continuity in the individual's life was severed when something happened to his sports participation. In every instance, maladaptation replaced the previously adaptive behavior.

Through sports the inevitable transition from boy to man may be delayed or sometimes, seemingly, even reversed. The tennis bum, who follows the sun, playing in tournament after tournament, achieves a temporary reprieve from entering the adult world. Old grads act like college students when they return to school for the big game, while parents relive youthful experiences with their children in Little League competition. At picnics sober adults romp in nostalgic competition with one another, only to be reminded of their age by next day's aches and pains. The professional athlete, if he is good enough, may drink from the fountain of youth and continue to play or stay in sports almost indefinitely.

In each of the cases, the athlete found it more comfortable to remain a player than to turn to the seeming vicissitudes of change. Some found the transition from boy to man so fraught with unacceptable consequences that they felt anxious and empty, and they developed symptoms. Some attempted to return to earlier, happier days through their fantasies. Sports became a way of maintaining the past while living in the present, representing a place where unfinished situations could be lived out again and again without social condemnation.

Sports provided meaning and substance to the lives of the seven athletes described. The following chapters will deal with broader observations of the millions of Americans who watch sports and participate in them, whose behavior is seen in the stadium or reported in the news.

11 THE RITUAL IN SPORTS

The case histories in Chapters 3 through 9 illustrate the significance of sports in the lives of the athletes and the fan who suffered from mental disorders. Now we shall consider the behavior of the average player, team, and spectator on the field as they engage in one of the few remaining rituals in American life carried out with the fervor and enthusiasm usually associated with primitive tribal rituals.

While the insights gained from the patients discussed offer a basis for the understanding of the behavior of masses of Americans participating directly or vicariously in athletics, it must be made clear that participation in sports is by no means considered an indication of psychiatric disorder. The masses of Americans in the athletic stadium, watching in the grandstand, or playing on the field are performing rituals which in every respect constitute an integral part of American life and are in no way deviant. In fact, if adjustment to prevailing institutions is taken as a criterion of mental health, one might conclude that the nonparticipant in sports is more likely to be disordered than is the participant.

Scientific thought and method have reached a state of development in Western civilization far beyond that of any previous societies. Resulting industrial and technological advances have made ours a society of affluence. Science has so dominated Western philosophy that it has emerged as perhaps the only consistent approach to understanding the life of Western man. It has been applied also to social and psychological attitudes toward life.

Scientific objectivity carries with it certain by-

148

products of great significance. It idealizes an attitude of dispassionate observation. The scientifically oriented person becomes more an observer than a participant, and he often experiences a sense of detachment from life as he emulates the very machine he has created. He suffers an alienation from the processes of living that has been described as the malady of twentieth-century man.

In scrutinizing his life processes, physical, psychological, and social, Western man has often inadvertently changed them. While his purpose was only dispassionate description, the result has been actually to change his institutions through noninvolvement and a blase attitude.

As the searching spotlight of science focuses on and tries to explain our traditional rituals, people have found them less appealing. As a result there is a lack of involvement or even open rebellion toward the traditional rituals of religion, politics, work, and family life. Attitudes toward authority, whether it be teacher, parent, or policeman, no longer involve blind allegiance; they have become detached and critical. The ultimate in detachment is the beatnik as he becomes a nonparticipant in any form of traditional institutions. It is clear that our culture has suffered from scientific progress as well as benefited from it.

The contemporary attitudes toward commemorative holidays typifies the changes. In the small American town at the turn of the century, the Fourth of July was eagerly awaited by the townspeople and everyone was involved in the celebration, either as participants or observers. Excitement enveloped the community, with parades, patriotic plays and speeches, fireworks and picnics. Today it has become just another holiday, except to a few residual romantics, the unsophisticated, or the very young. Similar changes have taken place in the celebration of Halloween, Christmas, New Year's, Armistice Day, and others. Today a blasé mass commercialism has replaced the sense of intense personal commitment.

These holiday rituals of bygone years were the nearest American counterpart to primitive rites. They served many purposes for the community, the individual and the interrelationships between them. They were activities of total involvement—of the individual, the family, the community, and the nation. Few such rituals remain in our culture today. Sports events, nevertheless, have defied analysis and have retained the appeal of excitement and commitment formerly associated with holiday rituals. The magnitude of sports interest has grown in proportion to the loss of involvement by Americans in other rituals.

We have seen, in the case histories, how a sport may represent, for an individual, a place of anachronistic refuge where he can comfortably retain his place in the world without facing some of the hazards of mature responsibility. Sports in general may represent a parallel anachronism for our society. They are the remaining stronghold of the archaic family structure, led by the strong patriarchal figure of the coach, with the intense sense of communal involvement of the team, and providing a place for everyone, whatever his age or station, whether fan or player. This aspect of American life has been left pretty much unsullied by analysis. It remains a locus for the expression of the competition, physical strength, and social rituals of a bygone era.

Despite disclaimers and the national denial to the effect that we don't really take our sports seriously, we Americans are deeply invested in our sports. Although there is a tendency to minimize the importance of sports as only a leisure activity not to be taken seriously, in writing this material, I am cognizant of the fact that I am analyzing that which is sacrosanct and that such analysis is likely to arouse vigorous denials and criticism from those who choose not to question the meanings of their enjoyment.

The lessons of ancient Rome should be sufficient justification for a close examination of America's athletic activity and its motivations. One can see many parallels between our sports and the sports of the declining years of that great empire. A single Coliseum served Roman spectators; today thousands of stadiums, great and small, serve the United States.

In the declining years of Rome, an increasing number of formerly productive rituals became focused on the sports arena. While Romans cheered their games and gladiators, their empire crumbled. Can our national drive and our productiveness be travelling a similar path today? Perhaps if Romans had been willing to examine the significance of their sporting interest, they would have found viable alternatives to decline. America's intense interest in games may signal a similar decadence, or, more hopefully, it may only represent a transition from the vestiges of the past to the birth of a new vitality.

12 THE PROBLEM OF WINNING

Those who challenge the gods will be destroyed.
Those whom the gods would destroy, they first drive mad.

In the pursuit of excellence in sports an athlete has many problems to face. These include his natural ability, learning the basic skills of the game, training routines, accommodation with coaches and team mates. Finally, there is the contest itself—the pregame anxiety, pacing himself to be ready for the crucial moment, and then going all out. These problems are familiar ones to coaches and athletes, and they have devised various methods of solution. In this chapter the focus will be on an aspect of winning not quite so familiar to sportsmen, yet one which is present in some degree in all contests. It is the psychological problem of winning—the mastery of one's aggression.

The sports stadium is a nearly ideal laboratory for psychological investigation. Games are played to be observed, and the investigator has an excellent opportunity for such observation just by attending an athletic event. In many experimental settings the presence of an investigator is foreign to the actual life circumstances, thus distorting the results. In most sports, however, for only the price of admission, studies can be made in the natural environment. The

152

observer is indistinguishable from other fans and has no perceptible influence on the results. The provisions for spectators, ranging from a single park bench alongside a neighborhood tennis court to hundreds of concentric rows of numbered seats in football stadiums, invite the psychologist to examine the life drama that unfolds there.

The explicit goal of all competitive sports, of course, is to win within the rules. Although the rules vary from sport to sport, this purpose remains constant. Sports like boxing and wrestling retain elements of the primitive combat from which they are derived. To win, the athlete must physically overpower his opponent. In other sports, such as golf and bowling, the competition is veiled so that there is no actual physical contact between competitors. Football, basketball, and baseball all contain certain elements of physical contact, but the winner is determined by comparative scores. In tennis and other games played with a racket, physical contact is removed from the hand-to-hand encounter of boxing and wrestling. The opponents are separated by a net and rather than striking one another, the players strike a ball with an instrument, the racket. Instead of hitting one's opponent in order to overpower him, as in the more elemental sports, the player hits the ball in such a way that his opponent cannot reach it. In track and field events an athlete attempts to run, jump, or throw faster, farther, or higher than his opposition. Since the course is the same for each contestant, the record of each may be compared with that of all of his competitors in the event.

The capacity of the human animal to perform in any sports event is obviously limited by his physical structure. But beyond these broad limits, psychological factors play the decisive role. Nevertheless, athletes and fans usually tend to consider as physical, all limitations which confront athletes in the pursuit of records or victory. There is ample evidence, however, that many of the human limitations assumed to be physical are actually psychological in origin. The skilled coach knows well the nature of these factors and intuitively works with his team to overcome them.

In track and field there have been a traditional series of so-called physical limits. These records were believed to represent the ultimate performance within the capability of a human being. Some of the well-known physical limits of the past two decades are the four-minute mile, the 9.4 second one-hundred-yard dash, the 15-foot pole vault, the 7-foot high jump, and the 60-foot shot put. For years performers competed at a level just below these limits, thereby confirming the theoretical assumption that the limits were inviolate.

Eventually, in each instance, someone broke through the barrier. The immediate reaction of athletes and fans to such record-breaking performances was one of disbelief. They were believed to be the result of errors in measurement or timing, of cheating or unfair tactics, such as pacers, or of secret scientific applications. An aura of magic and sorcery seemed to surround the transcendence of such records. But within a relatively short period of time other athletes equalled or bettered the unbelievable records, and surpassing the barrier has become almost commonplace.

Thus, for example, for 20 years the four-minute mile stood as an apparently unsurpassable limit. Great runners from many countries approached but could never break through the barrier. Like many of his predecessors, Roger Bannister, then a medical student in England, trained himself for this one ultimate performance. When he finished the record-breaking race he collapsed into the arms of friends. It seemed almost as if he had extended the record beyond man's limits. Strangely, within a few months after this memorable event, several other milers throughout the world had run under four minutes—without collapsing at the finish. When, in 1962, Peter Snell lowered Bannister's record by some 5 seconds he even continued jogging around the track. Stopping at a sportscaster's microphone to be interviewed, he hardly seemed short of breath.

Of course there have been technical advances which have facilitated the breaking of records; improved tracks, improved training regimes, and stronger and better equipment have helped greatly. But the final striking impression is that when a record is finally broken by one man it opens the way for others to do the same. The story of the breaking of the four-minute mile is not unique in the annals of sport but is, rather, characteristic of all such barriers. Within certain broad physical limits, the obstacles are in the minds of the performer and of the fans.

Psychological obstacles are to be found not only in the assault of man against a record in time or distance. They are even more prominent in man-to-man competition. The history of sports is filled with reports of bad-luck athletes who always faltered on the threshold of victory. Lady Luck, rather than psychological disability, is magically blamed for such faulty performances. They are not limited to the untalented, either, for among those who folded in the clutch have been the most skillful and able athletes.

Just as there are those who falter at the moment of victory, so there are renowned money players or clutch players. At the moment of greatest pressure they rise to meet these circumstances and gain victory. Such golfers as Arnie Palmer and, a decade before, Ben Hogan won such reputations. Ted Schroeder could be counted on for years to provide a pressure performance in the Davis Cup competition. Parry O'Brien, the great shot-putter, could always beat opponents with superior records in face-to-face competition. Bob Cousy in professional basketball and Jackie Robinson in baseball always seemed to be able to come through with the big performance at precisely the right moment.

Some fascinating studies have been made by Francis J. Ryan on some differences in the competitive ability of fine athletes.* Ryan is the field events coach at Yale University and a psychologist as well, who thus had a superb opportunity to make such studies. He has observed that some athletes give exceptional performances in competition while others

* Francis J. Ryan, "An Investigation of Personality Differences Associated with Competitive Ability," and "Further Observations on Competitive Ability in Athletics," *Psychosocial Problems of College Men,* ed. Bryant M. Wedge (New Haven: Yale University Press, 1958), pp. 113–139.

do poorly in spite of having at least equal potential. "To give a simple illustration of the pattern, two shotputters may both make practice puts almost daily of 45 feet. In formal competition one may achieve 48 feet and the other 42 feet. In practice sessions their performances may again converge, only to separate once more in competition—and in the same direction as before. As another example, there are high jumpers who have frequently bettered 6 feet in practice and never in competition; others may have cleared 6 feet only in competition, never in practice."

Ryan sent questionnaires to track coaches throughout the country asking them to describe one of the best and one of the worst competitors each coach had had under him. The men described included world-record holders and Olympic champions, all of whom were exceptional athletes with great natural talent in track and field events. The distinction was solely on the basis of their ability in competition. Some of the results will be summarized here.

Ryan points out that all athletes appear to compete poorly on some occasions and that there are distinguishing characteristics between the poor and the good competitors. A good competitor who has a poor performance does so because he is temporarily "overanxious." He appears to try too hard, disturbing his timing and coordination, or he expends too much effort. The poor competitor, however, who nevertheless may have much natural ability, does poorly in competition because he makes a feeble effort. Ryan observed that the prognosis for future competition in these two types is quite different. The performer who has failed because of an overanxious, violent try will eventually do well in competition. The chronically poor competitor who makes only a feeble effort has a very poor prognosis for improvement. Ryan observed that poor competitors may even negate an otherwise good performance by some unnecessary action. For example, a thrower may foul after a good effort, or a broad jumper may fall backward.

The good competitor, in the heat of battle, uses his opponent as a temporary enemy. He may even appear angry at him; some good competitors seem to require "grudge" opponents. They develop specific hostile rivalries with certain opponents. An observation of my own of the way one of America's great tennis players reacted toward his tournament opponents, gives emphasis to Ryan's statements. As a tournament would progress and he could see who his next opponent would be, he would undergo a strange personality change toward that opponent. He would avoid his potential opponent and not speak to him. If, as was inevitable, they met socially, he would glare angrily and utter hostile and sarcastic remarks. In a most unrealistic fashion he accused his opponent of unfounded and petty things. Because most tournament players are of necessity close companions, it would often happen that his opponent was actually a good friend. But for several days before the match the opponent was to him a bitter enemy. His anger would disappear immediately after the match, whether he won or lost, and once again he would be affable. Although his behavior reached paranoid proportions in the accusations he made against potential opponents, after a match he would completely disregard the whole affair.

This kind of behavior is also characteristic of the attitudes of an entire campus, both team and fans, before Saturday football games. As the big event nears, the students recall or invent more and more horrendous stories of how "dirty" or "unworthy" their opponents are. By the time the team comes on the field, the event has become a grudge game.

Among poor competitors Ryan observed the opposite reaction. Rather than whipping up their anger to meet the competitive challenge, they did everything possible to maintain an atmosphere of friendliness with their opponents. In the heat of battle they would even encourage or console them, going so far as to coach their opponents, doing everything possible to avoid recognizing the contest as a competitive one. Ryan further observed that any display of anger by athletes, coaches, or spectators disturbed the poor competitors.

After a poor performance, the chronically poor competitor is in good spirits and cheerful; he accepts his defeat philosophically. A good competitor, in contrast, is morose, surly, and angry at himself or others. Precisely the reverse is true after successful performances. If the poor performer by accident has made a good mark and won, he is often upset. His next competition will almost certainly be poor. Ryan cites fascinating examples of the extremity of the need to lose by the poor competitors.

"A poor competitor of great natural athletic talent was entered in two field events. The first effort of his first event went extremely well. Almost before he could prevent it, he had achieved by far the best performance of his career. He appeared pained and anxious. His remaining trials were incredibly poor but, of course, the first mark stood as his performance. When the time arrived for his second event, he was not to be found. Later it was found that he had left the athletic area in a panic. He could offer no explanation for his absence."

The second example is even more dramatic. "A pole vaulter routinely cleared 12'6" in competition. Just as routinely, he failed to clear the next height of 13 feet. His teammates noted that he usually had more than 6 inches of clearance at 12'6" and therefore reasoned that his inability to make 13 feet was 'only mental.' Thus they conspired to 'help him.' When his back was toward the take-off, they raised the bar from 12'6" to 13 feet. Unaware of the bar's true height, the vaulter made a successful attempt.

"A vaulter's first clearance of 13 feet is something of a milestone and traditionally calls for a minor celebration. Thus, as the athlete landed in the pit and the bar remained aloft, his teammates rushed toward him with cries of congratulations. When he realized his accomplishment, he was stunned, he left the area and never again vaulted."

In all cases these athletes expressed the conscious goal of winning. They directed all of their deliberate efforts to this end by preparing for competition through arduous training. But when the long-awaited opportunity was actually at hand, other forces appeared to work against victory. So strong were these forces that they overcame the expressed goal. A closer examination of the psychological forces which an athlete must master in order to win would appear to be warranted.

Competition in sports requires that aggression be focused on the goal of victory. The poor competitor has learned to fear aggression most of the time, the average competitor fears it occasionally, and the good competitor fears it only infrequently. Ryan observed that his poor competitors in field events avoided aggression in many ways both on and off the field. They spoke softly, and they avoided arguments. They tried to maintain friendly relations with their rivals under all circumstances. It is the nature of this aggression that we will now consider in trying to understand the problems faced in winning.

In the process of growing up a child learns that under certain conditions a display of aggression has unhappy consequences. To oversimplify the situation, an aggressive attempt to take something or to destroy something is likely to be met by disfavor from parents, teachers, or other adults. Their disfavor is expressed either by retaliation in the form of corporal punishment or by the withholding of love. These consequences are very serious for the child who is dependent on the parents or other adults for love and its material accompaniments. His small size and relative weakness make him especially vulnerable to any kind of retaliation which might result from his aggression.

He soon learns to think before acting and to consider the consequences first. This represents the beginning of the development of conscience and eventually is incorporated into the child's personality as a system of conscious and unconscious "shoulds" and "should nots." These parental admonitions to the child become translated into the rules of society as he grows older. The rules may be informal, as when he learns that he must be polite and "nice" or he will be unaccepted by others in certain situations, or formal, as in the case of laws, policemen, and religious teaching.

He also learns that "there is a time and place for everything," and, especially if he is a boy, he is sometimes expected to be aggressive. In certain situations, such as sports, he is looked upon with disfavor if he is not aggressive or assertive enough. Unfortunately by the time he has sorted out when he is supposed to be aggressive and when he is not supposed to be, there has been some contamination of the sanction with the prohibition. The "should nots" have largely gone underground; they have become unconscious and generalized. In a "should-be-aggressive" situation such as, let us say, a basketball game, a player may find himself, to his consternation, reacting as though it were a "should-not-be-aggressive" situation.*

These psychological prohibitions largely have their effect and take their toll outside of conscious awareness, so that the athlete, his coach, his teammates, and the spectators are at a loss to explain some of his peculiar falterings in quest of victory. They all tend to believe that it must be that he needs to train harder, change his diet, or alter some technical aspect of his performance. Unfortunately these changes are rarely successful, except as they may alter the emotional tone of his performance.

At the deepest levels of the unconscious, aggression may be equated with violence and murder. The reader will recall the case of our tennis player, "Killer Ken," who unconsciously equated long tennis matches with killing. He could only win quickly and put his opponent "out of his misery" swiftly and mercifully, for a long match recalled too vividly his father's agonizingly slow death, an event for which he felt responsible.

Some further verifications of the murderous nature

---

* The psychoanalytic term "superego" is technically applied to this learned guiding system. It includes the conscience, the common term for the conscious prohibitions and admonitions, as well as those elements which are unconscious.

of the unconscious component of aggression in sports can be seen in the description of an effective competitor. It is said that he must have the killer instinct. Although this is usually taken to mean that an athlete is able relentlessly and without inner prohibition or a sense of guilt to keep the pressure on his opponent while achieving victory, the language chosen to describe it suggests a criminal act rather than a sportsmanlike activity.

An interesting example which demonstrates the destructive nature of the fantasies associated with athletic competition appears in tennis. When two opponents enter the court for a tournament match they enter a very restrictive setting with a myriad of inhibiting psychological factors, both conscious and unconscious. Although the avowed purpose of each is to win and defeat his opponent, this must be done in a sportsmanlike manner. Sportsmanship dictates that outward signs of aggression toward one's opponent should be suppressed. Tennis, the gentleman's game, requires spotless white attire and polite praise for a rival's good shots; the loser is expected to congratulate the winner with a hearty handshake and a smile. Audience participation is limited by custom to applause for placements—but never for errors. This sedate atmosphere is rarely violated during a match. By contrast, in the locker room after a match where there are fewer social restrictions and the facade of politeness is removed, the intense competitive spirit of each player is clearly revealed in the language used: "It was murder," "He slaughtered him," "He killed him." One is struck by the contrast between such expressions of primitive carnage and the polite cultural setting in which the action took place and to which murder, killing, and slaughter would seem to be quite foreign. Yet the selection of these terms to describe the game betrays the latent implications of the controlled aggression of the match.

Sometimes situations arise unexpectedly, and the reality of the contest coincides with the competitor's latent destructive fantasies. Under such circumstances the athletes are suddenly confronted with a demonstration of the full

intensity of the violent wishes they hold, and they are ap-
palled by what they see. Their subsequent performances bear
testimony to the guilt they feel over the realization of their
destructive fantasies.

A few years ago in the finals match of the United
States Tennis Championships, two splendid Australian
players met to decide the championship. The same two
players had met the year before for the title, and the winner was again favored. The match was very close and the
competition intense. Soon the champion of the previous
year gained the upper hand and needed only a few points
to complete his second consecutive championship. Then,
during a particularly hard-fought point, the challenger fell,
apparently having sprained his ankle. The match was delayed while the officials rushed to see how seriously the
player was injured. The pained expression on the injured
man's face was far surpassed by the anguish on the champion's face. He hung his head and paced nervously back and
forth, the picture of dejection. As it happened, the injury
was minor and the match was quickly resumed, but now
the defending champion missed easy balls and was unable
to regain his former standard of play. Despite his earlier
commanding lead he went on to lose in a surprising upset.

Perhaps there were several determinants in the
sudden change in this match, but one of them was most
apparent. The turning point occurred when the challenger
injured himself, but the change was not in his play but in
the champion's play. The injury to his opponent produced
in the champion an appearance of dejection and anguish.
He hung his head, and his expression was one of guilt, as
though he had committed a serious crime. It was apparent
that this sense of guilt played a part in his losing the match.

An athletic injury is the calculated risk of anyone
who competes. Separated by a net, as is the case in a tennis
match, if one player turns his ankle, it is certainly not due
to an assault by his opponent. But man's unconscious is not
limited by the spatial arrangements of the game. In this case
the injury was so minor that play was quickly resumed.

However, the defending champion now behaved as if it had been his intent seriously to injure his opponent. His play was so disturbed that he lost the match.*

As in dreams, things that occur unconsciously are not bound by reality. For example, a dreamer may be an adult, but the dream may take place in a childhood setting and his parents who are dead may seem very much alive. In the dream he may fuse some elements of the home in which he now lives with his childhood home. Similarly, an athlete who could not actually have harmed his opponent may nevertheless unconsciously experience the opponent's injury as the result of his own deliberate act. His reactions which may appear illogical are not to the real situation but to its unconscious meaning for him.

An entire team may be similarly affected when an unfortunate event coincides with the team's violent wishes. The collective guilt experienced may result in a turning point in an important athletic contest. For example, a few years ago in a playoff game in the National Basketball Association, the Syracuse Nationals and the Boston Celtics were the two rivals. The great Boston team was overwhelming its opponent by a large score when, during a wild scramble for the ball, the Syracuse star and mainstay, Dolph Schayes, was knocked down and his wrist was broken. It was indeed a terrible blow to the Syracuse team, for without their leading scorer they seemed to have little chance. They might well have been expected to fold up, and the Boston team to display some subdued pleasure, for the loss of Schayes practically wrapped up the game for them. But instead, the Boston team appeared apathetic and unnerved rather than the Syracuse team. The Boston Celtics seemed to lose their will to win, throwing the ball away and missing easy shots.

In contrast, Syracuse, now in a mood of revenge, began playing better. The eventual result was an almost unbelievable finale as Syracuse beat the favored Boston team. An important factor contributing to the Boston defeat ap-

---

* Arnold R. Beisser, "Psychodynamic Observations of a Sport," *Psychoanalysis and the Psychoanalytic Review,* Vol. 48 (Spring 1961), pp. 69–76.

pears to have been the guilt experienced by the players upon the realization of their violent fantasies. Afterward, in an interview with a Boston star regarding the loss, he expressed over and over again how the injury to the Syracuse star had had a detrimental effect on his own team's morale. He said he could not explain why but that the injury had upset Boston more than it had Syracuse.

When one traces the turning point in a game one frequently finds events of this kind.* A team, seemingly on the way to victory, loses its spark under a cloud of depression when a member of the opposing team is injured. They appear to want no more violence. This, coupled with an attitude of revenge in the opposing team, often spells the difference between defeat and victory.

Sometimes the violence which is latent most of the time erupts into deliberate attempts to kill or to do violent bodily harm to the opponent. Rocky Graziano, with striking candor when talking about his fights with Tony Zale, said simply, "I want to kill him." In heated rivalries in football there are sometimes malicious and deliberate attempts to injure an opponent. A baseball pitcher, too, may turn a brush back into a bean ball. The fans, caught up in the excitement of the event, may yell, "Murder the bum!" or "Kill him!" Sometimes their violent wishes erupt, as was the case following a recent Latin American soccer event when many deaths resulted, or in the riots associated with the Stanley Cup in ice hockey several years ago. In these tragic moments athletes or fans act as though the limited aggression allowed within the rules is license to be violently destructive. Just as, in appropriate circumstances, the prohibitions against aggressive displays may inhibit the aggressiveness in competition, so may the freedom to battle within the rules sometimes be confused with freedom to kill.

These examples of naked violence are the exception, however, rather than the rule, and for most athletes the

---

* This occurs mainly in individual sports or small team sports where the players are intensely involved in the whole course of the game. It is infrequent in football, with platooning and plays called from the bench.

destructive significance of the competition remains unconscious. Instead, it reveals itself only in the inhibitions to aggressive expression within the rules, as in inexplicable
"blowing" or "choking" at the moment of potential victory.

Whenever there are seemingly mysterious forces
at play a tendency exists to attach magical significance to
them. The athlete whose competitive ability is blocked by
such unconscious forces looks to magic for explanation and
solution. The primitive tribesman attempts to deal with the
mysteries of nature, such as fertility and the weather, by
magical ritual and incantation. Strangely enough, the modern
athlete does the same. Unlike the primitive, however, modern
athletes, in keeping with the scientific society in which they
live, disclaim the importance of their rituals. Nevertheless,
they continue them.

It has been said that "baseball players aren't super-
stitious; they just don't want to take chances." They use
lucky pieces, lucky clothes, lucky equipment, refuse to shave
while winning, sit in special places in the dugout, and don't
mention that a pitcher has a no hitter going. Some athletes
seek Divine protection—a basketball player can be seen to
make the sign of the cross before shooting a foul shot, or a
boxer may kneel to pray in the ring before the bell. Basketball teams, before going into action, lay their hands together
to symbolize their solidarity. They try to fight the unknown
forces that lie within them with magical gestures.

When it comes to rituals, no one surpasses the
baseball player. As he steps to the plate for his turn at bat
he engages in a mixture of purposeful activity and obsessive
ritual. The same ritual is compulsively repeated to its com-
pletion each time before he takes a pitch. If it is interrupted,
he steps out of the batter's box and starts all over again. A
typical example is something like this: First, the player
knocks the dirt off his spikes, then he picks up dirt for his
hands, then he hitches up his trousers. He carefully places
his feet in the batter's box, he loosens his trousers around
his genitals, he pulls down his cap, digs in his feet, takes
back the bat—and behold, he is ready!

The order and the style of the routine may vary, but it must be repeated each time. There are many variations of the baseball ritual. For example, Dick Stuart, a veteran major league long-ball hitter, before he steps into the batter's box always bites off a piece of gum of designated size and throws it on home plate. The elaborateness of the rituals in ball players varies considerably. Gil Hodges of the Dodgers and later of the Mets, in his playing days, and Roger Maris, home run champion of the Yankees, are among the most careful in their rituals.

One of the interesting characteristics is the attention paid by hitters to making sure that their trousers are just right around the genitals. It seems doubtful that positioning the genitals should have much to do with hitting a baseball, but in the language of the unconscious the genitals are the symbols of potency and power. It appears in large part to satisfy unconscious, not physical needs, that a batter must pay close attention to his genitals.*

Pitchers, too, engage in standardized routines. A pitcher leans forward in exactly the same way each time to get his signals from the catcher and goes through the same characteristic motions before throwing. Of course, some of these rituals do facilitate the actual physical action of throwing, but many primarily offer the psychological safety of routine. There are some teams where it has become a custom for the players in the dugout to switch seats constantly when the team is losing but to keep the same seats when they are winning. Maury Wills, the Los Angeles Dodger shortstop, wears the same trousers when he is hitting

---

* If the person feels compelled to perform rituals of this kind and, when he does not, is flooded with anxiety, his behavior is classified in clinical psychiatry as an obsessive-compulsive symptom. As has been described earlier, psychological disorder is largely a matter of degree, and nearly all persons sometime in their lives perform similar rituals. For example, children commonly avoid stepping on cracks in the pavement or feel compelled to touch each lath in a picket fence. Analysis of obsessive-compulsive rituals has revealed that they are performed to magically ward off certain unconscious forces which are in conflict with the superego. The preceding discussion would suggest that those rituals served to protect the athlete against the implications of his own aggression.

well and will not change them until his streak stops. There are also certain subjects that he will not talk about as a magical remedy for specific competitive problems that are encountered.

Many baseball players deliberately try to avoid thinking when they are hitting. This appears to be an attempt to dispel any disturbing fantasies that might creep into the player's mind. The so-called no think school of hitting has a large number of adherents. Yogi Berra has been quoted as saying, "How can I think and hit at the same time!" If the player does not think, he cannot think anything bad that will come into conflict with his conscience. Not thinking thus serves as a protective mechanism.

I have described how guilt is one of the major difficulties an athlete faces in competing—that to win is, in the unconscious, tantamount to destroying one's opponent. One method of avoiding the guilt is to deny that one is winning at all. Denial is a common psychological defense mechanism, which is seen in many athletes in the pursuit of victory. For example, there are several world-caliber tennis players who exhibit a consistently predictable behavior when they are winning. As the match progresses, they begin to castigate themselves. They talk to themselves critically as though to someone else, saying out loud, "You're terrible," "You're lousy," "You can't play." This is indeed surprising to hear after a player makes a brilliant shot. It is incongruous to see a player behaving in this way on one of his best days, especially when on a bad day, in defeat, he seems to have no need to do so. This patently false denial of the true situation is a way of saying, in effect, "I'll conceal the fact that I'm winning and thereby avoid the consequences of guilt." I have asked a number of these players about their behavior, and they have told me that it is necessary for them in order to "keep the pressure on" and not to "let up." It would appear then that only by denying victory can they escape the anxiety and guilt of conscience.

One excellent tournament player, well known throughout the world, between points of important matches continually strikes himself on the leg with his racket. This is traumatic enough to produce bruises which can easily be seen. Beating himself is a magical gesture by which he equalizes the situation of beating his opponent. Since to beat his opponent in a tennis match has the latent connotation of physically beating him, he must satisfy his conscience by physically beating himself.

A famous Wimbledon champion regularly showed another variation of this same type of activity. Despite the fact that he was one of the best players in the world, he found it almost impossible to win an easy match. He had to struggle with each opponent and would barely win each time. His first round matches against weak opponents were just as close as those in the finals against the best players in the world, and he appeared equally disheveled. Among the other players it was wryly said that if his clothes weren't dirty from falling on the court and if he didn't look as if he had been beaten, he hadn't played at all. There are many players in many sports who behave in a similar manner; they can only win by a hairline decision, never by a wide margin. They persistently must demonstrate that there is little difference between the winner and the loser. If the distinction between the players can be nullified they are protected from the consequences of beating an opponent.

Another interesting variation of the attempt to deny the consequences of one's aggressive competition characterized a national tennis champion of some years ago. He was one of the most popular players with all other players, for he was always friendly with them even in the heat of battle. He would never say a harsh word about an opponent either on or off the court. In contrast, he was probably the most unpopular champion of all time with fans, for during a match he constantly berated the ball boys, linesmen, and umpires. Each of his important matches was held up by his loud and sometimes obscene criticism of them. On more than one occasion he was known to hit a ball boy with a ball or with his racket. Such unsportsmanlike behavior resulted in his being disqualified from several tournaments. He could, however, tolerate the displeasure of the fans, the tournament officials, and the ball boys, since it served a vital purpose for his personality. He accomplished a displacement of his aggression and his destructive fantasies to less threatening objects, allowing him to compete successfully against opponents. By this strange behavior he tried to demonstrate to himself that he was not engaged in combat with his opponent and that his only enemies were the ball boys and officials.

An athlete in a competitive sport must face his goal of winning. To accomplish this he must somehow master or overcome certain unconscious concomitants of winning. The aggression in the game may be tainted with implications of violence and mayhem and the athlete has learned restrictions of conscience against such murderous thoughts. These thoughts countermand his desire to win so that he unexplainably chokes or falters in the crucial moment. Since these forces opposing victory take place outside the player's awareness, they seem magical. Even though the player logically denies the existence of magic, he finds himself bound by superstition and employing elaborate rituals to defend himself against dire consequences.

SUCCESS AND FAILURE IN SPORTS

The magic and rituals described illustrate the problems that the athlete faces in trying to win and why it is often said that a player is "his own worst enemy." There are great differences in how freely athletes allow themselves to pursue victory. For some the ritual and magical gestures seem to be enough; for others no matter what kind of psychological manipulations they engage in, they still seem doomed to failure. All athletes experience difficulties sometimes, some frequently and some almost all the time. Personality is not static but dynamic, and a poor competitor may become a good one and a good one may become a poor one. Other factors, such as his coach, the crowd, or other changes in his life circumstances, may help or hinder a player's ability to win.

Early in his career he may have more difficulty winning than he will have later, especially in important contests. Lack of experience is often one of the reasons a youthful performer falters. A player must get the feel of winning before he can be successful. If he has the physical talent and skill there is a psychological obstacle which must be overcome. Coaches and fans are patronizing toward youthful failures and are apt to say, "All he needs is more experience" or "What he needs is a couple of victories under his belt" or "He needs confidence." An athlete has to "think he can do it" before he can win.

The four-minute mile, the 15-foot pole vault, and the 60-foot shot put are examples of how important it is for athletes to believe that it can be done. Once these records were broken it was commonplace to do so, but before that, they had seemed to be insurmountable barriers. The youthful performer who is uncertain whether or not he can win faces a similar problem. He must learn it is possible and that no disastrous consequences develop when he does win. If a player finds that nothing bad comes from victory the unconscious or only partly conscious destructive fantasies associated with winning are tempered by the reality.

The history of sports is filled with stories of athletes who could not live up to their potential. For years they seemed to have the talent and skill to defeat all opponents, but something always happened. For many of them a break finally comes, and once having tasted victory and found only sweetness, they continue on to be true champions. Others finally achieve that great victory, only to find themselves tortured by unexplainable forces of conscience, and they never again do well.

Sometimes fortuitous circumstances occur which seem to help a competitor over that important threshold between losing and winning, between challenger and champion. A few years ago there was a tennis Davis Cup final between United States and Australia. Team captain Perry

Jones had selected as a representative from this country a little-known Chilean player, Alex Olmedo, who was eligible only on a technicality. It was a surprising choice and one for which Jones was sharply criticized. The player had never won a major championship, and although there was no doubt about his natural ability and talent he could not seem to win important matches.

Sports columnists said he lacked the "killer instinct." But he astonished the tennis world by winning all of his matches, thereby also winning the Davis Cup for America. He defeated players who had always before been his masters.

The explanation which he gave for his brilliant play was most revealing. He took no credit for himself, but rather attributed his victory entirely to Mr. Jones. He stated that he had played for the captain alone because the captain had done so much to forward his career. Modestly he refused the accolades for his victory, directing them all toward Jones. The confidence of the team captain had obviously been a great boost to Olmedo. He had been unable to win the big ones before, but now Jones' demonstration of faith in him made it possible for him to win.

Beyond this interpretation lies a deeper one. By attributing his victory to the team captain Olmedo was able to transfer the responsibility for winning from himself. He was thus able to avoid the unconscious problems of conscience already discussed. These victories in the Davis Cup matches served as a turning point in Olmedo's career. In the next few tournaments, he won regularly and clearly established himself as a great player. Once having crossed the barrier which separated him from victory he had discovered that it was safe on the other side. In order to make the transition, he had needed the assistance of his intuitively wise captain who evidently recognized his potential.

This is not a unique story, for coaches often find themselves showing faith in the ability of an athlete to overcome the personal barriers that have kept him from winning. By encouragement and by assuming the responsibility for the player's efforts, the coach is able to spur the athlete on to victory. Often this is accomplished when the coach sets a specific training or game plan for the athlete. Although the emphasis is on physical performance, the most important part of the plan is the confidence the coach conveys in his "If you do this you'll win." The athlete is thus able to avoid his psychological inhibitions by "just following orders"— the coach handles the worries. Once the athlete has experienced victory, it is often no longer necessary for him to have such assistance.

The successful coach knows when to assume responsibility for the actions of his players and when to give them free reign. In a crucial moment sending in the play to a football or basketball team may relieve the players of the burden of responsibility and allow them to "just play." Often, I believe, it is not that the play itself was better than one the team might have used but the psychological relief it provides.

The opposite may also occur. Floyd Patterson achieved the heavyweight championship of the world under the guidance of Cus D'Amato. D'Amato expressed his boundless faith in Patterson, assuring the fighter that he was unbeatable. He encouraged Patterson to put his faith and trust in him and let him manage all the details. D'Amato accepted all responsibility for any unfortunate consequences of either winning or defeat.

Under this regime Patterson won the heavyweight championship of the world and appeared to be in for a long reign. But D'Amato became involved in a controversy with boxing officials, and Patterson's confidence in him became shaken. He began to assume responsibility for his own training and matchmaking. This was followed by a series of ignominious defeats. The former champion seemed, in these fights, especially against Sonny Liston, to lose all confidence and to be frightened of his opponents. He seemed to be waiting only for the inevitable defeat. Having some insight into the nature of this difficulty, Patterson has set himself on a course in which he hopes to regain his "pride" and confidence. Whether or not he can do it alone remains to be seen.

An athlete may work out his problems about winning outside of the athletic arena. A dramatic example of how one well-known athlete did this took place in golf. Lloyd Mangrum was known as the mystery man of golf, for although he had demonstrated himself to be a brilliant performer, he had also established the reputation for blowing the big ones. His sudden failures in competition were mysterious to his fellow players and to his fans.

Mangrum was inducted into the service and was in combat in the European theater in World War II. He faced the most difficult wartime conditions over an extended period during the Battle of the Bulge but was one of the survivors of that costly battle.

The first year, in the first major tournament after his return from combat he played in the U.S. Open, one of golf's greatest challenges. In this tournament, in contrast to his previous strange inability to win the big ones, he displayed exceptional coolness under fire. Although the tension was great during the match, Mangrum appeared to be able to tolerate the stress without difficulty and went on to win the tournament. This great victory occurred under amazing circumstances. Mangrum had not only had a long layoff from competition in golf but also had returned after war experiences that had in other ways exhausted him. This did not inhibit his ability to win, however, but seemed to enhance it. In the war he had experienced the threat and the realities of death and destruction. The dangers he had faced as a soldier seemed to clarify his competitive activities in golf. He was now able to pursue victory on the golf course without confusing it with destructive fantasies, for he had seen the real thing. Mangrum's war experiences had brought his golf competition into a more accurate perspective and made him into a cool competitor.

Among the other forces which may play a decisive role in an athlete's ability to win is the crowd. It is well known that if the crowd is with a team or a player, there is an advantage for that team or player. So widely recognized is this fact that in making up the season's schedules in sports, careful attention is paid to giving the teams equal numbers of home games. Sports experts say that a football team playing at home has a seven-point advantage and a basketball team playing at home has a five- to ten-point advantage.

It is not encouragement and support alone which make the crowd such an important factor to the player or the team; it is the knowledge that they share with him the responsibility for his aggression. It is not just public relations or sportsmanship that stirs players to pay tribute to the fans for their part in the victory achieved by the team. The fans shout "Kill 'em!" and "Murder 'em!" thus sharing with the players the violent impulses directed against the opposition. This sharing of unacceptable aggression allows the team or players to compete fiercely. The guilt which they might otherwise experience if they were alone is diluted and shared by the fans. The athlete may feel that he is only carrying out the mandate of the crowd and any evil conse-quences are therefore not his responsibility. Knowing the crowd is with him is comforting and removes some of the inhibitions from his aggressive actions.

On an international scale, the tragic consequences of crowd support were seen during World War II. Nazi soldiers and their sympathizers carried out the most dread-ful acts of murder and genocide against other humans. The support of the crowd gave license to many persons who probably would otherwise have retreated in horror from the ghastly crimes in which they participated. Today, without the support of the howling mob, many of these people look back in amazement at their complicity.

The player who faces a hostile crowd meets a con-verse situation. He may find it difficult to go all out because there are so many against him. For example, tennis fans in Italy do not generally observe the niceties expected of tennis audiences. They castigate foreign players who compete against Italians with jeers and profane comments. Many players find it so intolerable that they will not play in the famous international tournament in Rome. It is so unpopular for a foreigner to win there that it is almost impossible for them to compete effectively. They find themselves losing quickly just to get off the court.

In team sports an athlete is never alone. He always has his team mates to share some of the responsibility for his aggressive action. No doubt this plays an important role in the choice an athlete makes of his sport. The reader will recall the case history of the basketball player in Chapter 3. Although he displayed amazing natural ability in individual sports, he chose not to compete in them. He needed the support of team mates to share responsibility for his aggression. The athlete in an individual sport stands alone to face whatever consequences result from his action. Some athletes prefer this position and choose individual sports.

There are times when no amount of support or sharing of responsibility by coaches, team mates, or fans is sufficient to liberate an athlete to pursue his goal vigorously. This is not to say that athletes inhibited by conscience in their pursuit of victory do not have the same intensity of desire to win as do their freer fellow athletes. They want to win, they train to win, and they hope to win in the same way, but they are defeated by forces beyond their awareness.

Ryan describes the case of a young runner who never could reach his potential, always failing to win in important meets. In a particular event his performance meant the difference between victory and defeat for the whole team. Under great pressure the team was able to wring out a victory from him. Although successful for the team, the results were disastrous for the athlete: faced with the restrictions of his conscience, he dropped out of school.

Sometimes becoming a winner is so disastrous for an athlete that he develops a serious psychiatric disorder when success comes his way. There have been several examples of potentially great athletes who managed every time to fail at the moment of victory. A few, through either crowd support or other seemingly fortuitious events, did win a great event. Following this they underwent severe personality disorganization. At the moment when a player sees victory within his grasp he may feel the most exquisite conflict.

There was once a tennis player of international reputation who consistently managed to stay just below the top. Through a peculiar series of events he found himself in the final round against a champion who was sick that day. He was within a point of victory on several occasions, and each time he would either throw away the point or make a wild attempt to put the ball away. In either case, he lost the point. Following the match which he eventually lost, he played in only one or two more tournaments. After that he was an emotionally disturbed man and spent much of his later life in a mental hospital. He maintained the delusion that he had actually won this great championship match, but tragically it was only in his delusions of grandeur that he could allow himself to achieve the greatness which was his potential.

The reader of the sports page is aware of examples of this kind in every sport. It is the story of a promising career which fell apart at the very moment when success was at hand. Such a player is soon forgotten once he no longer competes. Athletes who fail to achieve in reality sometimes become broken men who finally rely on their fantasies for achievement. Winning is safer there. These psychodynamics of failure are not specific to athletes but can be found in other areas of life as well. It is not uncommon for the psychiatrist to meet patients in his office whose psychiatric problems are related to the athlete's problem in winning. These patients develop their psychiatric disorders at the very moment in their lives when they achieve a long-awaited and dreamed-of goal. Such psychological destruction can occur in the man whose lifelong ambition is realized —when a businessman becomes vice-president of his company, or a college professor becomes chairman of his department, or a man finally has enough money to retire.

Like the athlete who becomes disturbed when he wins, such men present at first a puzzling situation. The goal, long awaited and sought, when finally achieved, creates discomfort and anxiety rather then the expected happiness. The reader may recall that in certain of the case histories this was also the case. The basketball player became disturbed upon graduation from college, the football player became depressed when his son was born and he was offered the family business, and the tennis player became anxious when he married into wealth. All these events would appear to be signals for relief, joy, and pleasure, but instead they led to tragic and disintegrating personal consequences. Although each case had its own specific and unique background which led to the predicament, there are certain general principles which may help to explain the strange phenomena.

Sigmund Freud observed early in his career that there were "those who are wrecked by success." He related such misfortunes in the adult to the unfinished business carried over from childhood and expressed contemporaneously in the joke, "I spent the happiest days of my life in the arms of another man's wife—my mother." To the adult male certain successes are symbolic of the achievement of unconscious wishes representing the anachronistic displacement of his father and the sexual possession of his mother —the Oedipus complex. "The term, of course, has complicated matters in that it compared what is to be inferred in childhood with what is to be inferred from the story of King Oedipus. The name thus establishes an analogy between two unknowns. The idea is that Oedipus, who inadvertently killed his father and married his mother, became a mythical hero and on the stage is viewed with intense pity and terror because to possess one's mother is a universal wish, universally tabooed."* This statement of Erik Erikson's suggests the scientific and emotional controversy that prevails as to the use of the term. For our purposes it is

* Erik Erikson, *Childhood and Society* (New York: W. W. Norton, Inc., 1950) pp. 82–83.

sufficient to emphasize that there is almost always a rivalry between growing sons and their fathers. This rivalry is mainly on the child's part while he is too small to threaten his father physically, but as the boy emerges into adolescence the father becomes keenly aware that he has a competitor in the home. The adolescent struggle, over almost everything—money, cars, school, girls—obscures the historical roots of competition. The childhood statements of little boys who declare that they will replace their fathers and marry their mothers are patronizingly forgotten.

In the Victorian era when Freud began his work, the stereotypes of family members were very different from what they are today. Although they were a composite of fact and myth, they were clearly presented: The father was the dominant member of the family; he was the provider. He was hard-working, God-fearing, and powerful.* He expected and received obedience from his wife and children. It was in this context that the Oedipus complex could be seen in full force. The tremulous weak child, looking to the power and possessions of the forbidding father, was subject to a variety of problems that are not so obvious today. Contemporary models of father-son relationships are very different.

The Victorian dictum that children should be seen and not heard has given way to what has been termed the "century of the child." Today the child occupies center stage and his mother is the director. The boy and his father, as portrayed in fiction and television, are pals and the patriarchy of earlier days has been replaced by democracy—togetherness. The father appears as a good-natured, slightly befuddled buffoon, dominated by his wife, who actually holds the family together. He is no longer sole provider, for his wife too, may be working outside the home. The father's job is often sedentary and rather obscure. Such caricatures, although not entirely accurate, do illustrate the direction of family change since Victorian days.

* In modern sociological terms he was an inner-directed man. (See David Riesman's *The Lonely Crowd*.)

Whatever the weaknesses in the Victorian family, and they were many, the roles were at least fairly clear. It was easier for boys to identify with their fathers. But today, a boy rarely relies on his father for the example of the ideal male. The image is diffused, and rather than serving as the ideal for his son, father and son together share an admiration of an ideal, frequently a baseball or football player. Erikson has described this father-son relationship in the following passage: "If a father plays baseball with his son, it is not in order to impress him with the fact that he, the father, comes closer to the perfection of a common ideal type—for he probably does not—but rather that they play together at identifying with that type, and that there is always the chance, hoped for by both, that the boy may more nearly approach the ideal than father did."*

To be a winner, a champion, an athlete achieves a position similar to the Victorian ideal man: strong and powerful, for otherwise he would not have won; righteous and moral, for he is a good sport and potentially, if not in fact, a good provider. He achieves success as a man that his own father only dreamed of. He stands alone on unfamiliar ground, responsible for his aggression and its consequences.

Now this may not seem like a bad state of affairs at all. The fruits of victory include fame, admiration, and perhaps even financial success. The reader will also recall, however, that unconsciously the aggression is often tantamount to violent destruction of the opponent. So the athlete, although he basks in the glory of victory, also unconsciously stands convicted of murder.

In this unenviable position the contemporary youth does not have the security of continuity. His Victorian counterpart, and a small number of his contemporaries, matured in proximity to a powerful father image. Through a gradual identification process they assumed a familiar role of "the man." Today the role and duties of the man are

* Erik Erikson, *Childhood and Society* (New York: W. W. Norton & Company, Inc., 1950), p. 273.

clouded by change and a disturbing relativism. No clear continuity exists for a youth to follow.

The problem faced by the champion is familiar on the contemporary scene and is fabled in the modern western. The cowboy who becomes known as "the fastest gun in the West" is constantly plagued by vanquished foes, relatives of his victims, "two-bit gun slingers," and "reckless kids trying to make a name for themselves." He is the winner and champion and is thus the target of attack. "Once you've reached the top there is no place to go but down." The "High Noon" story has all of the elements of the problems of a champion in sports. The marshal (the athlete) who defeated the outlaws (his opponents) reigns (is champion) in peace only temporarily. He hopes to settle down with the girl (the prize) whose love he has earned. However, his retirement cannot be accomplished, for the outlaws (his opponents) whom he sent to jail (defeated) have been freed and will come after him (challenge again) to get even. It is futile for him to run because he knows they would only track him down in order to retaliate. He turns to the townspeople (the fans) for support. After all, he did it for them while they cheered. But they are not with him; he is alone, frightened, and disappointed. He must defend the town (his championship) by himself. In the Hollywood endings, he usually kills the outlaws (wins), but he is a bitter and disappointed man.

Of course the youngster, the athlete, meets many men—coaches and other athletes—other than his father who can serve as the image of the winner or champion. But the point is that these occur outside the home and the immediate family where he learned his first important lessons. His foundation may thus be weaker than the superstructure which it is required to hold.

An "also ran" in the game is like one of the fans, for he does not stand apart from the crowd, risking isolation from them. For him the competition may be filled with violent fantasies, but they are without the risk of their becoming a reality. He is like the child who may entertain the most destructive possibilities without the power and strength to carry them out. His safety comes from losing, as the child's comes from his weakness and impotence. He remains united with the others, the crowd, as the child is united with his parents, deriving his strength from their size. In his capacity for failure he receives comfort and the certainty of belonging.

It is the winner, the champion, who risks emerging from the crowd and who tangibly acts out their mutual desires. He bears responsibility for the collective aggression focused in sport. He may receive respect, awe, and deference, but great things are also expected of him and he is allowed no sign of weakness. Comfort and pity, the rewards of the child, are reserved for those he defeats. He is the man who stands alone. In America everyone cheers for and loves the underdog. When the underdog becomes champion, he loses much of his support.

If the loser is the child, and the winner is the man, society prepares a player for the former role better than for the latter. It is "the century of the child," and the world is organized for his benefit. His innocence and goodness are idolized by adults who hope his fate will be better than theirs. It is the paradoxes of adult life as much as the virtues of childhood which retard the maturation process. The experiences of youth are inadequate preparation for the shifting identities of adult life. Continuity from child roles to adult roles is disrupted by the possibility of social mobility and the paralyzing relativism of changing values. By comparison, the child's role seems stable and secure.

The athlete on the threshold of victory faces a dilemma in his renunciation of the comfort of the child for the responsibility of the adult, in his choice of the isolation of being outstanding over the mass solidarity of remaining mediocre. The champion is the man emerging from out of the crowd of all others into uniqueness. Winning is one aspect of the enigma of maturity.

13 ON SPORTSMANSHIP

When the one great scorer comes to write
   against your name—
He marks—not that you won or lost—
But how you played the game.

> ... Grantland Rice: Alumnus Football

The previous chapters have been devoted to a consideration of some underlying meanings in sports. Specifically we have discussed hidden unconscious forces in the psychology of the athlete which tend to inhibit or prevent him from achieving the logical goal of a sport—winning. By nature these underlying psychological factors are primitive and vicious, inappropriate to the competition within the rules of a sport, and subject to the restriction of conscience and guilt. We have emphasized the hidden, primitive, and socially unacceptable determinants of behavior and outcome in a sport. To balance this emphasis it must be noted that a sport or an athletic contest is a highly civilized activity, the result of thousands of years of increasingly complex culture, controlled by many social impositions.

We assume that families began living together for mutual protection. Perhaps the first step toward civilization was the realization that two heads and two pairs of hands were better than one. The advantages of communal living were obvious. Several men were more capable of warding off an attack than was one man. Several men could cooperate together and more efficiently catch game or fish, gather food, or move a stone. But community living raised new problems within the group even while it solved some of the problems with the outside world. Competition, rivalry, and jealousy within the community developed and became intensified. Material prizes—food, women, and security—were sought within the group, and the aggression which resulted had to be handled in a way that would not destroy the group itself. As community groups grew in size their structure became increasingly complex, and the opportunities for the overt display of aggression had to be limited. The "fight" as it became more subtle and symbolic had increasingly more restrictions, personal, intrapsychic, and social, placed on it.

In this increasingly complex social organization and necessary proximity in which man lived, sports evolved. The rules governing leisure and recreation developed to be as complex as other aspects of social interaction. Sports became one of the few acceptable areas in modern society in which physical competition and aggression among men is allowed, within limits, that is, within the rules of the game.

Living together in a community required that a certain code or set of laws be followed in the conduct among men. What were no doubt originally practical considerations have developed into the ideals of humane treatment of one's fellow men. An important part of these ideals is the reduction of uncontrolled expressions of violence and carnage.

There can be little doubt about the advantages of confining violence to the athletic field if it frees man to act in a humane manner at other times. Certainly to compete in a symbolic way in sports and thus to avoid wanton killing is consistent with the highest goals of civilization. If sports, as has been suggested, could, at least in part, be a substitute for some of the forms of aggression which are destructive to society, they would represent an important step along the way toward civilization.

With the development of technology has come a series of ever more frightening and destructive weapons, in the form of missiles and nuclear explosives so powerful that they have the potential of extinguishing human life from this planet. In primitive society, competition took the form of the fight for survival, with death the fate of the loser. At first, one man seeking protection from another found an ally. As a consequence, the enemy, now outnumbered, had to maintain the balance of power, and he sought his own ally. The size of coalitions grew to maintain a balance between threat and protection, and power blocs became aligned and realigned. Two men working together might be able to ward off the ravages of disease, hunger, and the caprice of nature. If they became opponents and fought, one might be killed, but the survivor would then have to try to protect himself alone from the jungle and might himself perish. Similarly, today, if men are able to work together in some sort of coexistence, they may survive. If they must fight, however, today's ominous weapons have reduced the outcome to precisely what it was in the primitive society when there were only two men—extinction.

For centuries, thinking men have sought some sort of substitute for the violence in man which leads to murder on an individual level and to wars on a national level. In 1932, Albert Einstein and Sigmund Freud, both recognizing the urgency of the subject, exchanged letters on how war might be avoided. Freud made this provocative summary statement of their correspondence. "In any case, as you yourself have remarked, there is no question of getting rid entirely of human aggressive impulses; it is enough to try to divert them to such an extent that they need not find expression in war."

Whether wars and violence can ever find a substitute is open to considerable question. It is interesting, though, that in time of war, the incidence of murder and suicide "back home" has definitely been found to decrease. This suggests a reciprocal relationship between various forms of violence and the possibility that one form may be substituted for another. If war has any influence on the aggressive, destructive impulses of the nonfighting citizenry it must be a vicarious influence. Possibly, some sort of symbolic violence may be a substitute for murder and war. Consistent with the emphasis in this book, it is conceivable that aggressiveness in sports could be a partial substitute. William James entertained this idea; law enforcement officers and social agencies who have dealt with delinquent boys, many of whom have been arrested for acts of violence, feel that sports may be a substitute for antisocial violence. The recent world heavyweight boxing champion, Floyd Patterson, believed that his career represented this successful transition from delinquent violence to sports champion.

It is a giant step, however, from individual psychodynamics to power politics between nations. In order to feel that sports competition on an international scale could substitute for war, governments and their leaders would have to be able to achieve in this at least a modicum of the goals ordinarily achieved by war. The citizens (fans) of a particular nation would need to achieve symbolic gratification for their hatreds of other people and nations. There have been suggestions of a relationship, perhaps even a reciprocal one, between sports and wars. Athletic competition is emphasized in peacetime armies and in the training of armies. At the end of each of the recent world wars military personnel waiting to return home were organized into intensive competitive athletic programs. It would be interesting to study the levels of aggressive feeling in nations at the time of international athletic competition. One might ask whether during the Olympic games competition, there is a reduction of aggressiveness and potential for war between the intensely competing Russia and the United States. Or, is the aggression strictly confined to the sports competition?

Perhaps the most famous expression on the relationship between sports and war is that which has been attributed to Wellington: "The battle of Waterloo was won on the playing fields of Harrow and Eton." It would be a felicitous event indeed for the human race if one could ever say that "The battle was not fought because there was competition on the same day on the playing fields of Harrow and Eton."

Most sporting events require strict adherence to the rules. The occasional transgressions of the rules, which receive much publicity and discussion, reveal the primitive anlage of sports. Breaking rules, however, is grossly subordinate to the high ideals of sportsmanship which pervade most contests. Webster defines a sportsman as "a person who can take loss or defeat without complaint, or victory without boasting and gloating, and who treats his opponent with fairness, generosity, courtesy, etc." Such are the highest ideals for relationships between men and could well serve as the ideals for relations between nations.

That behavior like this can occur in connection with vigorous, aggressive physical competition is the very essence of civilization. A football player knocks his opponent to the ground with a hard, well-executed block; when the play is over he assists his opponent to his feet. If injury should occur to his opponent he expresses his concern and offers his help. His act of aggression, the block, has been almost completely localized within the rules of the game. Some may see hypocrisy in boxing matches, for the two boxers battle each other mercilessly until the last round is over; then they embrace. This contradiction, the expression at the same time of fraternity and primitive aggression, of the restrictions of society and biologic urges, is the fundamental contradiction of civilization. Lack of integration of these two forces provides the base of many of the problems of the individual and society. Athletic contests highlight the conflict and dramatize it for both players and observers. The athlete who has truly become a "good sport" has achieved a high level of integration between his individual biological desires and the needs of the society in which he lives. Baron Pierre De Coubertin, the founder of the modern Olympic games, is said to have developed his interest in rekindling sports as a reaction against the violence of the Franco-Prussian wars. His succinct statement perhaps best describes the ideals of good sportsmanship: "The important thing is not winning, but taking part; the essential thing is not conquering, but fighting well."

There is among athletes, especially peer groups such as team players or weekend golfers, a strong feeling of fraternity based not on intellectual knowing but on strong, intuitive feeling. Athletic competitors have deep respect for each other since, they understand the mutual feeling of aggression towards one another while competing. They have thus shared something fundamental which is ordinarily concealed.

The essentials of sportsmanship can be summarized into three points: First, the athlete must adhere to the rules of the game and strictly confine his aggression to the way in which it is permitted. Second, he must believe that the loser is no less worthy than the winner, that the result is less important than giving the best effort and sticking to the rules. He demonstrates humility in victory and pride in defeat. Third, he must appreciate the "good play" whether it be his or his opponent's. He is like an art critic who judges not the artist but only the work.

Sportsmanship is an appropriate concept for generalization to man's whole life. For example, the handshake is the gesture which epitomizes sportsmanship and is traditional before and after such sporting events as football, basketball, track, tennis, and golf. Its meaning is that even though opponents compete against each other with vigor and aggression and will do everything possible within the rules to win, they respect each other, are friends, and have no personal animosity, both feeling that "the game is the thing." The pregame and postgame handshake thus symbolizes good sportsmanship throughout the world.

Similarly, in all walks of life, the handshake has been a traditional gesture of friendship. When friends meet and renew an acquaintance they shake hands; when a "business deal" is completed it is consummated by shaking hands to indicate good will; when strangers meet for the first time they shake hands to declare friendship. Considerable significance is attached to the kind of handshake that is offered. A firm handshake is said to imply sincerity and strength of character; a limp handshake, weakness or treachery. A warm hand is supposed to signify warmth of feeling; a cold one the opposite. The moist handshake suggests tension between the handshakers.

As with most symbolic gestures the handshake was once quite practical. When two men came out of the forest and met, each was concerned about the other's intentions, so a practical safeguard developed. If a man came in friendship he held his hands open so that it could be seen that he carried no weapons. This was further confirmed when the two men clasped hands so that they could be certain that the hands would not be used for some evil purpose. It was a protective device based on suspicion and mistrust and roughly equivalent to the present-day police technique of "frisking." The handshake represents an attempt to integrate man's trust and mistrust of his fellow man.

The historical significance of the handshake may seem far removed from present concepts of sportsmanship. We have learned, however, that even though an activity may have undergone considerable transformation, we must also pay heed to the archaic meanings of the act. An athlete may be aware only of the sportsmanlike characteristics of shaking hands with an opponent and the reassurance it brings to both. In line with our previous considerations of the murderous quality of some of the aggressive drives in sports, it is understandable that the athlete should attempt to protect himself psychologically from the violence he disowns in himself with rituals and magical gestures, such as the handshake. Thus this gesture takes on additional meaning.

Sam Snead, the great golfer, participated a few years ago in a series of nationally televised golf matches. Golfers were to challenge Snead, and if one was successful he would take over and continue to play against a succession of challengers. Winning thus gave a golfer not only monetary reward but allowed him to play before the largest golf audience ever to watch a match. Snead had won week after week and appeared invincible. His defeat came somewhat unexpectedly at the hands of a young but talented opponent. The young golfer, who at that time was relatively unknown, has since become famous and is now one of the most able golfers in the world. At that time, however, his reputation was not established and he was only a promising youthful challenger. When he dispatched the great "old pro" handily in their match, he stepped with Snead before the television camera. Both men received their prizes and were interviewed, in the best tradition of sportsmanship, which in this instance turned out to be almost a burlesque. Snead stood with head high and discussed the match in a matter-of-fact way, congratulating his young opponent. It was the young winner's appearance that was striking. He hung his head, looked down at the ground, and spoke in a voice so soft as to be almost inaudible. If, with the sound of the television set turned off, one had had to guess the winner, one would have chosen Snead. He appeared confident and composed, whereas his young opponent appeared despondent and beaten.

The moderator of the program inquired of the victor to what he attributed his success. He responded that it was entirely a matter of "luck," without which he could never have defeated so great a player as his opponent. The interviewer's attempt to find out how he had won met only with insistence that he could take no credit himself. He attributed what had happened not to his skill but to the good will and kindness of the managers of the golf club, those who had invited him to play, and even the television interviewer himself. He emphasized that he was not deserving, and his demeanor showed no evidence of happiness, either when he received his large prize check or when those around him enthusiastically offered congratulations.

The reader has already become acquainted with some of the obscure determinants of such a response. The psychological manipulation of denying a victory and act-

ing as if the game were lost serves to protect against deep
fears of retaliation and the guilt of "beating" an opponent.
In this instance the young golfer had beaten a powerful,
almost legendary figure in the game in which he himself
aspired to be champion. Certainly such a powerful opponent
should not be antagonized any more than necessary.

Of course some of the determinants of this young
golfer's behavior were social. Modesty and humility in a
conqueror are valued cultural traits—"Blessed are the meek."
Since he valued the approval of the crowd, he chose to conform to these social niceties. From the standpoint of the culture, he was complying with the highest standards of sportsmanship. He underplayed his victory, respected the excellence of his opponent, and was grateful to those who had
assisted in making his victory possible. From the standpoint
of his personal psychodynamics, he was protecting himself
from the potential vengeance of his powerful opponent by
disclaiming all responsibility for winning. He shared with
others the responsibility as well as the credit for winning.
By insisting that his opponent was really superior, he was
saying that it was all a mistake and that the "old pro" should
overlook this inadvertent victory. Perhaps the psychosocial
determination of his modesty is best demonstrated by the
fact that although willing to share the credit he was not
willing to share the prize money.

In subsequent victories this young golfer appeared
to have little need for such dramatic displays of humility.
He still maintained the attitude of the "good sport," but he
was not as obsequious as he had been on the occasion of
his first great victory. Having successfully survived the after-
math of this event, he felt safe in accepting the accolades
from later ones.

The dilemma facing the strong and successful person has been expressed eloquently by Frank Lloyd Wright
who said, "Very early in life I had to choose between hypo-
critical humility and honest arrogance." Wright chose the
latter and was forever branded as a social nonconformist.
But he was also secretly admired by people who felt a basic

hypocrisy in their own modesty. The majority of winners and champions choose social acceptance through the psychic protection of modesty.

To sum up, sportsmanship represents the highest ideals of civilization. It is a way of integrating some of the aggressive biological qualities of the human being with social necessity. The fact that a part of the motivation for modesty and sportsmanship comes from the latent barbarism in men does not detract from its value. For, from the standpoint of society, the value of an activity is not determined by its motivation.

14 FATHERS AND SONS

COACHES AND ATHLETES

The much maligned American ideal of "together-ness" can be seen most clearly in the relationship between fathers and sons. In literature, contemporary art forms, television, radio, and movies, the "good" father-son relationship is portrayed in a stereotyped manner: They play ball together, they go to football and baseball games together, and they fish together. This is the model of the suburban father-son encounter.

In previous chapters we have alluded to the importance of the father-son relationship in the development of the athlete and in his participation in sports. The cases of "The Boy Who Played the Game Too Well" and "Rock'm, Sock'm Jack" revealed intense father-son relationships which molded much of the subject's subsequent athletic participation. In Ryan's research on track and field athletes, the "poor competitors," those who in spite of outstanding natural ability ritualistically defeated themselves in competition, were found to have a particular kind of relationship with their fathers. They described their fathers as strong, standing for no "nonsense," perhaps even restrictive. In the consideration of the problem of winning, we saw a parallel in the difficulties that an athlete had to overcome in his pursuit of victory in his sport, and in his assumption of the adult role in life. Symbolically, winning in an athletic contest was experienced as replacing the father in the family.

Historically, the role of the father has undergone profound transformation. Based primarily on his greater physical strength the father in ancient times was hunter, protector, and the ultimate authority in his family. The traditional father of the Judeo-Christian cultures has been the strong authoritarian man, "master of his home," demanding and expecting obedience from his spouse and children. With the coming of the Industrial Revolution women were able to do what had been men's work. No longer was the man distinct because of his greater physical strength, for now, with machines, his wife could perform as well or almost as well as he could in many areas of the work world. This led to a series of social changes and greater equality for women in social, economic, and domestic spheres, with an apparently diminishing difference between the sexes.

Today in the American middle-class home both mother and father may have jobs, sharing in what was once exclusively the "man's world," as well as sharing the women's domestic tasks. Fathers barbecue and cook out, they may help with the housework and do the dishes. They have even invaded, by invitation, that most sacred of all feminine activities, infant care. Fathers today do many of the same things that were exclusively maternal activities in times past—they warm bottles, diaper babies, and give children their baths. This results in a great deal more physical contact between fathers and children than formerly.

In the authoritarian family, roles were more differentiated and more clearly separated. If a boy challenged his father's authority a spanking quickly set things into perspective. But sometimes even this vestige of the traditional father's strength has been undermined by misinterpretations of principles of child psychiatry. Sometimes misquoted and sometimes misinformed, these bootleg purveyors of morality have raised a forbidding finger against the age-old practices of the use of authority and have thus contributed further to the diffusion of roles within the family.

Not only are fathers and mothers more nearly equal, but so are fathers and sons. What may be called the infantilizing of adults and the adultizing of children has brought them much closer together. Fathers and sons are now "pals" and have more nearly the relationship of a younger and an older brother. Father's absolute authority has been challenged, and he has lost it.

Television, which appears to have usurped from the pulpit the job of setting ideals and standards, portrays the stereotyped father as bungling, well-meaning, slightly confused, and youthful, always learning from his wise and moral children. A refreshing throwback to the earlier traditional father was the popular program—one of the longest runs in TV—called "Father Knows Best." This succinct title caused Americans to flock around their television sets to watch this now extinct variety of father as if he were the last live dinosaur.

With the demise of the authoritarian father, fathers have become more available, life-size instead of godlike, and in closer, more intense contact with their sons. At the same time the prohibitions against physical contact between males have grown. Although a boy may have been nursed and mothered by the first man in his life, his father, as he grows up, intimacy with other males, even his father, will be branded as "queer." Just as Victorian women once had to deny their heterosexuality, twentieth-century American men must deny any physical affection for other men.

The extremity of American defensiveness against male closeness stands out in bold relief when one compares related cultures. In the French army a symbol of virility is the kiss on each cheek when a medal is awarded. Even the stolid, emotionally unexpressive Russians have nothing resembling the restrictions that are prevalent in the United States. It is an expected gesture for a Soviet premier to kiss national heroes, such as the cosmonauts, at the time of success. In a similar vein it is fascinating to watch an American in conversation with a Latin-American. Latins prefer to stand close to each other when talking, much closer than Americans deem safe. As the American retreats to keep his distance, the Latin moves closer, sometimes providing a ludicrous imitation of the minuet.

Because this is such a loaded subject in our culture, let us try to put the relationships between men into perspective. It is clear that genital sexual activity is most appropriate between the male and female of the species. This is a biological truism, an anatomical necessity, essential for procreation and the survival of the species. Attempts to perform genital sexual activities between males is an aberrant procedure beset with the most extreme difficulties, biologically, anatomically, psychologically, and socially. The spectrum of physical contact between males is broad, however, just as it is between male and female. The handshake which our culture permits is a very limited form of physical affection between males. Many gradations of affection between men are possible, ranging from the handshake to genital sexual contact. In our culture, confusion has developed between genital sexual contact and the more limited forms of expressing affection and love, so that any physical contact between men is branded sexual in nature. If a father hugs his son or if two old friends embrace they are on "thin cultural ice." The man who shrinks from a pat on the shoulder by another man, sincere as it may be, is shrinking from a perfectly understandable expression of affection because of a defensive cultural fear. It is not unlike global interpretations of good and bad, of which currently the most prominent is the conflict between the Western democracies and communism. Extremist groups in this country equate anything they dislike with communism, so that they brand as dangerous even some of the most benign activities, ranging from the Boy Scouts to mental hospitals. Similarly, the most frightened of American males see homosexuality any time two men get together.

The genesis of the American fear of homosexuality is diffuse, with an infinite number of determinants. But one which emerges consistent with present-day psychological theories is that the intensity of the wish for physical closeness between men is precisely what leads to the defensive reaction against it. Since the dissolution of their absolute authority in the home fathers, as already mentioned, have more close physical contact with their sons at the earliest ages through feeding, diapering, and bathing them. The wish for continued physical contact becomes a reality, but once the baby becomes a young boy physical contact becomes forbidden. The more intense the wish, the more intense the need to defend against it.

One of the striking methods of defending against contact between males is increasing pressure from parents toward having their children grow up and engage in heterosexual behavior. Children at younger and younger ages are encouraged to date. Youngsters whose major relationships have been to the nursing bottle are encouraged to go to "coke-tail" parties. Girls, before breast development, wear "training bras." Teen-age marriages, as a result, have become a national institution. Before puberty, children engage in various caricatures of adult mating behavior—long before they are emotionally or physically prepared to do so. Insufficient heterosexual interest in children is often viewed with alarm by parents who fear their children may show "homosexual tendencies." Even the passive boy who shows only modest aggressive behavior may concern his parents for the same reason. All of this leads to a premature encouraging of children to act in an adult heterosexual manner.

Perhaps some mitigation is to be found in sports and athletics. A football player who is a linebacker can encouragingly pat his lineman on the behind in full view of a hundred thousand people. Baseball players hug each other after an important play and may even kiss each other. A basketball player like "Cool Cal" can relive the feeding experience he had with his father by "feeding" to his teammates. Athletes and fans alike may shout ardent support to their team, "I love you!" Many of these activities are done in seeming jest, yet their sincerity does not elude an observer.

Sports provide an opportunity for the expression

of the historical relationship between father and son while at the same time bringing into perspective the biological differences between father and son. As "pals" they may admire the great athlete and in this way maintain the same ideal. Though the father may have resigned his role as ultimate authority, fountain of knowledge, and moralist, he may maintain it in his role as teacher and coach in sports. He can hit or kick a ball harder and farther and can show his son how to do it. In most physical sports it is unlikely that the son can beat the father, for the father is stronger and more powerful.

In the athletic arena the more traditional roles of male and female are also maintained, for the female athlete can never be more than "a pseudo male." The most limited acquaintance with records in sports shows that men maintain superiority in this one area where biology reigns supreme while the woman is largely relegated to the role of spectator and supporter. She occupies the same position as the women who for centuries have watched their men go to battle and who could help only by cheering them on. In sports activities the mother and father are clearly differentiated to the son. It is similar to those rare moments in the home when physical strength prevails and the mother is unable to screw the lid off the jar and has to call upon the father.

A culture which severely restricts a biological function must have a safety valve for its expression. If there is none, the biology returns as a neurotic or psychotic symptom. In Victorian days there was the theory that women had no sexual desires, experienced no pleasure in sex, and were merely passive sexual partners. Since there was no cultural opportunity for the expression of the sexual wish, the mental illness of the day was gran hysterie. A woman could express both her sexual desires and the restrictions against them only by symbolic movements or physical dysfunction. As we have seen, the mid-twentieth century male has a difficult time of it and is roughly in the position of the Victorian female. He must altogether renounce any affection for males, although in his childhood this very same feeling might have been stimulated. The American male experiences intense social pressure to avoid any close contacts that could be interpreted as homosexual while he is encouraged to express, prematurely, heterosexual feelings. Sports represent the cultural safety valve. Here is the great arena in which the historical traditional roles of the sexes can be played. Men compete in battle for fair maiden, fathers are stronger than sons, frowned-upon wishes for male closeness can be expressed, and forgotten competitive roles can be experienced.

*   *   *

Social critics and educators have expressed concern about the paucity of male teachers in the lower grades of school, since generally it is not until high school that a child begins to encounter a significant number of men in the teacher role. The concern is that this situation has deleterious effects on the intellectual and emotional development of boys.

If all teachers are women, learning and education may come to have a distinctly feminine connotation. We have seen the fear among American men of appearing feminine in any way. It has been suggested that many promising students have been discouraged from pursuing an education because learning implies femininity.

A boy who enters school may already have acquired a rather undifferentiated view of masculinity and femininity because of the diminishing differences in the roles of mother and father within the home. He may in fact be frankly confused. When he begins to attend school and finds women in the teacher's position of authority, the situation becomes even more complicated. If he identifies himself with the new authority he assumes feminine traits. If he rejects the new authority in favor of a seemingly masculine role he also rejects education. In this age when science and technology are closely related to survival, the danger exists that we may be defeating ourselves by not providing young students with male educational models.

As in the home, sports occupy a special position in the schools. In the home the father continues to be the authority in sports, and there is little confusion regarding his role in this field. In elementary school the first male teacher encountered by a boy is usually the coach. If a woman teacher has to substitute as coach this does not usually cloud the issue significantly, for ordinarily she can only tell her boys "how the men do it"—she does not, herself, provide the identification model.

The educational process in the schools in the early grades thus is divided, with academic subjects having a feminine tinge and sports having a masculine one. This split is probably responsible in large part for the intense interest and devotion to sports of young boys and for their rejection of academic subjects. American girls at this stage do not experience the same degree of rejection of studying. One of the saving factors is that often the coach also teaches a class in mathematics or the sciences, and thus these subjects may become a masculine concern.

This problem is illustrated by a boy I treated for some time in a child guidance clinic. One of the major presenting complaints was his truancy and poor learning ability, despite an extremely high natural intelligence. After a time he explained to me that if he studied he would be a "sissy." He described clearly how he had to embrace athletics and reject academic subjects in order to be a member of the "in group" of the "best boys" in school. A contributing factor to his problem was the inordinate amount of role confusion within his family. Much of therapy was related to clarifying what was "sissy" and what was "manly." An event occurred outside of his therapy which assisted in the resolution of his problem. He was promoted to a new grade, where for the first time he had a male teacher who was athletic coach and science teacher and admired by the students for both. This man was the symbol of the resolution of this boy's identity problem. My patient related warmly to his new teacher, wanted to please and emulate him, and began studying and enjoying it. He went on to become an outstanding student in college and incidentally a successful college athlete.

Coaches also fill some of the functions of the traditional father. The term "the old man" was once reserved exclusively for one's father. Today just as frequently it may be applied to the school coach or team manager. The model of the good coach is the same as the model of the good father. He is strong, tough, and virile, deserves and expects respect, is not punitive, but neither is he easy. Though firm discipline has almost disappeared in many homes it is still expected in athletics. The coach demands and receives obedience. He is the expert and the teacher. The errant athlete receives physical punishment, not in the traditional spanking given by fathers but rather in the form of extra physical demands—several laps around the track, additional calisthenics, or additional working on fundamentals. The successful coach is one who gains the respect of his team, and whom the young athlete generally obeys.

Alumni, fans, and parents also view the coach as a substitute father. Because of his unchallenged authority he is responsible for the "boys" and for the performance of the team. This holds true even in college and professional athletics. The athletes that make up the team are not ordinarily held responsible for a loss—they are to be excused for they are only "boys." It is the coach who carries the burden of responsibility. On a losing team, the team members are rarely replaced; rather, the coach or manager is "fired." This is a magical symbolic gesture, for often a team is simply inadequate and the coach may be doing the best possible job, nevertheless he is the one who is replaced.

The vicissitudes of the coaching profession are well known. The losing coach is subject to the most scurrilous insults, and he and his family may even be threatened with bodily harm, as has been the case with many college football coaches. Hanging a losing coach in effigy has become a tradition. Success is expected of a coach. If he has a good year, he is only performing as a good father should, protecting his family, providing for them, and carrying them through successfully. He receives no extra credit for merely doing his job.

Coaches capitalize on this paternal image to gain extra effort from the team. The inspired team which wins one "for the old man" may perform beyond their expected capacity. The great Knute Rockne was always able to get "a little more" from his team by giving an inspirational pep talk before important games in which he implied that the team should win the game for him. He used all sorts of pretenses to exploit such performances, implying that if they didn't win he would be fired, feigning illness, or suggesting that he was seriously ill and that the team had to win this one game for "the old man."

The strong, decisive baseball manager, from John McGraw to Leo Durocher, has enjoyed success. In considering the problem of winning, we discussed how the strong coach or manager, by assuming responsibility for the performance of the team, makes possible a better performance. Through his strength he protects his players from their unconscious fears of retaliation for their aggression and their guilt. As the person responsible for the "boys" he accepts the unpleasant consequences of victory or defeat and frees the team to perform at their best.

In some sports, such as baseball, the father image is split. The manager is the good father to the team, protecting his boys, advising them and encouraging them. Animosity which players might ordinarily feel toward the manager because of the restrictions and demands he makes on them are dissociated from him and projected on to the "black fathers of baseball," the umpires. These black villains can do nothing right; in the eyes of a ballplayer they are restrictive, stupid, capricious, and unnecessary. The cry from both players and fans is "Kill the umpire!" This split between the good and the bad father allows for strong loyalty toward the manager. The greatest delight of players and fans is to see the manager and umpire embroiled in a spirited argument.

Ryan has described how a coach may wring a good

performance out of an athlete through strong direct efforts. He points out that although the coach's pep talk is now out of fashion, a coach may occasionally resort to strong measures. Ryan describes a case of a high jumper who was able to do 6 feet 5 inches in practice and yet could never clear 6 feet in competition. Just before a critical meet the coach in exasperation gave the jumper a strong pep talk and told him that he was "letting down the team." He gave the athlete the alternative of either clearing 6 feet or turning in his uniform. On this occasion the jumper cleared 6 feet.

Ryan is pessimistic, however, of the long-term effects of such coercion on poor competitors. The high jumper just mentioned, for example, never again made 6 feet. Ryan found that none of those athletes he termed extremely poor competitors ever made the transition to becoming good competitors. He believes that they must defend so heavily against achievement that they cannot afford to win under any circumstances. This may be true of the worst competitors, but they represent a relative minority.

More often one sees the occasional bad performer or the athlete who has not yet found himself. With such men the coach's attitude may have a profound effect on immediate and subsequent performances. In discussing the problem of winning we described the cases of some athletes who, by sharing the responsibility for winning with a coach or manager, were able to compete successfully. Once these athletes got the "feel" of winning, under the protection of the coach, and found that it was not dangerous they became better competitors. The coach's role may therefore be critical in determining the success or failure of an athlete. The coach must provide him not only with the technical "know how" for successful performance but also with a psychological climate conducive to it.

A strong coach or manager is able to protect his athletes from the fears which inhibit their becoming winners. The coach, who, like a father, renounces the paternal role and becomes a pal, cannot provide such protection for the team. An athlete must know that he can depend upon his coach under all circumstances. Young performers need only a modicum of sympathy and understanding, but they require a great deal of protection and strength. Many coaches have fallen prey to the same influences that have caused the demise of the father, erroneously assuming the relatively passive "psychological" role of being neutral.

The athlete who has successfully overcome the barriers of winning no longer needs the protection of the strong coach. He has himself become strong and responsible in the image of the strong father and coach. Even though he may not, in fact, have switched roles, remaining the player, his experience, polish, and maturity may set him apart from those who have not yet arrived. The epitome of such an athlete is the "old pro." He is dependable, technically expert, and skillful, and he can be counted on to perform at his best. He no longer needs the emotional support or protection of a strong paternal figure.

The old pro occupies a special position of esteem in sports, commanding the respect of coaches, fans, and young athletes. It is, then, not surprising that the big test for the young athlete comes at the moment when he challenges the "old pro." Even when they they are beyond their prime, old pros are difficult for younger opponents to beat. We have already considered how the young athlete may expand the psychological size of the old pro to the point where he is impossible to defeat; how young golfers and tennis players who were clearly technically superior to older but established players could not defeat them. If the challenging athlete can get by the old pro successfully without undue guilt or fear of retaliation, he can become an old pro himself. The analogy has been pointed out between this transition and the one from boy to man.

It is in this crucial transition that the coach may play such an important part. If an athlete unconsciously experiences beating the old pro as destroying "the old man," he can be supported in this task by another old man, the coach. When a young athlete tries to beat an old pro he is attacking a symbol of his father. If he knows that in accomplishing this task he is supported by another symbolic father, his coach, who will not desert him, his task is made easier. Once he has achieved the goal he may intuitively know that neither the coach nor his experienced opponent were actually his father and that nothing drastic has happened. At this point he is a stronger and more realistic person.

Chapters 14 and 15 trace an individual's present behavior in sports to the roles within his family during his early years. The changing roles in American life, however, may change an individual's relationship to sports. Therefore, the findings here may need reevaluation in the future.

15 THE FRUITS OF VICTORY

SIGNIFICANCE OF THE LOVING CUP

Up to this point we have considered some of the psychological obstacles an athlete must overcome in his pursuit of victory. We have seen the destructive wishes which underly the competition which appears civilized. We have explored some of the relationships between the competition in sports, a boy's earliest competition within his own family, and his relationships with coaches and fellow athletes. We have examined some of the symbolic experiences, the satisfactions and vicissitudes which athletes have during the competition. It is now time to consider in some detail another feature of sports, the prize.

In his book on the evolution of the Olympic games, Webster speculates on the earliest sports competition.* "As time went on a quarrel arose in the tribe as to who should marry the chieftain's daughter, for the ruler had no son to succeed him. Now the chief was a crafty old statesman, and, not wishing to see his fighting tail diminished by internal strife and bloody warfare, he decreed that his daughter should be given to the tribesman who could outrun, out-wrestle, outthrow with the spear, outjump, and outswim all others who might come against him. Thus came about the first sports meeting, for surely never was a more sporting contest held, or one for a fairer prize."

* F. A. M. Webster, *The Evolution of the Olympic Games 1829 B.C.– 1914 A.D.* (London: Heath, Cranton and Ouseley Ltd., 1914).

This story is also a parable of one of the most common contemporary themes in movies, television, and magazine fiction. It is cogently paraphrased in the song "You've Got to be a Football Hero to Win the Heart of a Beautiful Girl." Various homecoming and bowl queens and attractive cheerleaders have become nearly as much a part of sports events as the contest itself. A kiss by one of these lovelies is often a public part of the reward for victory and is greeted by a roar of approval from the spectators. The prize thus has a strong sexual connotation.

There are other fruits of victory as well. There is the prestige and popularity which an athlete may acquire from the general public. For professionals, there is money, their source of economic livelihood. Yet the traditional symbolic prize given to the victor is a trophy. Interestingly, the trophy is called a "loving cup." It is ironical that an athlete, sweaty, bloody, and bruised as the result of vicious physical competition in what seems like mortal combat, should be presented with a "loving cup."

The "loving cup" is allegedly so called, because it used to be passed from friend to friend by the double handle.* The reason for its selection as the symbolic trophy of victory is not so clear, however. One might assume that there is a reference to love for the competitor. Certainly, fraternal spirit among athletes is very strong, with the tradition deeply embedded in the present and the past. The brotherly love among Greek athletes is legendary. It seems doubtful, however, that this is the whole story or even the most important part of it. The trophy is given to the victor to keep, not to share with the vanquished. It is given to him in recognition of his having defeated his opponent, and it is not a symbol of their camaraderie. It seems more accurate to judge that it is symbolic of the love object which has been won. The implication is the same as that in Webster's speculation that in the first sports contest the quest was for the heterosexual prize, the girl.

* Webster's *New World Dictionary,* Encyclopedia Edition (Cleveland and New York: The World Publishing Company, 1952).

The first feminine person for whom the boy competes is his own mother. Every boy has experienced feelings of rivalry toward his father or toward his siblings, for his mother's attention. No child wants to share his mother's attention and care; he would prefer it for himself. These jealous desires quickly become concealed, however, in the social expectations of the family. But as the boy grows older this relationship, the competitive one with his father and his brothers and sisters for his mother's favor, serves as the prototype for future competition for feminine prizes.

The importance to athletes of mother-son relationships has been described by one psychiatrist, Stephen Ward,* a former football star at the University of Pittsburgh. Dr. Ward is quoted as saying, "The most competitive athletes seem to be driven by a strong subconscious wish for mother's approval. Certainly they have other motives, but from the evidence I've seen they're out there striving for mom's love. I've told this to fathers and they've looked as though they'd like to punch me." In support of his hypothesis, Dr. Ward cites such examples as football star Mike Ditka bringing his mother to a testimonial dinner; Warren Spahn, the great Milwaukee pitcher, calling his mother before the game on his fortieth birthday; Dick Stuart, long time major league first baseman whose mother attended his games and shouted support to him; Gene Fullmer, former world middleweight boxing champion, whose mother watched regularly at ringside. It is Dr. Ward's opinion that in his childhood the future athlete received strong approval from his mother in his expressions of violence and physical exertion. He has further observed that "almost every football player I've talked to told me his mother didn't like the idea of his playing football, but in almost every case, the mother attended the games."

Dr. Ward further quotes Harvard anthropologist John W. M. Whiting. He has observed that many of the best professional athletes grew up without fathers in the home,

* Myron Cope, "This Week," *Los Angeles Times,* October 14, 1962.

due either to death or parental separation. Jimmy Brown of Cleveland and Paul Hornung of Green Bay, two famous contemporary football players, are outstanding examples of this. Detroit's great defensive player Joe Schmidt and Dr. Ward himself could also be included. Although the anecdotal evidence of Whiting and Ward certainly documents a few cases of outstanding athletes, no attempt has been made to study a large group of athletes under controlled conditions to determine how frequently they have grown up in a home without a father.

The hypotheses for the motivation of the athlete, such as the absence of the father, the athlete striving for his mother's love, and winning through physical aggression, may be correlated with some of the observations that we have made.

First let us consider the loss of the father through death or separation. This may seem to contradict the previous discussion in which we showed that a major psychological hurdle for the athlete to overcome is the feeling of guilt for outdoing or replacing his father. Athletic competition symbolically recapitulates the earliest competition between father and son, and if the son is successful, it is tantamount in the unconscious to doing away with father. The devastating effects were seen in the cases of the tennis player and the football player described earlier. In the case of Rock'm, Sock'm Jack each change in his life—marriage, the birth of a child, and the final precipitating event when his father turned over the business to him—brought him closer in fantasy to the feeling that he was doing away with his father.

There is a body of psychiatric literature which also documents the traumatic nature of the loss of a father to a boy. Wahl* examined the family background of 392 schizophrenic patients. He found that four times as many of these patients had lost a parent by death before the age of 15 years as is found in the general population. Although

---

* C. W. Wahl, *American Journal of Psychiatry,* 110:668, 1954.

the loss of either parent has far-reaching, serious consequences, the loss of the father was more frequent. Blum
and Rosenzweig* studied 147 schizophrenic case histories
and found that the frequency of death of a parent was high
and particularly significant if it was the death of the parent
of the same sex.

We have alluded to the nature of the problem for
the boy whose father is gone due to death or separation.
He is faced with a feeling of responsibility for doing away
with his father. This is especially meaningful, since as we
have seen it is almost inevitable in our culture that a
boy competes with his father for his mother's attention and
that he harbors open or secret aggressive wishes to get rid
of the father. Even though the son has nothing to do with
his father's departure, whenever an accidental event occurs
which coincides with a wish, there is a tendency to assume
that there is a causal relationship.

A son's guilt may be further amplified by the
mother's loving attention showered on him to compensate
for the father's loss. To the boy it may be an indication
of her preference for him over the father, thus increasing
his responsibility for his father's departure. In divorce, the
loss of the father, even with the knowledge that it is the
mother's doing, is still considered to be "because of" the
son. When the son is faced with a realization of his wish
and worst fear, he bears the burden of guilt for his aggression and aggressive fantasy.

One might expect, then, that a boy who had lost
his father would be especially cautious about his aggression
and be inhibited in the expression of it to the point that
any violent impulse would be replaced with passivity and
gentleness. Expression of anger, if any, would be tentative in nature. Dr. Ward's observation of athletes, however,
is just the opposite. He found that certain boys without
fathers actually seemed to seek violent expression in sports.

The boy who grows up without a father usually

* G. S. Blum and S. Rosenzweig, *Journal of General Psychology,* 31:3,
1944.

has an additional problem: He does not have the usual masculine model on whom to pattern himself and against whom he can differentiate himself. In this connection it has been observed that boys raised by women without a male identification figure tend to prefer activities which are like women's. They pattern themselves after the models to which they have been exposed and have feminine characteristics.

Since the possibility of deleterious effects on the boy from the loss of a father are so great and potentially lead to inhibition of aggression and even to mental illness, we must assume that such a boy who became a well-adjusted athlete has been exposed to special remedial circumstances. The boy without a father seeks a substitute. In present-day culture he can find a ready-made substitute in the coach, usually a strong, masculine man who is always available at school. Although the boy encounters an endless series of women teachers in school it is usually only in the gym or sometimes in the sciences that he finds a man. It might be expected, then, that if there were no other obstacles a boy without a father would have an affinity for the coach.

The boy and the coach are, in a very real sense, "made for each other." Not only is the coach often the most available father substitute, but he is the purveyor of a kind of unique play therapy for such a boy. In athletics a boy can find the vehicle for reenacting aggressively and violently the fantasy of having done away with his father. This is safe, too, for the structure of the game provides that no matter how vicious the assault, the opponent is not actually harmed but will rise again. The boy acts out his violent wish and is reassured by a symbolic victory without actual damage to the opponent. By practicing over and over he can achieve some mastery over what was potentially a devastating psychological blow to his personality.

Play therapy and psychodrama are two common psychotherapeutic techniques used by psychiatrists and psychologists. A child in play therapy, through the use of toys, can reenact situations which he has experienced or is experiencing which have led to maladaptive behavior. In a similar way, psychodrama allows adults who have psychiatric disturbances to act out the traumatic experiences which have led to their illness. Such reenactments are useful in that they allow and encourage expression of wishes or feelings which the patient fantasies would be met with condemnation or retaliation. He is relieved when the expected and feared reaction is replaced by understanding.

For the boy who experiences guilt and tension, feeling that his competitive wishes to get rid of his father have actually resulted in his father's departure, vigorous athletics are a near-perfect medium for his play therapy. The game itself encourages aggression. The fact that it's a game signifies that it's "all in fun." The coach, the reassuring figure of the substitute father, is not injured by the boy's aggressive display. The boy may thus be able in sports to achieve integration of the violent wish against the father with a variety of reassurances inherent in the structure, "It's all part of the game." Long ago Freud observed that the person who had suffered a traumatic experience may try repetitively to relive that experience in order to achieve mastery over it. For the boy who has lost his father, sports provide a socially acceptable, remedial measure.

The discussion in the chapter began by considering the role of the mother in all of this. She is crucial, since her attitude towards her fatherless son's athletic endeavors makes it either possible or impossible for him to use sports therapeutically. If she permits and encourages him, he may benefit; if she forbids his participation, she may deprive him of the remedial experience. Probably her most important attitude is not one toward sports per se, but toward men. To help her son see that she is not able to supply him with everything, and that the man's role which is absent in their home is as important as the woman's, is tantamount to giving her son permission to seek a father substitute and to participate in sports. Not uncommonly, one encounters the bitter divorced woman who is derisive of men and denies their importance. Such mothers may attempt to be all things to their sons, presenting a confusing picture of masculinity and femininity. Bitterness may crystallize the guilt which the son experienced at the loss of his father and may further inhibit any overt expression of aggression. It is in such instances that boys may become confused and develop overtly feminine traits.

In this connection I once examined a man for the Superior Court who had repeatedly been arrested and convicted of acts of violent rape. He was a huge, muscular man who had a promising athletic career in football, which, however, had been stunted. His pattern in sports had always been the same; throughout junior high, high school, and college he would start out fairly successfully playing on a team, but he never finished a season. His parents were divorced when he was quite young, and he had been raised by his mother, a bitter woman who had never remarried. Her son often witnessed her vitriolic attacks on men and well knew her derisive attitude toward them. He was the only male seemingly spared from her attacks. Since he was treated differently from other men, this raised for him the question of whether he was male or female. He was precluded from the opportunity of finding any suitable masculine substitute. He made initial attempts to seek out such contacts with his coaches, was extremely sensitive, and felt he could not trust them. Often his mother would purposely interfere with a budding relationship with a coach.

Although she despised men, in many ways she attempted to imitate them herself, and she tried to tell her son how to participate in sports. She frequently would set her son straight, urging him to disregard something a coach had told him. She instructed her son in football and in baseball. His sexual identification was very hazy, and it was in moments when he felt threatened and when this confusion reached a peak that he would commit acts of heterosexual violence.

Similarly, I have known a number of outstanding and even great women tennis players whose fathers had been the driving forces behind their careers. At crucial

points in their careers these girls suffered identity crises and
were flooded with anxiety. They feared that they were more
masculine than feminine. For one great woman tennis player
this actually became a delusion and she believed that she
had turned into a man. Their fathers had treated them like
sons and perhaps had even wished that they were sons.
Eventually a crossroad was reached. All of these girls with
whom I was acquainted found at least a partial solution to
the identity crisis by giving up tennis entirely and con-
tinuing to avoid it, dropping completely out of sight. For
the public it was inexplicable that they would quit the
game. Of course, for the majority of girls there is no conflict between playing tennis and being feminine. The woman
tennis player has, in fact, a very appealing feminine public
image. There is nothing inconsistent about being a girl and
a competent tennis player unless for the individual the game
symbolizes masculine expectations. Most girls find in tennis
wholesome exercise which may enhance their femininity.

For sports to have a remedial effect, the athlete
must have the privilege of reenacting those life situations
which were difficult for him. The privilege is his if he is
given both the freedom to compete with the men and the
pleasure of receiving the feminine prize. The mother who
approves of her son's aggressive display is also approving
of his male competitiveness and, more important, of his
being a man. It is easy to see how great athletes look for
and even need such approval from their mothers.

Returning then to the initial theme, Webster assumed
that love of a lady fair was the motivation for the very
first athletic competition. The way to get the girl by winning
in sports remains a popular theme in our society. The loving
cup as a symbol of the fruits of victory maintains this
theme, most basic to which is a boy's first love, his mother.

16 THE AMERICAN SEASONAL MASCULINITY RITES

Not all of the characteristics which are attributed to being male or female are to the same degree biologically determined. Some, considered to be basic to masculinity or femininity, are determined by the culture in which one lives rather than by obvious physical differences. In our culture athletics are considered the most masculine of activities. Let us turn now to a consideration of what part sexual orientation plays in the intense interest in sports in America.

Before puberty, boys can be distinguished from girls mainly on the basis of primary sexual characteristics. When puberty is reached, biological distinctions become more apparent. At that time, with the differences in hormonal balance, the distinct secondary sexual characteristics begin to develop. Boys begin to have hair on their faces, and their bodies and become more muscular and angular. Girls become more curvaceous and develop breasts. Primary and secondary characteristics are predictable and universal: girls' hips broaden; boys' shoulders grow wider.

Beyond these physical characteristics are others which are largely, if not exclusively, determined by the society in which one lives. These can be termed tertiary characteristics and are transmitted from generation to generation by the examples of the men and women in the culture. To suggest, as Margaret Mead does, that the nature of maleness and femaleness, outside the physical characteristics, is culturally determined, may be an extreme point of view. For differences must develop just from living in a male body which has greater physical strength compared to living in a female body which experiences menstruation and pregnancy. Nevertheless, it is true that many of the male or female characteristics which are taken for granted in our society are determined by social custom rather than genetics. for example, up to very recently in this country, boys wore short hair and girls wore long hair, but in other parts of the world the reverse is true.* Similarly, an American boy would hide in shame if he had to wear a skirt, but in Greece it is the attire worn by a particularly virile and courageous group of soldiers.

There is a story which, although of doubtful validity, nevertheless illustrates the importance of these tertiary sexual characteristics: "Two children were playing outside a nudist camp. One of them discovered a hole through which he could look in the wall surrounding the camp. While he peeked through the hole, the other child excitedly inquired, 'What do you see, are they men or women?' The peeper responded in dismay, 'I don't know, they don't have any clothes on'!"

Tertiary sexual characteristics, such as dominance, mannerisms, dress, and speech, are often considered unalterable, yet studies of different cultures reveal quite different ideas about what constitutes male and female behavior. Each culture assumes that it "knows" how a man or woman should act. The folklore is justified by a self-fulfilling prophecy, as parents transmit to children their cultural expectations.

To be considered feminine in Victorian society women had to be frail, passive, and the potential victims of aggressive, lecherous males. Yet, according to the stories of Greek mythology, women were as urgently sexed as men.

---

* Since the above comments were first written, a remarkable change has taken place in the dress and hair styles of American teenagers and young people. Boys often now wear long hair and bright attention-getting clothing making their dress more similar to the traditional feminine attire. Girls frequently wear trousers and male style shirts. These changes are consistent with the reduction of difference between the sexes in our society as discussed in previous chapters. For the purposes of this chapter it is sufficient to note that standards of dress can change depending on taste and are not inherently either male or female.

In our own age primitive tribes differ grossly in what we consider basic masculinity and femininity. Among the Arapesh tribes of New Guinea, for example, studies in the early twentieth century found that men as well as women showed such characteristics as concern, giving, protectiveness, which we in America associate with mothering. Their neighbors, the Mundugumor, living only a short distance away, had quite opposite attitudes, with both men and women being strong, tough, and aggressive, like the idealized pioneer male in the United States.*

Another tribe in New Guinea, the Tchambuli, showed a reversal of conceptions about masculinity-femininity in another way. The male job was head-hunting, war making, and war preparation. To carry out their plans the men congregated daily in the "men's house." The women on the other hand were charged with all of the economic responsibilities in the village, such as fishing, food preparation, pottery, basket weaving. When the British banned headhunting and imposed a peace upon these people, the men became essentially unemployed, while the women continued their traditional activities. These women were temperamentally stable, secure, and cooperative with others, but the men, having lost their important function, became insecure, capricious, and aesthetic. Although men could no longer make war, the preparation rituals were continued. Their interest in the cosmetic arts and in creating suitable costumes, previously an important part of war, was now used instead to make themselves sexually attractive in competing through charm for the favors of the "important sex," the women. The women were tolerant of their men whom they viewed as gossipy, self-centered playthings.

Among the Manus it is the father who is endowed

* The information in this paragraph and the following paragraphs about New Guinea is from Margaret Mead, *Sex and Temperament in Three Primitive Societies: Manus, Mundugumor, and Tchambuli* (New York: William Morrow & Co., Inc., 1939), 2, pp. 1–384, 3, pp. 164–244, 237–322; and from a lecture by the noted anthropologist, Weston LaBarre.

with what in America are considered maternal characteristics. While the women are occupied with the economy and have little time for children, the father cares for and raises them. When Dr. Mead brought dolls to the children of the Manus, she found that it was the boys who eagerly played with them, while the girls were disinterested. The boys in their play were emulating their fathers' activities.

Largely, then, the tertiary sexual characteristics of people, the ones which are most visible and apparent, are socially determined and subject to considerable change from one generation to another and from one culture to another. Sometimes, however, the roles assigned to certain members of a society are intolerable, and in order for such a society to survive and maintain stability there have to be safety valves through which those who are placed in ambiguous or deprecated positions can gain some satisfaction or status.

The Iatmul are a tribe of New Guinea natives who had such a culture. The men despised women, considered them unimportant, worthless, almost subhuman, allocating to them only the most menial and routine of tasks. Men, in contrast, were considered to be the "real human beings," strong, brave, and courageous; they, too, were head hunters. The men were expected to be proud, the women self-effacing. Everything in this culture was either all black or all white, all good or all bad. There were no shades of gray. To be a man was to approach perfection; women epitomized all that was to be avoided. If a man showed the slightest feminine interests or characteristics, he was considered to be sliding toward the subhuman. Such rigid standards of human behavior placed each man in constant jeopardy of losing his humanity. This dichotomy was hard on the women, but it was equally difficult for the men. Adjustment in the Iatmul society was precarious: men walked a tight rope and women were scorned.

A society like the Iatmul has doubtful durability, for the tensions and resentment engendered are at an explosive pitch. This tribe's "safety valve" was the ceremony of Naven,* an annual occasion in which bitterness and tensions were discharged in a convulsive reversal of the year's pressures. Naven was a ceremony of cultural transvestism, during which men and women exchanged not only their clothes but also their roles. Boys who had been rigorously taught the shamefulness of femininity were now contemptuously called "wife" by their maternal uncles. They were bullied in the same way that women had been bullied throughout the year. The women, during Naven, were given a vacation from their despised roles and identified themselves dramatically as men, wearing their clothes and assuming their actions, strutting and swaggering. They could enter the "men's house" and could even beat certain designated men. They could engage in a theatrical simulation of the war games that men played. The men, who had spent the year taking elaborate ritualized precautions to avoid anything feminine could relax during the ceremony. It was a great relief actually to assume, in deliberate fashion, the female role.

By the end of the ceremony the tensions and resentments accumulated during the year were dissipated. The women felt better about their position in the community and the men admired the women for having been able to assume the masculine position. For a short time the women had become human and the men could love them. Over the next year the tensions built up again and hatred pervaded community life until the next Naven.

The Naven ceremony of the Iatmul is not unique, for other cultures have similar festivals. Rome's ancient feast of Saturnalia served a related function in discharging the year's accumulated tensions between masters and slaves. In this ceremony, slaves were waited upon by their masters and enjoyed all the privileges which they were denied during the year. It is easy to understand the necessity for such rites and their vital function in preserving a culture.

* Gregory Bateson, "The Naven Ceremony in New Guinea," *Primitive Heritage: An Anthropological Anthology,* eds. Margaret Mead and Nicolas Calas (New York: Random House, 1953), p. 186–202.

Beyond a certain point, tensions and resentment would destroy any community life.

The Iatmul looked forward throughout the year to their ceremony of Naven. The Romans, both slaves and masters, eagerly awaited the festival of Saturnalia. In fact, in these cultures and others with similar rites, the populace lived from festival to festival. These were the most important events in their lives. Similarly Americans, particularly many American males, mark time by their own seasonal rites: football season, basketball season, baseball season, and so on. Many men live from one sports season to the next, with sports representing the most vital part of their lives.

Iatmul men and women were in a precarious psychological position as a result of the extreme demands which their culture placed upon them. The Naven rite offered an opportunity for the expression of strong feelings which had to be disowned throughout the year preceding the ceremony. For the women it was denial of self-assertion and aggression; for the men it was denial of passivity, with no opportunities for relaxation of their facade of superstrength. Naven saved the Iatmul people from the otherwise impossible demands of their culture and thereby saved the culture from extinction.

American men, as we have seen, are also on shaky cultural ground. Their position is precarious as a result of the contradictions in their lives. To an ever-increasing degree, American male children early in their lives have close physical and emotional experiences with their fathers. Fathers share almost equally with mothers in the maternal activities: feeding, bathing, cuddling, and comforting, which were once the exclusive domain of the American female. American parents are apt to take turns in getting up with the baby when he cries at night. When either parent has a "night out" the other serves as baby sitter. If the egalitarianism is disrupted it is likely for bitterness to develop.

"Togetherness" has largely meant the diminution of the uniqueness of the female position as well as the male position in the family. Father is no longer the ultimate authority; he has become a "pal"; he is now not a teacher but a co-learner. He has an equal, but not a greater voice in the collective activities of the household than have the children and his wife. The wife, who may have a job outside the home and may make as much as or even more money than her husband, quite naturally expects him to share the housecleaning, dishwashing, and caring for the children. The roles are diffused and the differences between male and female, between adult and child are diminished.

Like the Tchambuli, American men have had a change in status. The Tchambuli men lost their principal function, head hunting; American men have had to share with their wives their economic productivity as bread winners. Tchambuli men became superfluous; the authority and uniqueness of the American man has diminished. Previously, the main way men were superior to women was in their physical strength. Now, development of machines has caused male strength to be less important, almost obsolete. Machines are stronger than men, and the sexes are equally competent in running most machines. Dexterity has become more important than power, and women are at least as competent as men in this respect. The serious consequence is, that in their work, the new breed of factory and office workers are essentially neuter in gender.

While these changes in technology and in the family have taken place, the cultural expectations of masculinity have remained fixed as they were in pioneer days. Physical strength and agility were the qualities by which a man was measured, for then only the strong were able to survive. Obviously, such values are more appropriate to the frontier than to the office. Now, in order to fit this already obsolete image, men and boys must engage in artificial, nonproductive displays of strength.

As the real demands for what was considered traditional male strength have decreased, the expectation of show of strength has grown. Parents have a special concern that their boys are not aggressively masculine enough. Mothers are more apt to be concerned about passive, compliant behavior in male children than about their destructiveness. Often they are even relieved by, and subtly encourage, overt displays of aggression, for in that way, they are reassured that their sons are not "sissies." This is quite different from the concept of several decades ago that the quiet child was the "good" child.

As fathers and sons have grown closer together, an obsessive cultural concern with homosexuality has grown. In a counter move to avoid such taint, as already noted, children are pushed earlier and earlier into heterosexual relationships. The tragedy of this parental encouragement is that it is self-defeating, since the child in latency has other more important business to learn than sex appeal. In addition, his premature explorations in heterosexuality promote a sense of inadequacy within him as he recognizes his inability to perform as expected. This inadequacy, in turn, is interpreted as the "taint" and the parental efforts and encouragement towards aggression and heterosexuality are redoubled, the situation becoming a vicious circle.

Just as Naven helps to relieve the Iatmul tensions, American sports have a similar function. The first man outside the home that a boy encounters is usually a coach. In school he meets a series of female teachers who are the purveyors of morality, knowledge, and competence. The coach is not only a man among men but, more important, a man among women teachers. Boys try to model themselves after the coach and find security in imitating him. Their roles are clearer on the diamond than in the classroom, for it is on the athletic field in those seasonal masculinity rites that males become the kind of men their grandfathers were and their mothers want them to be. Strength is king; men are separated from boys, and boys, in turn, from girls. In the best tradition of the frontier, an athlete overpowers his opponent, and the sexual roles are re-established to conform with the expectancies of the culture. Male and female are relieved of their role discrepancy just as they are following the Naven ceremony. Fortunately, this can be accomplished, not only by participation, but by observation as a spectator who identifies with the players.

They can both then return to the office and the home with renewed respect for the uniqueness of the sexes and the re-establishment of their own identities, until the distinction gradually diminishes and another masculinity rite is necessary.

In a subtle way, these supermasculine "frontier rites" also allow for the expression of warmth and closeness among men which society compels them to disown. In sports, players huddle together; they caress, pat "fannies," shout affectionate phrases, and engage in activities which are scorned elsewhere but condoned in sports. In a recent heavyweight boxing match, the victor was embraced and kissed by his manager before several thousand fans in the sports arena and perhaps several million more on television. Such behavior anywhere but in the context of sports would be highly suspect. But here, with full cultural approval and without detracting from the supermasculine atmosphere, men can satisfy either physically or vicariously their needs for close male companionship like that which they experienced in childhood. In this context, physical contact, either aggressive or friendly, is applauded rather than condemned, and in the frenzy of American sports, males are purged of their femininity, and at the same time provided with an outlet for close male contact.

Among the Iatmul, Naven takes place annually, and a single festival appears to take care of a year's accumulated tensions between the sexes. Fifty years ago a single sports season, namely baseball, sufficed for Americans. Today each season of the year is occupied with a different sport. Sport seasons now fuse with one another into a continuous succession of ceremonial demonstrations. The fall rite, football, now overlaps with the spring rite of baseball and track. The vacant moments are filled with transitional rites: basketball, hockey, tennis, and golf, to mention a few.

Although the potential for wild celebration is always present, the pitch of these ceremonies is somewhat lower than the yearly Naven in New Guinea. This is consistent with the lower pitch of all activities in our sophisticated country. Very little can be termed a "special event," since we are bombarded daily with the spectacular and the overwhelming. Just as the differences between sexes have diminished, the difference between holiday and weekday has also. Activities converge into a more integrated (for the hopeful) or amorphous (for the pessimistic) mass of ongoing activities. The Fourth of July, once fraught with danger and excitement, is now closely controlled and tame. Similarly, other holidays such as Armistice Day, Flag Day, St. Patrick's Day have lost their appeal except to the most enthusiastic. Since the range of the pitch is lower, the exposure time must be increased. Thus, sports go on continuously from the beginning to the end of the year.

Among primitives, the transition from boyhood to manhood is accomplished in a single, brief ceremony—the puberty rite. A symbolic gesture, such as circumcision or knocking out a tooth, bears witness to the cliché, "Today I am a man." For American men the transition is quite different. Puberty, the time of traditional manhood when the secondary sexual characteristics appear, is now only the signal for the prolonged period of suspension between boyhood and manhood called adolescence. Biologically and sexually, manhood has been reached, but the technical complexity of our society requires an extension of many years of education and preparation before the productive work of life can begin. The preparation extends temporally toward mandatory early retirement, which advances from the other side, allowing only a relatively brief period for the adult work career.

The adolescent is thus in a state of moratorium, suspended in his choices of occupation and a wife, prohibited from sexual activity, prevented from making any firm commitment.* No true identity can be achieved in the face of such a moratorium. In the medical profession this problem is well exemplified. A boy who decides that he

---

* In the past decade young people have revolted against this state of suspension. They have adopted new and more permissive sexual mores and have often shown an unwillingness to delay gratification. They often choose not to wait the required period of time to achieve an occupational identity or traditionally defined marriage.

wants to be a doctor must make this decision at least a score of years before his goal is achieved. If, for example, he wishes to be surgeon he may not complete his training until he is past thirty. Failure at any stage of this process would force him to seek a new occupation and a new direction for his life. With the endless series of what can be likened to initiation rites—high school, college for four years, medical school for four years, residency—it is as senescence approaches that the moratorium is over and the man can say with some degree of finality, "I have an identity, I am a doctor."

Because of the nature of this moratorium, adolescence is a period of turmoil. Rebellion and confusion can be expected from the man who has not yet found a place for himself, who is suspended, seemingly for an infinite length of time, between his family of origin and his family of procreation.

But as we have seen, a culture with contradictions and ambiguities, if it is to survive, must have some way of relieving and integrating its tensions. Sports form an elongated bridge across childhood, adolescence, and adulthood for American males. Although the adolescent boy may have to suspend decision and commitment on most of his affairs until many years hence, he can enter athletics with full exuberance and play and work at sports with a dedication which satisfies his personality and his society.

Among my patients has been a successful attorney who came to treatment because his marriage was on the point of dissolution. The bone of contention between him and his wife was that in her eyes he was not "man enough." She was bitterly disappointed that he was not handy around the house, that he did not make the family decisions, and was not more assertive—all qualities she had admired in her father. Her husband's competence in a learned profession seemed unimportant, while her father's physical strength resulting from his being an unskilled laborer was important. She feared that their son would develop into a "passive man" like her husband. The husband, too, doubted his own masculinity, shared her fears, and so sought therapy in order to try to conform to her expectations of him. The bickering that went on between them always subsided when they engaged in sports or jointly watched sports events. This seemed to adjust the perspective and after such activity each respected the other for his or her distinctiveness.

This is not an unusual case. Wives are worried about their husbands not being aggressively masculine enough; mothers are worried about their sons being too passive; men fear that they will be dominated or thought to be effeminate.

In reality, men are larger and weigh more than women, they do have more powerful muscles, they do have bigger lung and heart capacities, and they do have a sexual organ which makes them different. They are built for physical combat, for hunting, as well as for a unique sexual role. In the work and social world, however, this combat strength is largely obsolete. A 200-pound man can easily lose a business encounter (symbolic combat) to a 130-pound man or to a 90-pound woman. Slender feminine fingers can push the buttons on a computer as well as can thick, strong, male fingers, perhaps better. Machines are stronger than either men or women, and to the machine it makes no difference if its buttons are pushed hard or lightly. Male strength has, at least in part, lost its function and its value in society.

In sports, male and female are placed in their historical biological roles. In sports, strength and speed do count, for they determine the winner. As in premechanized combat, women can never be more than second place to men in sports. They can cheer their men on, but a quick review of the record books comparing achievements in sports of men and women confirms the distinctness of the sexes here.

It is small wonder that the American male has a strong affinity for sports. He has learned that this is one area where there is no doubt about sexual differences and where his biology is not obsolete. Athletics help assure his difference from women in a world where his functions have come to resemble theirs.

17 SUMMARY: MODERN MAN AND SPORTS

The race is not always to the swift—
Nor the battle to the strong—but
That's the way to bet.

                                    . . . Damon Runyon

In a nation conscious of having a strong, efficient, capitalist economic system, there is less newspaper space devoted to financial matters than to sports. In a nation proud of its heritage as a political democracy, its citizens are often less interested in political contests than they are in sports competition. In the schools and colleges of a nation providing the greatest educational opportunity for all, the academic is often submerged by sports. In the mass communication media struggling with entertainment programming for the seemingly insatiable appetites of its consumers, nothing endures as well as current sports contests.

Each morning the American seats himself at the breakfast table, glances at the headlines in his newspaper, and turns quickly to the sports page where what he reads may seem more appealing than the food before him or the woman who serves it. He performs his weekly tasks in perfunctory manner, but when it comes time for sports he comes alive and is transformed by his enthusiasm. Perhaps ours is more nearly the sporting nation than an affluent nation, a capitalist country, a political democracy, or anything else.

What is the meaning of this national devotion to sports and why have sports achieved such an important position in the scale of human interest? Sports are played and watched because people want to play and watch them. They do it for pleasure, for the joy of exuberant movement of the body, for diversion from the tedium of life, for play, and for display before others.

Enjoyment may be the flame that lights the fuse, but much more is necessary to keep alive a fire which becomes a holocaust. Pleasure is not enough to account for the distance runner who drives himself beyond endurance and collapses. It is not enough to explain the repetitious gruelling practice of preparing for "the game," nor the brutal punishment and pain of boxing or football. Pleasure is not enough to explain the dedication of the loyal band of rooters who cheer the New York Mets, the major league's all-time worst baseball team, to victories that never come. Nor does enjoyment account either for the American preference for sports over other forms of play and recreation.

Is it victory? Is it money, fame, prestige? Perhaps all these play a part, but most of those who play or watch get no such tangible rewards. The participant himself does not have a satisfactory explanation for the frenzied interest in sports, in which he is a participant.

The reluctance to penetrate into comprehending the meaning of sports is understandable. We prefer not to know too much about what we treasure and that with which we are satisfied. The lover of a beautiful woman protects his cherished concept of her from anything which may detract from her beauty. "Better let well enough alone," he feels. This is the prevailing attitude of Americans towards their love affair with sports—but, in sports, unless more than the surface is explored men can become slaves, entrapped instead of being able to exercise free will.

A review of the case histories of athletes who developed psychiatric symptoms reveals something of the nature of the psychological issues which underlie sports. The problems that dramatically emerge in psychiatric illness are usually unique only in degree and are not qualitatively distinct from those experienced by most others in the same culture. The person who is healthy has, in many respects, traversed a similar life pathway and encountered similar road blocks as has the psychiatric casualty. It is the functional elaborations of a common core and not the core itself which lead to normality, to success, or to failure.

Studying the athletes who crossed the threshold from psychiatric health to psychiatric illness, sports have been found to be of central importance in the change which occurred—when a signal event indicated the end of their satisfying role in sports. As long as they remained players and could enjoy the satisfactions and meaning of that role, they were indistinguishable from other successful athletes. Sports provided the bond of union which integrated their personalities. Perhaps we might generalize and suggest that sports serve a similar function for others who play or watch. In sports they may be able to express feelings which, even though they are stimulated by the culture, are forbidden by it in most situations. Through repetitive experience in sports one may find personal solution, at least temporarily, to some of the generic problems of our culture.

The athletes described in this book developed psychiatric disorders when the continuity of their sports activity was interrupted. Why was it necessary for them to cling tenaciously to this thread of continuity? Were there not other interests which could provide it as well or better? What are the discontinuities for which sports compensate?

As already noted, among primitives the transition from boy to man is accomplished by single ceremonial act on a specified day in the life of the individual. There the knocking out of a front tooth or circumcision signifies that the transition is official and complete. There is little question to the boy or to those around him that the change has occurred. One day a boy, the next a man—beautiful in its simplicity.

How different it is for the twentieth-century American! The demands for increased technical skills have extended, seemingly almost beyond reason, the period of education and preparation. As preparation for life takes longer and mandatory retirement comes earlier, the convergence leaves a small and diminishing period of independence and productivity. But even though this is true, another conflict emerges. Although our youth remain in a position of economic dependence in the family of origin they often are physically stronger and able to supersede their parents. The speed of scientific advance precludes the father's being an expert on contemporary knowledge, the very thing which is of utmost importance to his son undergoing the educational process. The parent can no longer stand on his superior knowledge and strength as did the nineteenth-century craftsman who, once having mastered his craft, became the expert and was established for life. A modern-day social problem of increasing importance is the retraining of adult workers whose employment has become obsolete. When the strength and knowledge of the subordinate approaches and even passes that of the master of the household, tensions and confusion mount. Then, understandably, when the overdue liberation does occur, the intoxication of new freedom leads the liberated children to move as far away from their parents as possible. This amplifies the problem for the next generation who are deprived of the extended family members who could have served as objects for the dissipation of tensions.

The boy who looks to his father for a model of adult life may be disappointed. He may never see his father at work, and the father himself may be unclear about his own small part in the total picture—the work which he does is likely to be separated from its product by a large number of other jobs and intervening activities. All of this conspires to make it difficult for a boy to grasp the significance of adulthood.

It is easier to know more about the father's leisure activities. Again, in leisure which often takes the form of sports, the difference between fathers and sons is small. Although there may be differences in their abilities actually to play a sport, as spectators they are approximately equal and thus they become more like brothers looking toward an idealized distant figure on the field. They share the same idol, the "star athlete."

Erikson has described this elongated period of preparation for an adult role as the "identity moratorium." During this time the youth is in a cultural limbo without a clear place of his own, and denied supports. But even the direction of the preparation is clouded by the common dream of American youth. If he plays a sport well enough, he may drink from the fountain of youth and continue to play forever, even more profitably than if he were to work. In other words, he may become a star professional athlete.

In sports, the American boy has a chance to find an activity in which there is continuity between boyhood and adulthood. In the role of player or fan his interest may continue and be shared by multitudes of others, who all, as strangers in an anonymous society, can find almost immediate common ground for conversation in sports. As fans, in addition, they may share and express feelings of an intensity rarely experienced outside the stadium.

As the traditional guideposts to becoming a man have become obscure the intensity of interest in sports has risen. For the American male groping in a morass of ambiguity, sports serve as a guide rail to which to cling. The athlete who becomes a patient suddenly finds his guide rail disappearing and himself alone, bewildered. Most of those who play or watch sports do not need to cling so desperately. The guide rail is there, but it needs merely to be touched in getting from one place to another. Sports are used in the service of a broader interest and fuller life.

Some years ago an investigation examined some aspects of the lives of athletes after their playing days were over.* Troubled by claims and counter-claims, As-

* Edward H. Litchfield, *Sports Illustrated,* October 8, 1962, pp. 66–80.

sistant Athletic Director of the University of Pittsburgh, J. Clyde Barton, spent more than a year tracing the whereabouts of 1,678 Pitt lettermen who had performed between 1900 and 1960. He obtained 1,391 responses to a detailed questionnaire. It was shown that in the intervening years these former athletes had become amazingly successful in fields outside sports, although they still maintained a lively interest in sports. Their successes ranged from financial to academic. It is in the latter category that a most interesting statistic appeared. Five hundred and seventeen, of 37 per cent of those surveyed, went beyond the baccalaureate degree to earn an advanced degree, and this was in an era long before the current emphasis on graduate work. The most impressive evidence for success, however, came not from statistics but from the stories revealed in individual replies to the questionnaire. Many of these men had achieved positions of preeminence in their fields.

There are in sports many examples of athletes who could not win because of self-defeating behavior. Many continue to enact the drama of defeat. Others may, through practice and the support of teammates, coaches, and fans, eventually overcome such self-defeating behavior.

Whether the athlete succeeds in overcoming his psychological obstacles to winning or continues to enact his personal drama of defeat, sports provide the arena for the vigorous enactment conflict between responsibilities of victory and the exemption from responsibility of defeat, which is, in essence, the decision between maturity and childhood. Whatever the outcome, the potential does exist for mastery over this significant personal issue which occurs within a background of cultural ambiguity. Sports serve as the stage for the portrayal of modern-day, symbolic competition in archaic physical terms.

From Jean-Jacques Rousseau to Margaret Mead the antagonism between society and individual biological need has been expressed. Within the roles of everyday life there is diminishingly small space for the expression of some of man's physical characteristics. The male animal is physically stronger than the female; he is the primitive defender and aggressor. Modern technology has made physical strength partially obsolete. Yet in a contradictory way we still expect expression of strength and aggression from men. Women today are more apt to complain of a lack of aggression than of compliance in their men. The marvels of electronic gadgetry may equalize the sexes during the week, but on the Saturday athletic field, strength still prevails; that is, maleness prevails, for in almost no major competitive sport can female biology approach the male's. As the functional differences between male and female diminish, sports interest rises in a nostalgic return to premechanized days when physical strength was all-important.*

There is something for everyone in sports. Today women as well as men stagger under the burden of pseudo-equality. They labor under expectations consistent with masculine vestiges of Victorian patriarchy and yet are expected to integate masculine values with the older tradition of feminity. Except for time out for material activities, they are encouraged in the employment field to compete on an equal basis with men. But, as a sports spectator a woman may move freely among a variety of acceptable identification models. With the superfeminine cheerleaders, she can assume her historical place supporting masculine fighters. With the athletes on the field she can vicariously engage in aggression beyond her physical power.

The home is in transition, too. As women increasingly share with men the job-outside-the-home responsibilities they need the man's cooperation with household tasks—cleaning, washing, cooking. Of even more significance, perhaps, to personality development is the sharing by the father of the traditional maternal functions of infant care: feeding, diaper-changing, and bathing. Recognizing the para-

---

* Many teenagers and young adults today seem to have achieved a new and more relaxed attitude towards these contradictions. They seem less concerned about traditional definitions of male and female. They seem not to be so burdened by past traditions and perhaps, as a result, are less interested in sports.

mount significance of mother-child relationships in the development of personality, there is need to examine the effects of this increased amount of mothering done by fathers.

Although children today are highly stimulated by contact with their fathers in childhood, the most stringent restrictions exist regarding physical contact between men. Hart found that among college men the single greatest fear is of being considered homosexual.* The rules of American everyday life preclude any physical contact between men except the brisk handshake—and even a handshake is questionable unless it is manifestly an expression of strength.

Seemingly to defend against the possibility of boys and men engaging in close physical contact, there is increasing pressure for simulated heterosexual activities at earlier and earlier ages in children. "Going steady" and "coke-tail parties" for the pre-teenagers are premature and clumsy efforts to have the children comply to the adult conception of approved physical contact.

According to Erik Erikson, in most cultures the social expectations of adulthood tend to support what has been experienced and learned in childhood. But when a society sends out contradictory images of expectation, the individual and the structure as a whole are undermined. "Human nature is flexible, but it is also elastic—it will tend to return to the form that was impressed upon it in earliest years."†

The one place that allows and encourages close physical contact between males, and paradoxically this is in the service of the most masculine of activities is sports. Far from being considered "queer," male physical contact on the athletic field is sanctioned. The team goes into a huddle, the

* Henry Harper Hart, "Fear of Homosexuality in College Students," *Psychosocial Problems of College Men,* ed. Bryant M. Wedge (New Haven: Yale University Press, 1958), pp. 200–213.

† Margaret Mead, *Sex and Temperament in Three Primitive Societies: Manus, Mundugumor, and Tchambuli* (New York: William Morrow & Co., Inc., 1939), p. xiii.

linebacker pats his linemen on their buttocks, scantily dressed men collide, bump into, and hit each other in basketball, boxing and wrestling. Home-run! Touchdown! Victory!— and the players embrace! The thousands who watch roar their approval. Such actions outside the stadium, on the street, for instance, would be viewed with suspicion, a knowing glance, and perhaps even the summoning of the vice squad. Sports provide a culturally acceptable, useful, and vital place for such expressions.

But it is not only affectionate display that is sanctioned in sports. The tabooed area of man's aggression and violence is also released. Yablonsky has shown that the restrictions on the expression of aggression are a factor in the development of a new breed of criminal, one who is relatively unconcerned about the actual gains from his crime. His burden of suppressed aggression is unpredictably discharged in crimes of violence which are orgastic "kicks."*

The rules in competitive sports make certain kinds of physical aggression allowable. Referees and umpires are employed not only to forbid fouls but to enforce the rights of the athletes to assault one another during the contest. In boxing, one of the two principal reasons for stopping a fight is when there is insufficient display of aggression; the other, when one of the fighters is so badly beaten that his life is in danger. The distinction between the rules of everyday life and of the sports arena are clear in boxing, where it is actually demanded by the referee and the crowd that a boxer fight. On the street, if a boxer were to hit a man it would be felonious assault and a crime. In a paradox of terms, the way a base runner in baseball can be "safe" is by "cutting down" the second baseman with his spikes. In ice hockey, the rules display a refreshing frankness. Major fouls are distinguished from minor fouls on the basis of whether or not blood is drawn. Even in noncombat sports where no actual physical assault occurs between

---

* Lewis Yablonsky, *The Saturday Review,* February 2, 1963, p. 54.

players, vigorous physical aggression is expected in order to accomplish victory. The description of a wide margin of defeat in a sport like tennis, with phrases such as "He murdered him" or "He killed him" throw light on the symbolic content of this seemingly genteel competition.

Society applauds the aggressive male but allows fewer and fewer opportunities for him to be physically aggressive. Man attributes some of his problems to the increase in population and the consequent necessity of living in close proximity to others. Proximity itself may have only a limited effect; more significant is the requirement for restrictive regulation in a society which nevertheless emphasizes competition. Sports are one of the last outposts where physical aggression has an established, acceptable place in our culture.

It is clear that cultural ambiguities and contradictions make the personal development of the individual more difficult. When the cultural expectations are obscure or contradictory there are insufficient sign posts to guide the individual in his progress. Ideally the progress of the individual should be steady and gradual, in successive steps.

The burden of guiding the young is thrown onto family, but since the family itself is a product of the same culture, it is ill-prepared to meet this challenge. The son's succeeding the father is impaired by the father's being unsure of his own role and finding it similar to the son's. The son, in turn, has a vague sense of guilt over succeeding the father who never quite made it himself. There is a resultant longing on the part of both sons and fathers for the strong father against whom one could compete more freely.

This longing also finds its expression in sports where the coach or manager is the absolute patriarch, and the "star" is the hero. Any question about what is expected or forbidden is interpreted by the umpire who dispenses his justice without prejudice or favor. In much of contemporary life the opponents against whom one competes are vague, but in sports the opponent's image is sharp. Boys are encouraged and taught how to struggle successfully against an opponent using all of their physical, mental and emotional resources.

A special moment of truth, paralleling the succession of fathers by sons, appears in the moment of victory or defeat. It is, as it were, the threshold from boyhood to manhood. To the victor go responsibilities as well as the spoils. He must protect what he has attained and must face the assaults of competitors or of the defeated who wish to retaliate. The loser is exempt from these responsibilities and receives the sympathetic comfort accompanying defeat. The transition from boy to man made abstract by the ambiguities of cultural definition becomes concrete on the athletic field and may be pursued with the certainty of what the task is, even if not with the certainty of achieving it.

In watching, the spectator, too, may experience the competition with greater clarity than he may find elsewhere in family life, at school, or at work. He may engage vicariously in the same pleasures and struggles as the players on the field, yet with greater safety and the support that may be necessary for him. Sitting in the stands, he may be stimulated by the action on the field and by those around him to feel with an intensity greater than he can experience when he is actually taking part.

In the confusion of obscure identities, sports occupy a unique position. They are a socially accepted activity cutting across consecutive levels of development and of social class. They provide an activity suitable to nearly all ages. Baseball can be a peak interest to an eight-year old Little Leaguer, a turbulent adolescent, an adult fan, or a professional player. It is a continuous interest and activity which any American can grasp, whatever his occupation or class or background. From early ages the coaches emphasize the masculinity of sports, and they themselves are easy identification figures. Sports provide familiar experiences within the anonymity of change. They provide continuity in a series of otherwise disturbing discontinuities in our cultural conditioning.

Work and play were once traditional opposites. Work was productive, necessary for survival. Play was unproductive, free, and an end in itself. The relationship between work and its products has become more obscure to the worker as his function has become increasingly specialized and fragmented. In our complex social order one does not grow his own food, build his own house or weave his own cloth. Instead, work is divided into a series of seemingly isolated activities which serve as steps towards the ultimate product. In our society man's right to the necessities for survival have been firmly established whether he works well or poorly or not at all. Individual survival is no longer dependent upon the individual's productiveness. It is predicted that automation will cause work as we have known it in the past to be carried out by only a privileged few while large numbers of others will have to find meaning for their lives in other ways.

Work has already lost many of its traditional characteristics and so has play. Play has been increasingly transformed into organized sports, and sports, in turn, increasingly resemble work in the arduous practice and preparation they require, in the intense involvement of coaches and athletes in the spirit of work, and in their actual economic productivity. In a final paradox, only those sports which began as work, that is, hunting and fishing, are now dominated by the spirit of play.

Sports have become a transitional social institution, neither work nor play, but somewhere in between. Transition implies change, and although the direction of the change is not entirely clear at this time, it seems doubtful that the traditional distinctions between work and play will reappear. Hope rests in the possibility that a new satisfaction may come to be associated with the spirit of production and that greater freedom may be allowed for individual selection of activity. This may come as society provides for the individual's basic needs independent of his work.

Sport is transitional between the social institutions of work and play. It also serves a transitional purpose for the individual. Work was once the responsibility of adults and play the prerogative of children. Confused by the functional ambiguities, the twentieth century American may find in sports a useful bridge in his individual transition from boy to man.

In sum, sports may bind together the fragments and contradictions of the culture for the individual by providing a unique group of functions:

1. They provide an arena for the expression of many physical actions stimulated by the culture but precluded by the rules of everyday life.

2. They provide an opportunity for the symbolic or actual repetitive enactment of problem situations for the individual, with the possibility of achieving some mastery through such avenues as the teaching by coaches, the support of teamates and fans, and rules which allow for a change of roles, activity instead of passivity, and the possibility of victory.

3. They provide for the individual continuity of interest at various ages, in a culture filled with ambiguity of role function.

4. They provide a transitional institution between work and play for the individual in his personal development, and for society.

The child seeks the arena which allows, by its rules, overt physical expression; the youth confused in his role clings to the familiar; the adult nostalgically returns to a place of definite roles where he can allow himself to feel intensely. The nostalgia is not only for the individual but for all of mankind which is increasingly separated from its physiology and estranged from the elemental.

A patient recently told me of a recurrent fantasy which has been troubling him. He pictures a family—father, mother, and children—sitting motionless in a semidark room. They appear unaware of one another as their collective gaze is transfixed on the lighted TV screen before them. Without looking, their hands, holding forks, move mechanically upward to their mouths and down again from TV trays on which rest TV dinners. They do not taste the food they eat, and they appear entirely occupied with the picture on the lighted screen. On the screen is a family—father, mother, and children—sitting motionless in a semidark room. They appear unaware of one another as their collective gaze is transfixed on the lighted screen before them. . . .

My patient's fantasy is a grotesque metaphor of contemporary life in which reality is elusive. To the family seated before the TV screen their own activities and relationships seem insignificant compared to the activities of the family on the screen. But the family on the screen is only carrying on a mimicry of the viewers and is an illusion within an illusion. For them, reality and illusion are a matter of arbitrary definition.

The work world which is socially defined as real may not feel that way when it has become superspecialized and seemingly separated from its products. The individual performing a function not in harmony with his biology may do it in perfunctory manner. The pushbutton world is defined as real but may seem more like a fantasy. Which is more real, a consensually defined abstraction or a game which is more consistent with man's biological nature? The fantasy of the game becomes not a game at all.

BIBLIOGRAPHY

Baldwin, James. Nobody Knows My Name. New York, The Dial Press, Inc., 1961.

Beisser, Arnold R. Psychodynamic observations of a sport. Psychoanl. Rev., 48, Spring 1961, 69-76.

Blum, G. S., and Rosenzweig, S. The incidence of sibling and parental deaths in the anamnesis of female schizophrenics. J. Gen. Psychol., Jan., 1944, 3-13.

Cope, Myron. This Week. Los Angeles Times, October 14, 1962.

Erikson, Erik. Childhood and Society. New York, W. W. Norton & Company, Inc., 1950.

Freud, Sigmund. In the Basic Writings of Sigmund Freud. Translated and edited by A. A. Brill. New York, Random House, Inc., 1938.

Komarovsky, Mirra. The Unemployed Man and His Family: Effect of Unemployment Upon the Status in 59 Families. New York, Dryden Press, Inc., 1940.

Larrabee, Eric, and Meyersohn, Rolf. eds. Mass Leisure. Glencoe, Ill., The Free Press, 1958.

Litchfield, Edward H. Saturday's hero is doing fine. Sports Illustrated, Oct. 8, 1962, 66-80.

Mead, Margaret, and Calas, Nicolas. eds. Primitive Heritage: An Anthropological Anthology. New York, Random House, Inc., 1953.

Mead, Margaret. Sex and Temperament in Three Primitive Societies: Manus, Mundugumor, and Tchambuli. New York, William Morrow & Co., Inc., 1939.

O'Hara, John. Appointment in Samarra. New York, Random House, Inc., 1934.

Riesman, David. Individualism Reconsidered. New York, The Free Press of Glencoe, 1954.

———— et al. The Lonely Crowd. New Haven, Conn., Yale University Press, 1950.

Rose, Arnold M., ed. Human Behavior and Social Processes. Boston, Houghton Mifflin Company, 1961.

Scorecard. Sports Illustrated, Oct. 8, 1962, 6.

Wahl, C. W. Some antecedent factors in the family histories of 392 schizophrenics. Amer. J. Psychiat., Mar., 1954, 668-676.

Webster, F. A. M., et al. The Evolution of the Olympic
  Games, 1829 B.C.—1914 A.D. London, Fleet Lane, 1914.
Webster's New World Dictionary of the American Language,
  Encyclopedia Edition. Cleveland and New York, The World
  Publishing Company, 1952.
Wedge, Bryant M., ed. Psychosocial Problems of College
  Men. New Haven, Conn., Yale University Press, 1958.
Yablonsky, Lewis. The new criminal. The Saturday Review,
  Feb. 2, 1963, 54.